HUMAN SECURITY IN A BORDERLESS WORLD

Human Security

in a

Borderless World

DEREK S. REVERON

KATHLEEN A. MAHONEY-NORRIS

WESTVIEW
PRESS

A MEMBER OF THE PERSEUS BOOKS GROUP

Westview Press was founded in 1975 in Boulder, Colorado, by notable publisher and intellectual Fred Praeger. Westview Press continues to publish scholarly titles and high-quality undergraduate- and graduate-level textbooks in core social science disciplines. With books developed, written, and edited with the needs of serious nonfiction readers, professors, and students in mind, Westview Press honors its long history of publishing books that matter.

Find us on the World Wide Web at www.westviewpress.com.

Every effort has been made to secure required permissions for all text, images, maps, and other art reprinted in this volume.

Westview Press books are available at special discounts for bulk purchases in the United States by corporations, institutions, and other organizations. For more information, please contact the Special Markets Department at the Perseus Books Group, 2300 Chestnut Street, Suite 200, Philadelphia, PA 19103, or call (800) 810-4145, ext. 5000, or e-mail special.markets@perseusbooks.com.

Designed by Timm Bryson

Library of Congress Cataloging-in-Publication Data
Reveron, Derek S.
  Human security in a borderless world / Derek S. Reveron, Kathleen A. Mahoney-Norris.
    p. cm.
  Includes bibliographical references and index.
  ISBN 978-0-8133-4485-0 (alk. paper)
  1. Security, International. 2. National security. 3. National security—United States. I. Mahoney-Norris, Kathleen. II. Title.
  JZ5588.R496 2011
  355'.033—dc22
                          2010032268
E-book ISBN: 978-0-8133-4522-2
10 9 8 7 6 5 4 3 2

Governments understand that they cannot address today's threats, or seize today's opportunities, on their own. They need the private sector, civil society groups, philanthropic foundations, academic institutions—all those with the capacity to contribute—to do their part. And they need to cooperate with each other and with all stakeholders as never before. This is—and must be—an era of partnership.

—UNITED NATIONS SECRETARY-GENERAL BAN KI-MOON, "REMARKS TO THE HOUSE OF REPRESENTATIVES IN MALTA," APRIL 22, 2009

CONTENTS

LIST OF ILLUSTRATIONS

Boxes

Figures

Images

Maps

Tables

PREFACE

Collectively, the authors have been thinking about or promoting U.S. national security for more than sixty years as military officers and educators focused on security studies. In both professions, we have continually confronted biases oriented toward studying great powers and big wars. That logic made more sense during the cold war when Soviet and U.S. foreign policies under the shadow of nuclear exchange kept both countries on the verge of World War III. But as we commemorate the twenty-year anniversary of Soviet collapse in 2011, both professions need to move beyond a doomsday scenario to fully understand the new (albeit twenty-year-old!) security environment. Blindfolding ourselves to this increasingly complicated and ambiguous contemporary world will only delay our ability to address today's security issues where human security is truly national security.

Human Security in a Borderless World is designed to be a textbook for those students, researchers, and practitioners thinking about international and national security. While this work is developed from a U.S.-informed security perspective, we believe that the analysis stands on its own. We offer a detailed examination of the challenges that threaten most human beings, their societies, and their governments today, along with an alternative approach to thinking about national security, encapsulated in the concept of *human security*. As the influential United Nations Development Programme has phrased it, "Security is a child who did not die, a disease that did not spread, a job that was not cut, an ethnic tension that did not explode in violence, a dissident who was not silenced."

Instead of protecting against the most catastrophic possibilities (rogue states and nuclear attack), we think it is important to think about the most likely threats (nonstate actors and transnational challenges). We must educate ourselves about the many issues that have often been decades in the making and are now demonstrating their capability to threaten all human beings. These include issues such as climate change, pandemic diseases, endemic poverty, weak and failing states, transnational narcotics trafficking and criminal gangs, and vulnerable information systems. Engaging in critical thinking now will enable governments, militaries, nongovernmental groups, and individual citizens to better provide for national and international security, while improving good governance and social and economic prosperity for all.

ACKNOWLEDGMENTS

We are both grateful to Toby Wahl for his confidence in us and for sharing our vision for rethinking national security. This reassessment of international security is not only essential but long overdue. We also thank the editorial and marketing staffs of Westview, PublicAffairs, and the Perseus Books Group who turned our ideas into this textbook. For generous use of images, we thank Jennifer Doyle and Babak Parviz.

Individually, Derek would like to acknowledge the support of his colleagues at the Naval War College who research national security and develop future strategic leaders for sixty-five countries. In particular, Derek is grateful to Joan Johnson-Freese, Roger Nolan, Tom Nichols, Paul Smith, James Kraska, Paul Matthews, Mark Gleason, and Nick Gvosdev. Outside of Newport, Derek is grateful to Chris Fettweis and Jeffrey Murer.

Individually, Kathleen expresses appreciation to her colleagues within Air University who have stimulated her thinking about national security along nontraditional lines, especially John Ackerman, Mary Hampton, Chuck Costanzo, Bart Kessler, Elvis Davis, Judy Gentleman, and David Sorenson. Additionally, Kathleen is grateful to her mentors and colleagues from the Center on Rights Development at the University of Denver.

1

Human Security in a Borderless World

When it comes to security challenges, fortunately, we do not see any conventional military threats to the United States developing in the [Latin American] region, nor do we foresee any major military conflict between nations. . . . However, public security threats—such as crime, gangs, drug trafficking and use—pose the principal near-term security challenges to the region. . . . In many cases, the underlying conditions of poverty and inequality provide fertile soil for the principal security challenges in the region. . . . [N]early 80 percent of the entire region lives on less than $10 per day. When you add these poverty figures—which represent millions of people trying to provide for their families—to the world's most unequal distribution of wealth and a high level of corruption, you have a strong catalyst for insecurity and instability.

—ADM. JAMES STAVRIDIS, U.S. SOUTHERN COMMAND
2008 POSTURE STATEMENT

What U.S. Navy admiral James Stavridis noted for much of the Western Hemisphere is increasingly true across the globe: Nontraditional or human security challenges are increasingly relevant for countries throughout the international system—including the United States. It appears that traditional war as a way of settling grievances between states or advancing national interests is disappearing.[1] At the end of 2008, the Uppsala Conflict Data Program tracked zero interstate conflicts, twenty-nine intrastate conflicts (e.g., Sudan), and five internationalized internal conflicts (e.g., Congo).[2] Of these, only five reached the state of war where more than 1,000 battle deaths occurred.

While major conflict is important, incidents such as Russia's invasion of Georgia in 2008, the U.S. invasion of Iraq in 2003, or Israel's invasion of Lebanon in 2006 are rare. The absence of major war is also evident in the proliferation of UN peacekeeping missions around the world: In 2010, 90,000 blue helmets separated former warring factions and worked to ameliorate underlying conditions to prevent future conflicts.[3] Further, militaries that were once trained and equipped to defend their countries' borders are increasingly used in ways to promote peace, provide disaster assistance, and improve human development. This led well-known scholar John Mueller to conclude that war among great powers has almost ceased to exist.[4] Instead, illegally armed groups, pandemic disease, cyber hackers, and environmental degradation occupy the concerns of many national security professionals.

The implications of a changed security landscape are profound for every human being. Security concerns over the past twenty years have been shifting away from state-focused traditional challenges to human-centered security issues such as disease, poverty, and crime. These newer security concerns entail different ways of looking at issues, which is reflected in the diversity of ways by which the United States protects its national security (see Table 1.1). Although there are remnants of cold war conflicts on the Korean Peninsula and in the Persian Gulf region, these are largely the exception. Instead, the U.S. military no longer has a singular emphasis on defending the United States and preparing for major combat, but also provides security and other types of assistance to more than 150 countries ranging from Afghanistan to Zambia. It does so not out of imperial ambition but as a means to protect the United States from transnational challenges. American military forces usually do not engage

TABLE 1.1: CONTRASTING FORMS OF SECURITY

	NATIONAL SECURITY	HUMAN SECURITY
PRIMARY ACTOR	States	Individuals
PRIMARY CONCERNS	Regime stability and security	Economic status, health, personal security, and liberties
PRIMARY THREAT(S)	Forms of economic, military, or diplomatic coercion	Disease, poverty, and crime
ORIGIN OF THREATS	Unfriendly states, weak states, and rival states	Non-state actors, transnational issues (e.g., climate change), repressive regimes, and illegally armed groups
MEASURE OF STRENGTH	Military power, economic productivity, control of borders, and appeal of values	Human development index that captures quality of life, educational opportunities, and life expectancy
BASIS	National interests	Universal human needs and values
ULTIMATE ENDSTATE	National Sovereignty, territorial integrity, vitality of government, institutions, and society	Freedom from want, freedom from fear, freedom of expression, and freedom of beliefs
LEGAL BASIS	United Nations Charter and International Law	Universal Declaration of Human Rights and Responsibility to Protect doctrine

in combat; instead, they train and equip partners' militaries, lead civil engineering projects, and provide medical assistance. All of these activities are designed to strengthen partner nations' capabilities, sovereignty, and stability, which are increasingly threatened by intrastate and nongovernmental challenges. In a world where a Nigerian can travel to Yemen for explosives training, transit through the Netherlands to board a U.S.-bound flight, and attempt to destroy a civilian plane over Detroit, as happened on Christmas Day 2009, the implications of a borderless world are sobering. Significantly, these challenges are not entirely new. The 9/11 terrorist attacks occurred ten years ago. Two years before those attacks, the federally chartered U.S. Commission on National Security/21st Century (the "Hart-Rudman Commission") predicted:

> New technologies will continue to stretch and strain all existing borders—physical and social. Citizens will communicate with and form allegiances to individuals or movements anywhere in the world. Traditional bonds between states and their citizens can no longer be taken for granted, even in the United States. Many countries will have difficulties keeping dangers out of their territories, but their governments will still be committed to upholding the integrity of their borders. Global connectivity will allow "big ideas" to spread quickly around the globe. Some ideas may be religious in nature, some populist, some devoted to democracy and human rights. Whatever their content, the stage will be set for mass action to have social impact beyond the borders and control of existing political structures.[5]

Just as the Hart-Rudman Commission foresaw, technological changes and increased information flows have helped to stimulate new transnational challenges that are creating widespread insecurity across the civic, economic, environmental, maritime, health, and cyberspace realms. Examples are numerous. The proliferation of small arms and light weapons, often linked to narco-trafficking and criminal gangs, undermines government legitimacy and social stability in Latin America and the Caribbean, as individual citizens do not feel secure. International migrant smuggling and trafficking in humans challenge traditional notions of sovereignty and human rights in West and North Africa. Development inequities and systemic corruption foster unrest within, and between, societies in Europe and Asia alike. Cyber criminals and malicious code threaten information and cyber security for governments, businesses, and consumers throughout the world.

To ensure national security in a world characterized by these threats without borders requires new ways of conceptualizing security. Unfortunately, the Hart-Rudman Commission's concerns and specific recommendations were not immediately taken to heart by policy makers in 1999, even while the United States was floundering in the search to (re)define its national security interests after the cold war.[6] This is unfortunate. We argue here that the factors and issues fueling conflict and a pervasive sense of insecurity over the past twenty years will only accelerate in the next twenty years, requiring an increasingly nuanced understanding of these issues. Traditional analyses that focus on challenges to national security in the form of competitor states like China fail to take into account growing security challenges at the subnational and transnational levels or consider how the world has changed during the past two decades.

Far from ushering in a new era of peace and security, the end of the cold war actually exposed and accelerated transnational forces that challenge traditional ideas about power and security. While developed countries like the United States are often the *targets* of transnational actors, developing countries and poorly governed regions are frequently the *sources* of these challenges. Because of this, the United States enshrined in its 2002 *National Security Strategy* the conclusion that it was threatened more by weak states than by powerful ones, realizing that weak states allow domestic threats to become larger transnational ones. In recognition, the United States now finds itself engaged around the world in military operations and initiatives that have little to do with fighting but everything to do with providing humanitarian assistance, training foreign militaries, and building security, justice, and law enforcement institutions to improve domestic stability. Yet traditional conceptions of national security cannot account for this phenomenon of assistance, while conventional perspectives on world politics such as realism, which focus on the preeminent role of states, offer little insight into the growing American preoccupation with transnational issues.[7] Likewise, traditional conceptions of security are severely strained to explain today's security environment, where potential peer competitors or possible adversaries like the United States and China are transforming into cooperative partners to combat common transnational challenges such as pandemic diseases, maritime piracy, and terrorism. Neither can realist conceptions of security make sense of the growing influence of nongovernmental groups and activists who work across state boundaries to tackle human rights abuses, poverty, the spread of HIV/AIDS, and climate change.

THE NEW SECURITY ENVIRONMENT

Given the preeminent military position of the United States, the dominant international relations school of realism predicts that a new power must emerge to balance the United States. From 1945 to 1991 the Soviet Union filled this role, as persuasively demonstrated by prominent (neo)realist scholar Kenneth Waltz.[8] But contrary to realist expectations, since 1991 no new country has emerged to challenge the United States. Countries with sufficient economic resources like the United Kingdom, Germany, and Japan are allies of the United States and spend too little on national defense. Powerful emerging economies like China, Brazil, and India lack the strategic rationale to balance the United States. Finally, competitors like Russia lack the economic independence and conventional military might that the former Soviet Union once possessed. Instead of increased international competition among states, this new era of globalization is characterized by economic interdependence that makes traditional war seem highly unlikely. The increasingly prevalent phenomenon of contemporary globalization—characterized by high levels of worldwide economic trade, the movement of people, and information exchange—appears to be a critical factor in ameliorating conflict and preventing more military challenges to the United States. Journalist Thomas Friedman is well known for having popularized this concept of globalization, proposing in the late 1990s that the dynamic phenomenon "has replaced the Cold War as the defining international system."[9] For Friedman and other observers, globalization has appeared on balance to be a positive development, as it fosters integration and even similar cultural ideas. Thus, disputes seem more likely to be resolved peacefully, either bilaterally or through multilateral organizations like the World Trade Organization and the International Court of Justice.

At the same time that great power conflict has not occurred, this new era of globalization has brought together many of the world's countries that face similar security challenges such as climate change, illicit trafficking of drugs and people, and computer viruses. Given the transnational character of these challenges, international cooperation is recognized as essential and thus bound to increase. This positive assessment of globalization is generally shared by the international relations school of liberalism, the major competing worldview to the school of realism. For international liberals, whether scholars like John Ikenberry and Joseph S. Nye or policy makers such as former president Bill Clinton, the forces of globalization are projected to lead to beneficial economic development for all peoples, along with the spread of democratic and human rights ideals—all of which translate to a more peaceful international system.[10] (Table 1.2 contrasts the perspectives of the major international relations schools; constructivism is introduced below.) However, others point to potential dangers and new concerns in this age of globalization as some societies are not well situated to benefit from rapid change. In fact, Jonathan Kirshner sees the United States attracting "more violent resistance and political opposition to its international ambitions."[11]

It is unsurprising to find that developed states are more immune than developing states to the negative aspects of globalization. As the 2009–2010 influenza pandemic illustrated, the United States has the resources to manufacture vaccines, stockpile antiviral medicines, and inoculate tens of millions of people in a short period of time. Developing countries are not so well equipped. The same is true when it comes to illegally armed, violent groups or criminal gangs. In the United States these gangs are a problem for law enforcement. But in Central America gangs outnumber and overwhelm law enforcement and even militaries. There, gangs are a national security threat and have benefited from globalization through

TABLE 1.2: INTERNATIONAL RELATIONS THEORIES: PERSPECTIVES ON SECURITY

THEORY	REALISM AND ITS NEO VARIANTS	LIBERALISM AND ITS NEO VARIANTS	CONSTRUCTIVISM
PRINCIPAL CONCERN	Power where the strong dominate the weak	Order and justice regardless of relative position in the international system	Shared ideas continuously shape interactions between humans and institutions.
THEORISTS	Thomas Hobbes Niccolò Machiavelli Kenneth Waltz John Mearsheimer	Immanuel Kant John Locke Joseph S. Nye G. John Ikenberry	Sigmund Freud Michele Foucault Alexander Wendt Martha Finnemore
VIEW OF HUMAN NATURE	Individuals are greedy, aggressive, and will seek power	Individuals are social and perfectible through learning, and will seek cooperation	Individuals are thinking, adaptable, and will create environments to suit their needs
GOAL FOR FOREIGN POLICY	Maximize national security	International peace and justice (or prosperity)	Mutually determined by society
MEANS TO SURVIVAL	Military and economic power used to reward or coerce other states	International order through non-coercive diplomacy and economic cooperation	Shared values to enhance the well-being of all
PRIMARY ACTORS	States	States in intergovernmental organizations (e.g., United Nations) and nonstate actors	Individuals and groups

ANTAGONISTS	Great powers (regardless of type of government)	Non-democracies (according to "the Democratic Peace Theory")	Policy entrepreneurs who shape norms
MEASURES OF POWER	Hard power: Military capabilities and economic resources	Soft power: Appeal of political, economic, and cultural norms	Pervasiveness and acceptance of ideas
WORLDVIEW METAPHOR	Jungle: international system is anarchic; strong governments make the rules and dominate weak governments	Country club: international system is constrained by rules so strong and weak governments have more equal access	Blogosphere: density of connections and prevalence of transnational ideas matter
CAUSES OF WAR	Anarchic international system; all states amass power as they fear for their survival. For Thucydides, causes are fear, honor, and interests	Misperception among states; the absence of enforceable international law to punish aggressor states and wrongdoers. Democracies do not go to war with each other	Enabling security discourse where government leaders can manipulate populace to adopt aggressive behavior toward other peoples
PATH TO PEACE	Balance of power; powerful states constrain one another from going to war	Collective security, international law, democracy, and economic interdependence	Liberalization of thought; shared human rights and values and peaceful norms

weapons procurement and new markets, enabling them to compete with traditional state institutions and security forces.

Unfortunately, in almost every country of the world, transnational actors wage "wars of globalization," which Moisés Naím encapsulates as the illegal trafficking of drugs, small arms, and humans; violations of intellectual property; and money laundering. Svante Cornell and Niklas Swanström argue that among transnational criminal activities, illegal drug production and trafficking pose a full-spectrum threat to both state and human security. For example, narcotics trafficking affects societies through addiction, crime, and disease.[12] Drug production also undermines or weakens effective governance by fostering corruption and powerful criminal networks, and it may provide financial support to terrorism and insurgency. Prominent examples include the resurgence of the Taliban in Afghanistan, enabled by profits from the heroin trade; the FARC insurgent movement in Colombia, which sustains itself through cocaine trafficking; and competing drug trafficking organizations that are challenging the Mexican state's ability to govern. The issue of drug trafficking also highlights the fact that traditional distinctions between foreign and domestic policies are fading when it comes to many transnational concerns. Clearly, Mexico's violent internal battle with its drug cartels spills over into the border regions of the United States, affecting the security of U.S. citizens and the demands on local law enforcement officials. In turn, this affects U.S. foreign policy toward Mexico and U.S. willingness to become involved in Mexico's domestic campaign against its drug cartel problem.

The U.S. National Intelligence Council has somberly forecast that "weak governments, lagging economies, religious extremism, and youth bulges will align to create a perfect storm for internal conflict in certain regions."[13] Unfortunately for developed countries like the United States, weak states are assessed to have a comparative advantage in generating international crime and terrorism.[14] Because of this, transnational security issues have emerged as key challenges for all states and their citizens in the twenty-first century. Paul Smith has defined these challenges as "non-military threats that cross borders and either threaten the political and social integrity of a nation or the health of that nation's inhabitants."[15]

These threats are very different from conventional threats. In many cases nonstate actors such as terrorist groups or criminal enterprises cause these threats, and they find either sanctuary or support within weak states. For example, most law enforcement agencies regard West African criminal networks as dangerous adversaries with global reach.[16] Similarly the transnational gang Mara Salvatrucha (MS-13) challenges the viability of Central American governments, even as it has links to sister gangs in Los Angeles. Or witness the meteoric rise of Somali piracy in 2008 that has since forced dozens of countries to deploy warships to the Gulf of Aden.[17] These transnational security issues often represent the "dark side" of globalization, where individuals and groups compete with governments on a regional or global scale.

Turning specifically to Africa, many of the continent's fifty-three countries have been plagued with famine, disease, internal conflict, and population displacement that cross national borders to generate further security destabilization. Even the once-isolated trans-Saharan arc is increasingly seen as a breeding ground for violent conflict, terrorism, and regional instability. Notably missing from this list of concerns is peer competition, nuclear proliferation, or territorial ambition. In response to these complex security challenges, the United States created a new military command to assist African governments in developing their security institutions, including capabilities against threatening subnational groups or transnational networks. In general, these nonstate actors have some inherent advantages, especially over weak governments. Small private groups can more readily harness off-the-shelf technology such as satellite phones, encryption, and transportation technology. (For example, across the world in the Caribbean Sea, semisubmersible vehicles—the "poor man's submarine"—carrying cocaine are increasingly common. These vessels can carry several tons of cocaine thousands of miles while escaping detection). And in Nigeria, organized criminal groups illegally trade 100,000 barrels of stolen oil every day, which requires an elaborate system of transportation and financing. Whether they are local, transnational, narco-terrorist, radical Islamist, or neocommunist, these groups have access to a variety of underground economies, suspect religious charities, and often illicit government sponsorship.

Image 1.1—Semisubmersible vehicles in Colombia. Photo credit: Derek Reveron.

With so many nongovernmental and illegal groups operating at a subnational level, many police forces in developing countries are underequipped to effectively confront them and too frequently are co-opted through corruption. Further, military forces largely lack the capabilities, doctrine, and culture to confront these transnational security challenges. Militaries tend to prepare for defending their borders from invading forces and not for improving how they work with police or enforce domestic law and order. However, this is beginning to change, as military forces in many countries are beginning to think beyond warfare as they develop core competencies to meet the challenges of transnational threats to better address nontraditional human security concerns. From the U.S. perspective, formerly distant internal security concerns have now been elevated to the status of international security concerns, as they threaten national unity, stability, and internal peace within states— but also have much larger implications for regional and global security. Given these transformational changes in the security environment, we contend that traditional notions of security have little to offer in terms

CONTEMPORARY CHALLENGE

The Concept of Human Security

It should not be surprising to find that it was the United Nations—and specifically the United Nations Development Programme—that first conceptualized, and then systematically promoted, the concept of human security. In its benchmark *Human Development Report, 1994*, the UNDP provided an explanation, justification, agenda, operational indicators, and policy recommendations centered on the concept of human security. UNDP associates were clear that the concept of security had been too much associated with military conflict and arms and that human security involved such concerns as "job security, income security, health security, environmental security, security from crime." Fifteen years later the UNDP's *Arab Human Development Report, 2009* defined human security more broadly as "the liberation of human beings from those intensive, extensive, prolonged, and comprehensive threats to which their lives and freedom are vulnerable." The report helpfully distinguishes state or national security from human security by pointing out that the threats to state security are military ones, the actors who threaten states are usually located outside those states, and the state itself is the object that is threatened. By contrast, with human security the threats are varied in nature, as are the actors who threaten humans, and "the object of threat in the case of human security is *individuals'* lives, freedom, or both." Additionally, the necessity for collaboration between all sectors of state and society to address human security concerns was extensively documented by the independent Commission on Human Security in its influential *Human Security Now* report of 2003. Several related concepts are almost always part of the discussion on human security, including "the responsibility to protect," the inherent nature of human rights for all human beings, and the concept of "development as freedom" as popularized by Nobel Prize laureate and economist Amartya Sen.[1] All these concepts are addressed throughout this book.

---

1. United Nations Development Programme, *Human Development Report, 1994* (New York: Oxford University Press, 1994), 3; United Nations Development Programme, Regional Bureau for Arab States, *Arab Human Development Report: Challenges to Human Security in the Arab Countries* (New York: United Nations Development Programme), 23, 19 (emphasis added); Commission on Human Security, *Human Security Now: Protecting and Empowering People* (New York: Commission on Human Security, 2003), available at www.humansecurity-chs.org; Amartya Sen, *Development as Freedom* (New York: Alfred A. Knopf, 1999).

of understanding threats without borders. Instead, a *human security* construct is necessary to make sense of these threats and to develop viable policy options.

HUMAN SECURITY

In this book we propose that the only effective way to grapple with U.S. security concerns is to move beyond the traditional state-centric focus of *national security* to the organizing concept of *human security*, which is a people-centered approach focused on individual human beings and their rights and needs. In fact, the national security of states cannot be achieved without first achieving human security. Arguably, this belief is reflected in the steady shift in U.S. foreign policy, increasingly focused on combating threats without borders and placing development on an equal footing with the traditional tools of diplomacy and defense. This was already acknowledged under the George W. Bush administration and has progressed with the Obama administration. As Hillary Rodham Clinton proclaimed on her very first day as the Obama administration's new secretary of state, "Robust diplomacy and *effective development* are the best long-term tools for securing America's future."[18]

Furthermore, human security concerns have clearly become an essential component of U.S. foreign policy. In his first year as president, President Obama reiterated these themes when, upon accepting the Nobel Peace Prize in December 2009, he declared:

> It is undoubtedly true that development rarely takes root without security; it is also true that security does not exist where human beings do not have access to enough food, or clean water, or the medicine and shelter they need to survive. It does not exist where children can't aspire to a decent education or a job that supports a family. The absence of hope can rot a society from within. And that's why helping farmers feed their own people—or nations educate their children and care for the sick—is not mere charity. It's also why the world must come together to control climate change.[19]

Image 1.2—Women in Uganda wash clothes in the Nile River. Photo credit: Derek Reveron.

President Obama's chief diplomat fully embraced this notion. Secretary of State Hillary Clinton testified before the House Foreign Affairs Committee on February 25, 2010: "We're developing a new architecture of cooperation to meet global challenges that cross national boundaries like climate change and the use of our planet's oceans. In so many instances, our national interests and the common interests converge. And so from the Western Hemisphere to Africa, Asia, and the Middle East, we're promoting human rights, the rule of law, democracy, and internet freedom. We're fighting poverty, hunger and disease, and we're working to ensure that economic growth is broadly shared."[20]

In turn, we are convinced that it is essential to understand contemporary challenges through a more interdisciplinary, inclusive approach focused on human security that "equates security with people rather than territories, with development rather than arms."[21] The dynamic forces transforming human interactions at the international, transnational, regional, and domestic levels all have profound implications for the (human) insecurity perceived by individuals, groups, and states. Indeed, much of this dynamism is fueled by the process of globalization, which is constantly accelerating change. As Thomas Friedman noted, this type of rapid change can "breed enormous insecurity as well as enormous prosperity. [It] can breed in people a powerful sense that their lives are now controlled by forces they cannot see or touch."[22] Therefore, examining globalization as an ongoing process affecting human security is essential to our analysis. While we deal in large part with the negative aspects of globalization—for example, how it contributes to the growth of transnational threats—it is equally important to consider the positive, cooperative aspects of globalization referenced above. Thus, we review the growth of the transnational human rights movement with its many facets and the development of such human-centered international concepts or norms as the responsibility to protect (R2P). Only with this broader perspective can the human security construct be understood. In fact, the increasingly influential constructivist school of international relations scholars would argue that the type of broader perspective reflected in the human security construct is necessary to appropriately analyze and make sense of the changing international system. For constructivists, people's views and beliefs on trends such as globalization are formed through mutual give-and-take as human beings and societies adapt their ideas and build new norms of behavior. Not surprisingly, these ideas and norms are equally influenced by cultural and religious values and traditions, a point that is very evident when considering the condition of women worldwide.

Of note, one of the most important critical perspectives related to a constructivist mode of analysis is increasingly being offered by feminist, or gendered, analyses of international relations and security. Cyntha Enloe has argued that "how one thinks about national security not only affects global relations but determines who is even allowed to sit at the table to take part in the security conversation. The more militarized the understanding of what national security is . . . the more likely it will be that the conversation about national security—and international security—will be a largely masculinized affair." Significantly for purposes of human security, Jill Stearns proposes that "there is a great deal of overlap between feminist interests and concerns and the human security approach. . . . [F]eminists point out that the fate of women is a crucial determinant of the fate of whole societies and countries. The achievement of global security is tied up with the need to improve the status of women around the world."[23] This is a central point explored below.

Another logical consequence of shifting from a traditional state-based territorial definition of security to a human-centric view of security is recognizing the importance of nonstate actors (as both liberals and especially constructivists would doubtless agree). From a negative perspective, this means acknowledging that individuals like Osama bin Laden and the various al Qaeda franchises can pose serious threats to human security as terrorists target civilians. But from a positive perspective, it also means that individual activists like Jody Williams, philanthropists like Bill and Melinda Gates, or nongovernmental organizations (NGOs) like Greenpeace can act as catalysts to change government policies, improve people's lives, and incrementally transform the international system. The case of Jody Williams exemplifies these possibilities. She successfully organized a diverse network of people around the world against land mines and was the spokesperson for the International Committee to Ban Landmines. With the knowledge that more than 100 million land mines are scattered across the developing world, the group fought to change how militaries and governments behave with respect to their indiscriminate use. Jody Williams's efforts brought together more than 1,000 different groups in sixty countries to pressure governments to adopt a ban on land mines known as the Ottawa Treaty. The Nobel Peace Prize was awarded in 1997 to Jody Williams and the coalition of groups' contributions to international security. The Nobel Committee specifically recognized the power of nongovernmental organizations and expressed hope for similar models in the future for disarmament and peace. This example illustrates how governments can benefit from individuals' and civil society's efforts to improve international security, or conversely find their own efforts constrained, as the United States has found with its use of land mines on the Korean Peninsula increasingly called into question.[24]

HUMAN SECURITY AS NATIONAL SECURITY

Over the past few years, it seems fair to say that human security concerns have gained currency in U.S. defense circles and have now become the basis for more nuanced thinking about national security. In our view this is particularly significant because if the most powerful state in the international system acknowledges the importance of these concerns, then the human security construct will gain increasing traction. To be sure, the Pentagon largely trains and equips military forces for major war, but the U.S. military increasingly finds itself operating in non-war-fighting environments attempting to alleviate human suffering brought on by natural disaster, civil war, or insurgency.

Even climate change cannot escape discussions of national security and intervention by defense experts. The military advisory board National Security and the Threat of Climate Change, which is composed of distinguished retired senior U.S. military officers, concluded in 2007, "Climate change can act as a threat multiplier for instability in some of the most volatile regions of the world, and it presents significant national security challenges for the United States." The group's findings envision the United States as intervening to minimize the impact of disaster areas, provide stability operations, or deny sanctuary to extremists who may exploit weakened states. In thinking about the future, the group concluded that "the U.S. government should use its many instruments of national influence, including its regional [military] commanders, to assist nations at risk build the capacity and resiliency to better cope with the effects of climate change."[25] This connection between climate change and military intervention is based in part on the assumption that extremists can gain sanctuary where governments are weak and that climate change will weaken already fragile states that lack capacity to provide basic services and security for their populations.

RESPONSIBILITY TO PROTECT

Interestingly, what is relatively new to military and national security circles is not considered new in diplomacy and development circles. In fact, human security concerns have been gaining traction among international

THINK AGAIN

Human Security Is Not National Security

Over the past twenty years, human security has gained increasing acceptance as a concept, and improving human security is a critical goal for many governments' international assistance efforts. Yet in spite of this, conventional international relations theory does not adequately embrace human security as national security. For traditional realist (and neorealist) scholars, only nation-state threats constitute the basis for national security, as individuals or groups lack the capacity to significantly challenge the United States. Thus for realists, terrorists, pirates, and illegally armed groups are little more than a nuisance and should not rise to the level of national security concerns. Likewise, pandemic influenza is regarded as a public health issue, and computer viruses are a private concern. In sum, for realists, only countries that have large militaries and possess nuclear weapons and the delivery systems to reach the United States should be considered the objects of national security.

As an example, realists point to the limited effects of the 9/11 terrorist attack on security in the United States. Certainly, al Qaeda's attack was a tragedy that claimed the lives of nearly 3,000 Americans and altered New York City's skyline. But in their view the attack did little lasting damage to the United States. In fact, prominent members of the realist school have declared that the United States' subsequent invasions of Afghanistan in 2001 and Iraq in 2003 did more damage to the United States politically, militarily, and economically than the al Qaeda attack did. As evidence, they point to the more than $1 trillion spent on those wars, thousands of military personnel killed, and tens of thousands of military personnel wounded.

More broadly, many scholars are concerned that everything characterized as human security is at best a waste of precious national resources. Roland Paris argues that "as a new conceptualization of security, or a set of beliefs about the sources of conflict, human security is so vague that it verges on meaninglessness—and consequently offers little practical guidance to academics who might be interested in applying the concept, or to policymakers who must prioritize among competing policy goals."[1]

---

1. Roland Paris, "Human Security: Paradigm Shift or Hot Air?" *International Security* 26, no. 2 (2001): 102.

experts since at least the early 1990s. When he was secretary-general of the United Nations, Boutros Boutros-Ghali set forth an agenda for peace, "to enhance respect for human rights and fundamental freedoms, to promote sustainable economic and social development for wider prosperity, to alleviate distress and to curtail the existence and use of massively destructive weapons."[26] Unprecedented levels of UN peacekeeping operations accompanied this strategic outlook. Additionally, many countries, including the United States, conducted humanitarian interventions in the Caribbean, West Africa, southeastern Europe, and Southeast Asia. Whether it was the Australians leading efforts in East Timor or the British in Sierra Leone, developed countries largely acted for altruistic reasons to provide stability and improve living conditions for those who found themselves in unstable and violent countries.

In the wake of continuing internal and regional conflicts and violence against civilians—including the tragedy of genocide in Rwanda—the United Nations formalized its prevention activities in 2004 by appointing a special adviser on the prevention of genocide. Soon afterward, in 2009, Secretary-General Ban Ki-moon of the United Nations outlined three key elements of this recently acknowledged *responsibility to protect*. First, he noted that states have the primary responsibility to protect their populations against genocide, war crimes, ethnic cleansing, and crimes against humanity. Second, the international community should provide assistance to states in building capacity to protect their populations from catastrophe by addressing underlying conditions. Third, the international community should take timely action when states fail to protect their populations. As the 2009 *Report of the Secretary-General* on this responsibility to protect notes, "The strategy stresses the value of prevention, and, when it fails, of early and flexible response tailored to the specific circumstances of each case."[27] The key to prevention lies in identifying states at risk and developing appropriate responses to aid governments' efforts to promote development and improve standards of living. In short, waiting until war breaks out or masses of people become internally displaced or refugees is now considered too late and unacceptable. The R2P construct clearly rests on human security as being the central concern.

Based on these converging trends and assessments, we believe that it is clearly not possible to understand the complex threats to U.S. national security—or how to develop strategies and policies to deal with those threats—without a deeper understanding of the component issues that underlie human security. Thus, in this work we consider how best to attain human security for states, groups, and individuals by examining the continuum of interrelated issue areas that we conceptualize in specific chapters as civic security, economic security, environmental security, maritime security, health security, and cyber security. The first two issue areas, civic and economic security, are of necessity quite broad and conceptual, while the other four areas are more threat specific in nature. Yet in every chapter devoted to these issues we explore each area to provide a basis for understanding the problem and its challenges for human security, the issue's relevance for U.S. national security and individual citizens, and key policy recommendations. Fundamentally, we believe that states and their inhabitants are most threatened by subnational or transnational actors, that national instability can quickly develop into regional or global instability, and that international and transnational cooperation are essential to strengthening efforts at every level to improve human security. Although we appreciate the contributions that both the realist and the liberal international relations schools of thought may offer in terms of thinking about national and human security, our approach here would likely fit most comfortably within the constructivist school in terms of the primacy we accord to transnational issues, actors, and analysis.

CHAPTER OUTLINE

Surely, the most basic of human needs is to feel secure in one's person. Traditional national security perspectives have long focused on the security threats posed by *states* to one another as they engage in conflict or war. Implicit in this type of analysis is recognition that individual citizens of those states will be endangered, but that is not the key concern. Some analysts do explore the targeted violence that citizens may face in the context of civil war or insurgencies within the state, but the analysis is still state focused. And even in the wake of the *nonstate* attacks against the United States on September 11, 2001, the U.S. response was to target the *state* of Afghanistan for providing safe haven to al Qaeda. The human security construct of this book requires additional perspectives that are not dictated, or constrained, by the state.

POLICY SPOTLIGHT

Institutionalizing Humanitarian Operations at the Defense Department

When the world's attention shifted away from traditional security defined by presumed conflict between the United States and the Soviet Union to encompass human security, the U.S. military largely avoided adapting to the new security landscape. With an emphasis on planning for two major wars in the 1990s, the Pentagon simply outsourced humanitarian and peacekeeping missions to allies, nongovernmental organizations, or reservists and national guardsmen. This was reinforced by broad support for President George W. Bush's campaign promise in 2000 not to continue the nation building that had occurred in the 1990s in Haiti, Bosnia, and Somalia. Nevertheless, the U.S. military soon discovered in dealing with conflicts in Iraq and Afghanistan that supporting political, social, and economic stability, in addition to conducting counterinsurgency operations, was essential to achieving overall national security objectives. Although the Pentagon had initially hoped for the United Nations, allies, or the non-war-fighting departments of the U.S. federal government to assist with urban planning, local governance, and economic development, it soon learned that conflict zones were simply too dangerous for civilians and that the civilian agencies of the U.S. government were not funded adequately to support these efforts. The UN mission in Iraq was cut short in 2003 when its top diplomat was killed, which effectively shut down UN operations in Iraq. Consequently, U.S. military officers found themselves serving as town mayors, private investment coordinators, and public works managers.

Thus, in Chapter 2 we are concerned with the type of threats to individuals that may be caused by repressive and authoritarian governments, or, conversely, by ineffective and failing governments, both of which threaten the *civic security* of citizens in those societies. In the first case an individual's physical security and integrity may be threatened because

Policy Spotlight (*continued*)

Based on its diverse peacekeeping and nation-building military experiences over the past two decades, the U.S. military has essentially (if sometimes grudgingly) come to accept its role in non-war-fighting activities. In fact, in 2005 the Department of Defense mandated that the importance of stability and reconstruction activities be considered on par with preparation for major combat. And in 2008 the U.S. military accepted that irregular warfare against non-state actors is as important as warfare with rogue states and peer competitors. As both President Bush's and later President Obama's secretary of defense, Robert Gates, observed, "One of the most important lessons of the wars in Iraq and Afghanistan is that military success is not sufficient to win: economic development, institution-building and the rule of law, promoting internal reconciliation, good governance, providing basic services . . . along with security, are essential ingredients for success."[1] As of this writing, however, it is the U.S. military that still finds itself filling the gap that civilian experts from the federal government should fill.

Image 1.3—A U.S. Army engineer discusses building a water reservoir in Afghanistan. Photo credit: U.S. Army sergeant Teddy Wade.

1. Robert M. Gates, "Landon Lecture," November 26, 2007, available at www.k-state.edu/media/newsreleases/landonlect/gatestext1107.html.

the government is actually abusing his or her human rights, whereas in the second case the government is incapable of providing public security and protecting the physical integrity and way of life or cultural values of each citizen. The latter problem is attaining increasing importance as globalization empowers domestic and transnational criminal gangs, drug traffickers, smugglers, and others who flourish in weak and poorly governed societies to prey upon ordinary citizens. The gravity of this issue is reflected in the UN finding that of the some 750,000 people who are estimated to die yearly from armed violence, the majority of deaths (close to 500,000) occur from criminal acts of violence and not due to conflict.[28] What is more, this type of criminal violence is not contained by state borders, as U.S. citizens living on both sides of the U.S.-Mexican border have found to their detriment.[29]

As Chapter 2 also demonstrates, civic security entails the right to express one's cultural values and identity, to include such concepts as ethnicity, race, and religious identity. The fact that human beings value, and identify, themselves in a number of societal ways beyond national or state identity is a critically important piece of understanding why so many threats today are transnational in scope, such as that posed by violent political Islamists. Furthermore, the fundamental attachment that we all have to our cultural identity must be grasped in order to comprehend why globalization can provoke such a serious backlash and conflict, while it also helps trigger Naím's wars of globalization. On the other hand, in this chapter we argue that globalization equally acts in a positive fashion by enabling transnational social movements such as the human rights movement, which has made notable strides in advancing human rights standards for the world's people—particularly women. Only with these deeper insights can policy makers devise appropriate multilayered solutions to civic security issues generated at least in part by transnational actors and cultural identity concerns.[30]

Many would consider *economic security*, in the sense of being able to provide food and shelter for oneself and one's family, as critically essential to human security as is civic security. Thus, in Chapter 3 we explore the grim reality of inequitable development and severe poverty that predominate in much of the world today. This is plainly revealed in the Human

Development Index (HDI, compiled by the United Nations Development Programme), which highlights the staggering differences in life expectancy and child mortality around the world.[31] National and regional economic and social developmental issues have the clear potential to stoke instability, violence, and conflict—making weak states weaker, helping to produce failing states, and imperiling civic security.[32] In fact, many scholars would argue that it is socioeconomic factors and inequities that first fuel insecurity and conflict between different groups of people and not cultural differences or transnational actors and trends. Inequities will often be exacerbated by the lack of good governance, especially when accompanied by corruption. These failures may all be important factors in enabling criminality, extremism, and even terrorism to grow, whether domestic in nature or transnational in scope. Specific topics in Chapter 3 address many key aspects of development, especially the crucial concept of sustainable development as evidenced through the UN system. Particular attention is paid to the central role of women in the struggle for development. Additionally, the chapter examines the tragic problem of failing states and the necessity to address systemic poverty and implement good governance to overcome this phenomenon.

In Chapter 4, we take up *environmental security*. There is strong and growing worldwide consensus that climate change is real and will have profound effects on international security. According to the UN Intergovernmental Panel on Climate Change's conclusions in 2009, "By the end of the century, sea levels may rise twice as much as was predicted two years ago . . . [which] means that the lives of some 600 million people living on low-lying islands, as well as those living in Southeast Asia's populous delta areas, will be put at serious risk." Although there are climate change skeptics, the implications of relocating literally millions of human beings in areas threatened by climate change are staggering, and people are already moving internally from low-lying areas in Bangladesh and the Philippines. For some island countries, like Kiribati and the Maldives, abandoning low-lying areas is not an option, as their entire countries may become uninhabitable. Clearly, "ecomigration" is a growing trend, one triggered not only by rising seas but also by desertification and a lack of fresh water in areas like the African Sahel region bordering the Sahara.[33]

Image 1.4—Humanitarian
assistance in the Democratic
Republic of the Congo.
Photo credit: USAID.

Whereas the United States may have the resources to at least mitigate the effects of climate changes such as this in the future, developing countries and their populations will obviously be most at risk, as they lack adequate resources. Climate change will weaken already feeble states, contributing further to regional and global insecurity. And as populations are further stressed, the potential for instability, conflict, and even resource wars grows, especially where traditional societies may be already prone to clash with Western modes of development and modernity.

Key among resource wars are those that may take place in the maritime domain, which is the subject of Chapter 5. Considering this domain is essential, since 70 percent of the earth's surface is covered by water, 80 percent of the world's population lives on or near a coast, and 90 percent of international commerce travels by sea. Thus, it is important to increase awareness of the many dangers to *maritime security*. Illegal, unreported, and underreported fishing devastates fish stocks and undermines developing countries' food supplies. Piracy costs international shipping millions of dollars and threatens key shipping lanes connecting Europe and Asia. And pollution at sea—unintentionally through oil spills like the one in 2010 in the Gulf of Mexico or intentionally through toxic-waste dumping—threatens sustaining oceans as a vital resource. Finally, illicit groups increasingly benefit from maritime insecurity by exploiting trade routes to traffic drugs, people, and weapons. As new maritime routes open because of the retreating Arctic ice sheets, countries must resolve competing claims for these new routes and the natural resources that likely exist in the "High North." To consider these issues, Chapter 5 explores new legal agreements, international conventions, and initiatives to improve maritime security.

As the 2009–2010 H1N1 influenza pandemic made clear, disease knows no boundaries, making the United States vulnerable to chronic and infectious diseases prevalent in many parts of the world. These include HIV/AIDS, malaria, hepatitis, tuberculosis, the highly publicized Ebola hemorrhagic fever, and influenza. On average, three pandemics per century have been documented since the sixteenth century, occurring at intervals of ten to fifty years. If an influenza pandemic virus were to appear similar to the one that struck in 1918 (killing an estimated 40 million people), there would be serious consequences for international and human security. Air travel and international commerce would stop. Disease outbreaks could trigger massive human migrations, disrupting social orders. Chapter 6 on *health security* discusses the security aspects and lessons to be learned from past outbreaks of other epidemics and the challenges of preparing for the next pandemic. It also provides a brief overview of other widespread diseases such as HIV/AIDS and malaria, which multiply the already serious development problems in many weak states in sub-Saharan Africa.

The previous chapters explore security in the material world, yet citizens in developed countries like the United States increasingly inhabit the virtual world. Thus, Chapter 7 deals with the constantly accelerating issue of *cyber security*. Within just the past decade, human beings, along with their governments and militaries, have become as dependent on the virtual world for their daily activities as they are on the physical world for human activities. The International Telecommunications Union of the United Nations found that nearly one-quarter of the world's 6.7 billion people use the Internet, while more than half of the world's population pay for mobile phone access.[34] This interconnection of the world's population within and across societies holds tremendous implications for economic growth and development, particularly for impoverished areas. For example, global fiber-optic networks have enabled communication in an unprecedented manner, propelling the emergence of India as the world's "back office." On the other hand, just as with globalization generally, there is a dark side of the information age wherein hackers, phishing scam artists, and transnational criminal groups harness the technology, too. Through Trojan horses, criminals and spies gain access to government and private computer networks. Through viruses and denial-of-service attacks, individuals and groups can bring down government and corporate Web sites. And through spyware, the cherished civil liberty of privacy is subverted. Ultimately, cyberspace may prove to be the arena for future military conflicts, too. Recent conflicts in Europe and the Middle East included cyber operations, and the U.S. military is developing cyberwarfare capabilities.

In the concluding chapter, we reiterate that exclusively state-based approaches to understanding national security are no longer viable in an era marked by globalization, a revolution in information technologies, economic integration of states and regions, and a host of transnational challenges and threats. Instead, a new conceptual framework is necessary to understand the spectrum of challenges and the variety of actors and capabilities necessary to address national and human security. This framework places the individual citizen at the heart of national security not only to protect himself or herself but because individuals are literally on the front lines fighting disease, hunger, and malicious software. Further, this framework explains the rationale for growing American preoccupation with nonstate actors ranging from pirates and terrorists to criminal gangs and drug traffickers. Formerly considered a nuisance to national security professionals, nonstate actors have emerged over the past two decades as the principal challengers to U.S. national security and explain much of contemporary U.S. foreign policy. As our human security construct predicts, U.S. foreign policy is prominently focused on subnational and transnational groups, which operate in and across weak states.

Consequently, the United States has been seeking to bolster the security capacity of nearly every developing country in the world. Yet given the finite limits of defense and military assets, increasingly U.S. foreign policy articulates a "3-D approach," which incorporates defense, development, and diplomacy. In fact, both the U.S. State Department and the U.S. Defense Department have deliberately attempted to integrate their efforts through this 3-D approach, which is premised on improving national— and to some extent human—security in all its multifaceted aspects. Although this approach is a step in the right direction, we believe that it is still too state- and government-centric, and does not adequately address the underlying challenges ranging from civic security to cyber security. Ultimately, as examined throughout this book, any plan to advance human security on a global level must equally account for the transnational actors and forces that are shaping the international community, for better or worse. The Commission on Human Security eloquently warns us of the dangers ahead if we refuse to deal with these issues: "Today's global flows of goods, services, finance, people, and images spotlight the many interlinkages in the security of all people. We share a planet, a biosphere, a technological arsenal, a social fabric. The security of one person, one community, one nation rests on the decisions of many others—sometimes fortuitously, sometimes precariously."[35]

To Learn More

In 2003 the highly regarded, independent Commission on Human Security published its landmark report, *Human Security Now: Protecting and Empowering People* (New York: Commission on Human Security, 2003), at www.human security-chs.org.

Paul Collier analyzes the challenges of promoting sustainable human security in *The Bottom Billion: Why the Poorest Countries Are Failing and What Can Be Done About It* (London: Oxford University Press, 2008).

Shahrbanou Tadjbakhsh and Anuradha Chenoy present relevant case studies in *Human Security: Concepts and Implications* (New York: Routledge, 2008).

Roland Paris challenges the value of human security in "Human Security: Paradigm Shift or Hot Air?" *International Security* 26, no. 2 (2001): 87–102.

Derek S. Reveron explores how the changed international security environment is impacting the U.S. military in *Exporting Security: International Engagement, Security Cooperation, and the Changing Face of the U.S. Military* (Washington, DC: Georgetown University Press, 2010).

The United Nations special adviser on the prevention of genocide acts as a catalyst to raise awareness of the causes and dynamics of genocide, alert relevant actors when there is a risk of genocide, and advocate and mobilize for appropriate action. See www.un.org/preventgenocide/adviser/.

Alexander Wendt presents a constructivist account of international relations in his *Social Theory of International Politics* (New York: Cambridge University Press, 1999).

Cynthia Enloe argues that accurate understanding of the militarized nature of national security is impossible without considering a feminist perspective and the role of women in *Globalization and Militarism: Feminists Make the Link* (Lanham, MD: Rowman and Littlefield, 2007).

John Mueller sees the end of war but the inadequacy of governments to provide for human security in *The Remnants of War* (Ithaca: Cornell University Press, 2007).

Notes

1. Ted Robert Gurr and Monty Marshall, *Peace and Conflict* (College Park, MD: Center for International Development, 2005).

2. Uppsala codes "internationalized internal armed conflict" as conflict "between the government of a state and one or more internal opposition group(s) without intervention from other states" (Uppsala Conflict Data Program, Centre for the Study of Civil Wars, International Peace Research Institute, *UCDP/PRIO Armed Conflict Dataset Codebook* [Oslo: Uppsala Conflict Data Program, 2008]).

3. In 2009 about 80,000 peacekeepers were serving in twenty operations (www.un.org/Depts/dpko/dpko/bnote.htm).

4. John Mueller, "War Has Almost Ceased to Exist: An Assessment," *Political Science Quarterly* (Summer 2009): 297–322.

5. U.S. Commission on National Security/21st Century, *New World Coming: American Security in the 21st Century* (Washington, DC: U.S. Government

Printing Office, September 1999), 5, available at www.au.af.mil/au/awc/awc gate/nssg/. The U.S. Commission on National Security is also known as the Hart-Rudman Commission for its two principal authors, Gary Hart and Warren B. Rudman.

6. Ibid. The commission worked in phases to produce three separate reports.

7. See Derek S. Reveron, *Exporting Security: International Engagement, Security Cooperation, and the Changing Face of the U.S. Military* (Washington, DC: Georgetown University Press, 2010).

8. The core principles of neorealism (also known as structural realism) are laid out in the classic work by Kenneth N. Waltz, *Theory of International Politics* (New York: McGraw-Hill, 1977).

9. Thomas L. Friedman, *The Lexus and the Olive Tree* (1999; reprint, New York: Anchor Books, 2000), 7.

10. In their 1977 pathbreaking work, *Power and Interdependence: World Politics in Transition* (Boston: Little, Brown), Robert O. Keohane and Joseph S. Nye provided the foundational analysis for what would come to be known as the "transnational relations" approach and the neoliberalism school.

11. Jonathan Kirshner, "Globalization, American Power, and International Security," *Political Science Quarterly* 123, no. 3 (2008): 363.

12. Moisés Naím, "The Five Wars of Globalization," *Foreign Policy* (January–February 2003); Svante E. Cornell and Niklas L. P. Swanström, "The Eurasian Drug Trade: A Challenge to Regional Security," *Problems of Post-Communism* (July–August 2006): 10–28.

13. National Intelligence Council, *Mapping the Global Future: Report of the National Intelligence Council's 2020 Project*, NIC 2004-13 (Washington, DC: National Intelligence Council, December 2004), 14, available at www.cia.gov/nic/NIC_globaltrend2020_es.html.

14. Paul Collier, *The Bottom Billion: Why the Poorest Countries Are Failing and What Can Be Done About It* (New York: Oxford University Press, 2007), 31.

15. Paul J. Smith, "Transnational Security Threats and State Survival: A Role for the Military," *Parameters* 30 (Autumn 2000): 78.

16. Gail Wannenburg, "Organised Crime in West Africa," *African Security Review* 14, no. 4 (2005).

17. J. Peter Pham, "The Challenge of Somali Piracy," *New Atlanticist*, September 29, 2008.

18. Hillary Rodham Clinton, "Arrival at the Department of State: Remarks to the Department Employees at Welcome Event," Washington, DC, January 22, 2009, available at www.state.gov/secretary/rm/2009a/01/115262.htm (emphasis added).

19. The White House, "Remarks by the President at the Acceptance of the Nobel Peace Prize," December 10, 2009, available at www.whitehouse.gov/the-press-office/remarks-president-acceptance-nobel-peace-prize.

20. Hillary Rodham Clinton, Secretary of State, "Promoting Security Through Diplomacy and Development: The Fiscal Year 2011 International Affairs Budget," Opening Remarks before the House Foreign Affairs Committee, Washington, DC, February 25, 2010; available at www.state.gov/secretary/rm/2010/02/137280.htm.

21. In its landmark *Human Development Report, 1994*, the United Nations Development Programme noted that it was introducing "a new concept of human security, which equates security with people rather than territories, with development rather than arms" (UNDP *Human Development Reports*, http://hdr.undp.org/en/reports/global/hdr1994).

22. Friedman, *Lexus and Olive Tree*, 336.

23. Cynthia Enloe, *Globalization and Militarism: Feminists Make the Link* (Lanham, MD: Rowman and Littlefield, 2007), 40; Jill Stearns, *Gender and International Relations*, 2nd ed. (Malden, MA: Polity Press, 2006), 64.

24. Mark Landler, "White House Is Being Pressed to Reverse Course and Join Land Mine Ban," *New York Times*, May 7, 2010, available at www.nytimes.com/2010/05/08/world/americas/08mine.html.

25. CNA, *National Security and the Threat of Climate Change* (Alexandria, VA: CNA, 2007), available at http://securityandclimate.cna.org, 7. The group is composed of Adm. Frank "Skip" Bowman, Lt. Gen. Lawrence P. Farrell Jr., Vice Adm. Paul G. Gaffney II, Gen. Paul J. Kern, Adm. T. Joseph Lopez, Adm. Donald L. Pilling, Adm. Joseph W. Prueher, Gen. Gordon Sullivan, Vice Adm. Richard H. Truly, Gen. Charles F. Wald, and Gen. Anthony C. Zinni.

26. Boutros Boutros-Ghali, United Nations Secretary-General, *An Agenda for Peace: Preventative Diplomacy, Peacemaking, and Peacekeeping* (New York: United Nations, 1992).

27. United Nations General Assembly, *Implementing the Responsibility to Protect: Report of the Secretary-General* (New York: United Nations, 2009), 2.

28. According to the United Nations Development Programme Newsroom, "Armed Violence Threatens Progress on Millennium Development Goals," May 11, 2010, available at http://content.undp.org/go/newsroom/2010/may/armed-violence-threatens-progress-on-millennium-goals.

29. In March 2010 three U.S. consulate employees in Ciudad Juárez were killed by masked gunmen, presumably in the context of ongoing drug wars. That same month an Arizona rancher was killed by an individual who then escaped to Mexico and was allegedly involved with drug smuggling. For a short overview of U.S.-Mexican border issues, see David Danelo, "How the U.S. and Mexico Can Take Back the Border—Together," Foreign Policy Research Institute "E-Note," April 22, 2010, available at www.fpri.org/enotes/2010004.danelo.usmexicoborder.html.

30. As an example, in *Radical Islam in East Africa* (Santa Monica, CA: RAND, 2009), Angel Rabasa analyzes "the complex ethno-religious landscape in East Africa . . . that [has] produced failed or weak states susceptible to exploitation by extremist groups. . . . Building sustained national resilience that is intolerant of terrorists and extremists . . . can only be accomplished by linking hard security initiatives with a broader array of policies designed to promote political, social, and economic stability" (www.rand.org/pubs/monographs/MG782/).

31. The Human Development Index can be accessed online through the United Nations Development Programme Web site, http://hdr.undp.org/en/statistics/.

32. Mary Kaldor, *New and Old Wars: Organized Violence in a Globalized Era* (Stanford: Stanford University Press, 2001).

33. Jean-Marie Macabrey, "Researchers: Sea Levels May Rise Faster than Expected," *New York Times*, March 11, 2009; Shankar Vedantam, "Climate Fears Are Driving 'Ecomigration' Across Globe," *Washington Post*, February 23, 2009, A1.

34. Chris Tryhorn, "Nice Talking to You . . . Mobile Phone Use Passes Milestone," *Guardian*, March 3, 2009, available at www.guardian.co.uk/technology/2009/mar/03/mobile-phones1/.

35. Commission on Human Security, *Human Security Now: Protecting and Empowering People* (New York: Commission on Human Security, 2003), 2, available at www.humansecurity-chs.org.

2

Civic Security

America's experience as a great multi-ethnic democracy
affirms our conviction that people of many heritages and
faiths can live and proposer in peace. . . . When we see
democratic processes take hold among our friends in
Taiwan or in the Republic of Korea, and see elected leaders
replace generals in Latin America and Africa, we see
examples of how authoritarian systems can evolve,
marrying local history and traditions with the principles
we all cherish.

—PRESIDENT GEORGE W. BUSH,
THE NATIONAL SECURITY STRATEGY OF THE
UNITED STATES OF AMERICA, SEPTEMBER 2002

There is no doubt that President George W. Bush spoke for the majority of his countrymen when he declared in 2002 that not only was democracy the preferred model of good governance for the world, but differing ethnic groups and differing religions could coexist peacefully and cooperate in a democratic state. As President Bush's remarks indicate, the vast majority of U.S. policy makers and U.S. citizens believe that globalization (including modernization and economic progress) and the worldwide information revolution promote greater understanding and tolerance of people's differences, thus contributing to peaceful relations, democratization, and

protection of everyone's civic security. In fact, Thomas Friedman has argued that the dominant and homogenizing culture of globalization *is*
Americanization.[1] Although there might be some disagreement about the
desirability of spreading all facets of American popular culture (especially
as portrayed in certain controversial Hollywood movies, television shows,
and popular songs), most U.S. citizens would undoubtedly view the
spread of American values such as democracy and respect for individual
freedoms and human rights as entirely beneficial for human beings
around the world. They would find it hard to imagine that these cherished
American ideals might exacerbate divisions and conflict within certain
regions of the world, except perhaps for fanatical extremist groups such
as al Qaeda.

This positive perspective is also reflected in President Barack Obama's
speech to the United Nations General Assembly on September 23, 2009,
when he declared that "democracy and human rights are essential to
achieving each of the goals that I've discussed today [nuclear nonprolif-
eration, the pursuit of peace, preserving the planet from climate change,
and a global economy with opportunity for all], because governments of
the people and by the people are more likely to act in the broader interests
of their own people, rather than narrow interests of those in power."[2] President Obama's remarks highlight his firm belief that the basic security
needs of every human being can best be, or perhaps can only be, protected
under a democratic government. Of course, it is worth emphasizing here
the key point that providing this security requires that democratic governments actually have adequate resources and capabilities to protect and
sustain their people, along with effective and stable institutions of governance. This is a debatable proposition, as many of the new democracies
face challenges from powerful separatist groups—often religious or ethnic
in nature—terrorist ideologues, and increasingly sophisticated criminal
networks. These are all themes explored in this chapter.

Perhaps in recognition of difficult lessons learned by the United States
since September 11, 2001, President Obama also acknowledged the continuing relevance of cultural factors when he warned that there was no
one-size-fits-all democratic model that could be imposed; each country
has to follow its own path that will reflect its people's values and traditions.

Of course, President Obama could have pointed out, too, that ethnic- or religious-based cultural traditions may be manipulated by authoritarian governmental or religious leaders such as Robert Mugabe of Zimbabwe or Mahmoud Ahmadinejad in Iran to abuse the rights of their citizens in order to maintain their grip on power. Equally, extremist groups in civil society may use culture as a rallying call to rebel against a perceived unjust, corrupt, or ineffective government, especially if that government is supported by outside powers.

In this chapter we unpack a set of interrelated challenges to each human being's most basic civic security concerns, conceptualized as protection of one's physical safety and integrity, and equally respect for one's personal identity and dignity. Although it is still the reality that governments are simultaneously the principal protectors and the principal abusers of human beings, the process of globalization referenced in Chapter 1 clearly affects governments' abilities both to protect and to abuse. On the positive side, globalization may empower governments when it assists their development efforts and strengthens their abilities to institutionalize democratic government and to rule humanely and justly—often aided by other governments, international organizations, and activist groups. Yet globalization can also empower authoritarian leaders to persecute targeted opposition groups more easily and to use information technologies to incite culturally based dissension to remain in power and prevent change. Globalization can foster, too, the illegal actions of transnational criminal networks and gangs who seek to undermine public security and even rival the authority of weak states. Finally, globalization can enable terrorist groups based in weak or failing states to spread their extremist ideologies around the world with relative ease and few resources. All of these occurrences help generate challenges to human security, from poverty to disease to cyber crime.

THE CHALLENGE OF CULTURAL EXTREMISM

In the twenty-first century most would probably agree that the gravest threats to U.S. national security arise from terrorist groups, especially those manifesting extremist ideologies. In fact, a representative Gallup poll from 2009 shows that U.S. citizens ranked the threat of international terrorism first in their concerns (almost 90 percent were very to moderately concerned), followed closely by concerns about Iran's and North Korea's nuclear capabilities.[3] The ideologies of international terrorist groups tend to be linked to fundamentalist, frequently intolerant perspectives rooted in religious and ethnic cultural factors.[4] These ideologies are typically found within the developing, non-Western regions of the world. This includes certain regions and areas that contain unstable or failing states, or even ungoverned areas, not only in Southwest Asia (Afghanistan, Pakistan) and the Middle East (Iraq, Iran, Yemen) but also in Africa (Somalia in the Horn of Africa, parts of Sudan and Chad). Yet it is equally important to realize that religion and nationalism can motivate conflict, instability, and threats to American security as well in more developed and putatively Western areas of the world, such as the Balkans region in Europe or European-based extremist cells like the German cell that conducted the 9/11 terrorist attacks.

Extremist ideological threats can actually develop within the United States itself and among U.S. citizens, as a number of well-publicized cases in 2009–2010 demonstrated. These ranged from U.S. Army major Nidal Malik Hasan allegedly shooting thirteen individuals at Fort Hood, Texas, for religious reasons to a Pakistani American's alleged attempt at a car bombing near Times Square, New York City, in April 2010. In fact, while for all of 2009 there were some thirteen cases of domestic terrorism recorded,[5] the concern for many counterterrorism experts is whether radicalization of Americans will accelerate, fueled in part by the continuing U.S. involvement in certain Muslim countries and by the ability of U.S. citizens to receive indoctrination and training from terrorist groups in venues ranging from Yemen to Pakistan to Somalia.[6] Of course, as the Fort Hood case demonstrated, it is not even necessary to travel outside the United States to receive indoctrination in view of the ability of extremist groups to reach out via cyberspace to attract recruits worldwide.[7]

For most Americans, it is shocking to accept that someone raised within the United States could be won over to a fundamentalist, intolerant ideology that challenges the core principles of U.S. democratic and pluralist ideology. Most Americans tend to find evidence of cultural conflict disconcerting in general. Yet regardless of any discomfort, if the United States is to protect its national interests and the security of U.S. citizens, the country must improve its ability to understand how and why human insecurity may fuel diverse individuals and groups to turn to culturally based extremism. At the most basic level, it is important to understand that people tend to resist, and often fear, change, especially when their fundamental values appear to be challenged by other cultural traditions. President Obama emphasized this point in his first *National Security Strategy* when he warned of democratic values being linked with modernity and thus seen as a threat to traditional cultural identities. In fact, most scholars and regional experts do not find it surprising that different cultures—whether distinguished by such factors as ethnicity, religion, language, or common history and traditions—are prone to fear one another and often experience misunderstanding and conflict. History is replete with relevant examples. Renowned political scientist Samuel Huntington provided probably the most well-known (and controversial) arguments related to reasons for this proclivity, although he envisioned entire "civilizations" clashing, placing primary emphasis on religious differences.[8] (On the other hand, it should be noted that many scholars have disputed Huntington's argument on both theoretical grounds and through detailed case studies of various conflicts.)[9] Furthermore, Huntington and numerous others have predicted that these incidences of conflict would increase as cultures inevitably interacted and became more aware of their differences because of accelerating globalization trends. In other words, contrary to prevailing wisdom, modernization and even democratization and integration of the world community would actually have detrimental effects, including increasing the feelings of insecurity for many human beings and their desire to remain, or to become assimilated, with their own cultural communities. Since many cultural groups, especially ethnic communities, are separated by state borders such as in Africa, the implications for intrastate and interstate conflict are obvious.

Even proponents of globalization like Thomas Friedman acknowledge how globalization processes can foster fear of change and the unknown, as pointed out in the previous chapter.[10] This type of reaction helps to explain violent episodes such as in Nigeria in 2009 when a fundamentalist

Islamic sect attacked police stations primarily in reaction to Western influences. As a senior member of the sect stated, "We do not believe in Western education. It corrupts our ideas and beliefs. That is why we are standing up to defend our religion." Weak and ineffective governments may only exacerbate these divisions, as is evident from Chad to Yemen to Pakistan to Afghanistan. As Secretary of State Clinton commented in 2009, "It is important for us to have a combined civilian and military strategy in Afghanistan, because so many of the problems that are feeding the presence of the Taliban are rooted in people not feeling secure, not feeling that they have a solid future for themselves and their children, the government not being able to really provide the kind of control and support that people expect."[11]

Cultural appeals can be easily manipulated not only by terrorists or warring groups within a state but also by authoritarian leaders who may use them to attain, or keep, governmental power. Unfortunately, what Friedman has termed the "globalization backlash" makes it even easier for these "backlash demagogues" to offer traditional, if unworkable, solutions to societal problems because these types of solutions tend to appeal to those who feel most insecure and threatened by the changes fostered by globalization.[12] Individuals and groups who refuse to support authoritarian leaders and their policies tend to be marginalized and deliberately discriminated against by state officials. At the worst, they may be singled out for violation of their most basic human rights, up to and including imprisonment, torture, rape, and death. This was clearly the course of action followed by such despots as Serbian nationalist Slobodan Milošević, who helped ignite the Yugoslav civil war and then attempted ethnic cleansing of the Kosovo Albanians; recently indicted war criminal and Sudanese leader Omar al-Bashir, who has encouraged and funded interethnic, tribal, and religious rape and murder in his country; and the ruling military junta in Myanmar (Burma), which has imprisoned the democratic opposition and waged a steady campaign of forced assimilation and destruction of minority groups.

Regardless of one's opinion about how large a role culture may play in particular situations, there is little doubt that it can be a decisive factor in setting the stage for, or providing the proximate cause of, human rights abuses, violence, and war. Whereas in the past the United States might not have seemed to be that threatened by interethnic and religious conflicts in faraway states or regions, in today's globalized society the danger is clearly evident. Failing states that may form after years of conflict and instability can offer enabling conditions for ideologically driven nonstate actors such as terrorist groups to find support, expand their operations, and launch attacks—as shown by the deadly mix of the Taliban government and al Qaeda in Afghanistan and the growing mixture of terrorist and extremist groups destabilizing Yemen. Furthermore, conflict within a state may easily spread to neighboring states, particularly where ethnic and religious communities are not confined by recognized state borders (again, Afghanistan and Pakistan provide sobering examples). Refugees may flee from one state to another, seeking security with their perceived countrymen. In turn, this may generate further instability in the state now housing those refugees, especially if there are different national and religious groups who are already at odds within the host state. This phenomenon has occurred numerous times in areas of Africa, particularly in the Great Lakes region (Rwanda, Burundi, and the Democratic Republic of the Congo). Finally, the existence of culturally based grievances among groups within a particular state may skew access to, and control over, government power and resources, thus negating the possibility of equitable development and the chances of creating a viable (and democratic) state. In the worst case this can lead to massive human rights abuses, targeted killings, and war, as the breakup of Yugoslavia and the genocide in Rwanda in the 1990s demonstrated, along with numerous conflicts ongoing now in the twenty-first century.

It would be entirely too easy, and mistaken, to attribute most of the instability, conflict, or even terrorism to religious differences. First, many of the recent conflicts were fueled primarily by ethnic and not religious differences. Rwanda's genocide, led by its majority Hutu ethnic government, killed some 800,000 Tutsi ethnic minority members (and some Hutu moderates). Even in the Yugoslav conflicts of the 1990s, it would be difficult to conclude whether religious (Muslim-Christian) or ethnic (Serb-Croat-Bosnian) differences were most responsible for the perhaps 100,000 estimated killed. Second, with reference to the United States, it is very significant to note that although there are some 3 million Muslims in the United States (both legal residents and citizens), a mere 100 of them have been associated with radical Islamic or jihad-type terrorism. A RAND terrorist study concluded in 2010 that the U.S. Muslim community remained "unsympathetic" or even "hostile" to these religious-based appeals.[13] Third, intraethnic conflict often poses the greatest threat in terms of generating instability and terrorist threats within the Muslim world, whether these originate from Afghanistan, Pakistan, Somalia, or Yemen. Thus, while all four of these countries are overwhelmingly Muslim in religion, they feature different ethnic, tribal, or clan groups that have traditionally been in conflict with one another. For example, to highlight this factor, the young Somali Americans from Minnesota who were recruited to go to Somalia in 2007 to fight with the extremist al-Shabaab group are believed to have been motivated by Somali nationalism, wanting to unseat the fragile government that had been installed by the neighboring rival nation of Ethiopia.[14] Furthermore, there have been reports of a struggle within the al-Shabaab group itself, between Somali nationalists and "foreign jihadis" who want to expand the international struggle with the West.[15] The Somali case is particularly ironic since religion, nationality, and ethnicity are common to all Somalis, rendering Somalia more a story of civil war than religious or ethnic conflict. Yet regardless of the causes, the effects of this internal conflict are still being experienced beyond its borders through smuggling, piracy, and terrorism, threatening U.S. citizens.

The fact that Americans would not be inclined to understand, or accord much importance to, nationalism as triggering security threats is not surprising to historian Jerry Muller. As he observes: "Projecting their own experience onto the rest of the world, Americans generally belittle the role of ethnic nationalism in politics. After all, in the United States people of varying ethnic origins live cheek by jowl in relative peace. Within two or three generations of immigration, their ethnic identities are attenuated by cultural assimilation and intermarriage. Surely, things cannot be so different elsewhere."[16] It is these types of optimistic assumptions that underlie much of U.S. international assistance policy geared toward promoting elections and building modern democratic societies and economies in the developing world. These types of assumptions are also implicit in the American belief in globalization and the free exchange of ideas, goods, and education as benefiting all groups and countries. Yet as explored further in this chapter, and indeed throughout this book, we need to ask whether these assumptions are correct. If not, are policy prescriptions based on these assumptions actually enhancing U.S. national security? Are these policies even addressing the key human security issues in the world?

THE CHALLENGE OF CRIMINAL VIOLENCE

For many human beings in the world the most serious threat to their daily lives and physical safety arises not from cultural extremism but from common criminal violence, often associated with illegal drug trafficking, smuggling, and human trafficking. Globalization has empowered not only extremist and terrorist groups and authoritarian leaders but also *criminal* transnational networks of nonstate actors who are primarily motivated by financial gain.[17] In fact, UN law enforcement and drug control officials consider these transnational networks to be one of the major threats to human security, negatively impacting the possibility of development for many in the world.[18] UN experts have even seen linkages between crime syndicates on different continents, such as between East African gangs and drug-related operations in Thailand and Laos, and Mexican drug cartel members engaged in smuggling activities in the Golden Triangle area where Thailand, Laos, and Myanmar join.[19] Not surprisingly, international drug trafficking is viewed as the most serious criminal concern, as it may generate an astounding $400 billion in profits each year, a figure that clearly dwarfs the gross national product of many countries in the world.[20]

Particularly alarming is that criminal drug gangs and terrorist groups are associating, too. The head of the United Nations Drug Agency warned at the end of 2009 that "50 to 60 tonnes of cocaine were trafficked every year across West Africa while another 30 to 35 tonnes of Afghan heroin was being trafficked into East Africa every year." Furthermore, he pointed to criminals, terrorists, and other antigovernment forces in the

Sahel region (a huge area encompassing northern Africa, just south of the Sahara) who were using "resources from the drug trade to fund their operations, purchase equipment and pay foot-soldiers." And according to a high-level U.S. Drug Enforcement Administration official's testimony before the U.S. Congress in March 2010, at least eighteen of the forty-

THINK AGAIN

Globalization Has Minimal Influence on National Security

Although the concept of globalization seems to have attained near-universal scholarly and popular acceptance as a critical phenomenon affecting states' security and the international system, not everyone agrees with this assessment. Realist scholars in particular are prone to argue that powerful countries like the United States actually shape processes affecting the international system such as globalization, and not the other way around. Precisely because these states have more resources, they can resist global pressures that are perceived as unfavorable, while also taking advantage of any favorable trends and promoting them to their benefit.[1] For example, since the United States has long believed that a worldwide free trade system is to its material benefit, it has actively pushed international economic organizations, policies, and use of increasingly robust communications and other technologies to further advance the liberal movement of goods and services across states and regions. And in many instances the United States has actively encouraged the transnational forces of democratization and human rights—especially civil and political rights—because of a widely accepted view that democratic states do not fight one another. In other words, whereas some might paint U.S. actions on behalf of democracy and human rights as being inspired by ideals, others would view it as the United States pursuing a pragmatic strategy to protect its own national security.

1. Norrin M. Ripsman and T. V. Paul, "Globalization and the National Security State: A Framework for Analysis," *International Studies Review* 7, no. 2 (June 2005): 199–227.

four groups labeled as being international terrorists have some connections to transnational drug trafficking. As one specific example, in December 2009 federal prosecutors charged three West Africans with planning to transport tons of cocaine across Africa in league with al Qaeda. This was the first time the U.S. government had made use of a

---

Think Again (*continued*)

Another argument denying much influence to globalization would be to demonstrate that states still devote the vast majority of their defense budgets and related policies, planning, and training to the traditional threats posed by other states or, in some cases, insurgent or extremist groups. For instance, the "United States Department of Defense Fiscal Year 2011 Budget Request" highlighted the traditional and continued U.S. focus on nuclear and conventional weapons systems and personnel.[2] This is further reflected in the large number of United Nations–sponsored peacekeeping operations, which wealthy UN members like the United States support largely to defuse interstate conflicts (or sometimes intrastate wars) and not nonstate human security threats supposedly propelled by globalization.[3] Finally, a multifaceted analysis by well-known security studies scholars Ripsman and Paul found little evidence that states were transforming their national security structures or activities away from traditional state-centered threats to new globalized threats. At most, they concluded that the powerful, stable states were taking note of new security concerns at the margins as an additional, "complementary" security mission rather than a "replacement" for traditional security missions.[4]

---

2. Department of Defense, "United States Department of Defense Fiscal Year 2011 Budget Request," available at http://comptroller.defense.gov/budget.html. Ripsman and Paul's analysis of data also supported the finding that "defense budgets continue to reflect strategic conditions rather than the pressures of globalization" ("Globalization and the National Security State," 220).

3. The state-centric focus of current UN peacekeeping operations is evident at the United Nations Department of Peacekeeping Operations home Web site, www.un.org/en/peacekeeping/currentops.shtml.

4. Ripsman and Paul, "Globalization and the National Security State," 220.

2006 law aimed at punishing drug trafficking linked to terrorism. Most worrisome of all to U.S. authorities is this evidence of an emerging alliance between narcotics traffickers and al Qaeda, which is clearly interested in using drug profits to fuel its terrorist campaign. In fact, since the Taliban was removed from power in Afghanistan in 2001, its continuing efforts to foment insurgency there in spite of U.S. efforts have been increasingly funded by profits made from controlling much of the trade of poppies grown for opium and heroin and smuggled out of the country. According to the U.S. Office of National Drug Control Policy, Afghanistan has essentially become "the exclusive supplier" of this deadly drug.[21]

All governments are naturally concerned about transnational crime, including the United States, which views it as a national security challenge that can weaken the stability and governmental institutions of states, increase corruption, and destabilize commercial markets and the international financial system.[22] Yet a stable and wealthy government like the United States has the capacity to confront this type of challenge and control its most pernicious effects. But in poor, weak states with lawless or ungoverned areas, the actual viability of the government may be threatened, and, ultimately, so may the ability of the nation itself to survive intact. This situation is clearly occurring in states as varied as Afghanistan, El Salvador and Guatemala in Central America, Jamaica in the Caribbean, Yemen in the Persian Gulf, and numerous states in West Africa, such as Nigeria and Guinea-Bissau. Consider the specific situation of El Salvador, where estimates range from 30,000 to 40,000 youths belonging to what some experts term "third-generation gangs," meaning those sophisticated gangs that usually operate in more than one country, or at least have alliances with gangs in other countries, and who are involved in a transnational network of illicit criminal activity.[23] All analysis attributes the majority of El Salvador's extremely high homicide rate of 53 per 100,000 inhabitants to gang activity, which involves not only murders among gang members but also public officials and ordinary citizens—essentially to intimidate the government and its citizens to allow the gangs to operate unhindered.[24] Considering that El Salvador is a poor and weakly institutionalized state, still recovering from years of civil conflict and with limited law enforcement capability, intimidation is certainly feasible.

It is too easy to forget that it is usually individual human beings who bear the direct consequences of criminal violence and insecurity, ranging from being forced to pay for protection to criminal gangs to intimidation, rape, torture, and murder. In the very visible and violent drug war being waged between the Mexican government and various drug cartel families since 2007, it is estimated that at least 28,000 have died, including many civilians—not to mention an extensive number of kidnappings and extortion attempts. Whereas both U.S. and Mexican government officials usually blame all incidents of violence upon the gangs—whether through intragang warfare or the gangs targeting local officials and citizens—a number of reports trace at least some of the violence and human rights abuses to the police or even the 45,000 soldiers who have been deployed to help in the war.[25] Award-winning journalist Charles Bowden's exposé of the violence in Ciudad Juárez, across the border from El Paso, Texas— and rated by many as the most violent city in the world in 2009, with some 2,500 dead—carefully documents the large numbers of civilians killed in suspicious circumstances and the almost total lack of investigation or charges in any of these cases.[26]

However, the realization that this problem of criminal violence is not just Mexican but also concerns U.S. citizens' security became glaringly apparent by at least 2009, especially for Texans and Arizonans. In fact, a Gallup poll in the spring of 2009 indicated that not only were 51 percent of Americans "very concerned" about drug violence in Mexico (with 28 percent being "somewhat concerned"), but the violence in Mexico was rated on a par with concerns over the international threat of North Korean nuclear capabilities and only a few points below Iran's nuclear capabilities and international terrorism. In March 2010 the concerns became personified for many when a rancher in Arizona was murdered, allegedly in connection with Mexican drug smuggling operations in the area. Additionally, local law enforcement officials in Arizona have reported that burglaries and even home invasion robberies by armed Mexican criminals are on the rise.[27]

While the U.S. State Department has issued travel advisories against Americans visiting the border regions of Mexico, even more Mexican immigrants are fleeing to the United States either illegally or in pursuit of political asylum. Police in El Paso, for example, estimate that since 2008 some 30,000 Mexicans have moved across the border into their area. Ominously, the U.S. Justice Department believes that Mexican drug cartels have an established presence throughout the United States, as "the cartels now have operations in at least 230 American cities [in 2009], up from 50 in 2006." In fact, in its largest strike ever against a Mexican drug cartel (La Familia Michoacana), in October 2009 the U.S. Justice Department staged raids in thirty-eight cities and nineteen states across the country, arresting more than 300 alleged members of the cartel.[28]

Clearly, even with all its resources the United States has been unable to stop illegal drugs and criminals from entering the country, or to ensure physical security for its citizens along the Mexican border. Thus, it should not be surprising that the still-developing country of Mexico has been experiencing even more severe problems, along with its neighboring, very poor Central American countries. When organized criminal networks link up to do business together, they may easily overwhelm fragile or failing governments and threaten civic security in entire regions. While the U.S. government has been at pains to declare that Mexico is not a failed or even a failing state,[29] nonetheless in 2010 Mexican president Felipe Calderon warned that the drug traffickers were now attempting to dominate everyone, to defy the state, and were even attempting to replace the state.[30] There are complex political, economic, and social reasons for this vulnerability. But in common with most developing states where public officials are poorly or even intermittently paid, Mexico exhibits the crippling problem of corruption, which further enables criminal activity.

Governmental corruption is one of the most serious problems weakening effective law enforcement and thus affects good governance and stable economic growth in developing states. It impedes the ability to fulfill human security needs ranging from institutionalizing the rule of law to providing effective development assistance and public health needs. Afghanistan is a case in point, where a 2010 UN report found that entrenched corruption in Afghanistan was key to the persistent poverty there, in spite of the country's receiving extensive international aid.[31] Not surprisingly, corruption also breeds resentment among citizens, distrust of governments, in many cases support for vigilante justice and private militia groups and gangs, and in the worst case rebellion and insurgent or terrorist activities against governments. This finding is confirmed when considering how public support for the already struggling Afghan government has been seriously weakened by perceptions of corruption, with a corresponding rise in support for extremist groups like the Taliban. The gravity of the problem was underscored by U.S. Army General Stanley McChrystal, then commanding troops in Afghanistan, when he labeled corruption as a cancer and the greatest threat for the Afghan government. In fact, McChrystal declared that corruption was an even greater threat than the insurgency, because corruption was more "corrosive." These same conclusions have been echoed with regard to the near-failing state of Yemen as the United States has ramped up its assistance to help the ineffective and corrupt Yemeni government overcome the conditions that have enabled al Qaeda extremists to flourish there and threaten U.S. citizens, along with a rebellion and potential secessionist movement.[32]

THE CHALLENGE OF TRANSNATIONAL SOCIAL MOVEMENTS AND CIVIL SOCIETY

Although the analysis here often seems to reflect detrimental effects of globalization on human security, there are undoubtedly positive effects, too. It is important to emphasize that extremists and criminal networks are not the only ones who have reacted to, or taken advantage of, the information and technological advances propelled by globalization. Numerous individuals and groups arising out of civil society—in other words, those unconnected to governments and with generally altruistic motives—have responded in ways that many would view as constructive for human security. In fact, the 2010 *National Security Strategy* labels the increasing influence of these actors as "a distinct opportunity for the United States." For most people human rights groups may be the most widely known example, but the list of more than 3,000 nongovernmental groups that now have consultative status with the United Nations' Economic and Social

CONTEMPORARY CHALLENGE

Transparency International and the Struggle Against Corruption

According to its Web site, "Transparency International, the global civil society organization leading the fight against corruption, brings people together in a powerful worldwide coalition to end the devastating impact of corruption on men, women and children around the world. TI's mission is to create change towards a world free of corruption."[1] Although TI is a global network, it claims some ninety nationally established chapters. National chapters are accredited in three stages via a set of objective standards, and accredited chapters go through a review process every three years. There is an international board of directors with an international secretariat headquartered in Berlin, a global Advisory Council, and senior advisers who range from former presidents of nations to high-level corporate, university, and influential nongovernmental organizations.[2] All members are motivated by consensual beliefs, such as corruption both causes poverty and is a major obstacle to overcoming poverty. Furthermore, TI members understand that corruption undermines democracy, the rule of law, and effective governance.

Transparency International publishes an annual *Corruption Perceptions Index* (*CPI*), which measures and rates public-sector corruption for almost all countries in the world. This is achieved by compiling a composite index that "draws on 13 different expert and business surveys, to measure perceived levels of public sector corruption in a given country." The *CPI* scores countries on a scale from 0—highly corrupt—to 10, meaning the country is very clean. It is interesting to note that no country has received a perfect 10; for 2009 New Zealand and Denmark had the highest scores, at 9.4 and 9.3, respectively, while the United States was ranked 19

---

1. Transparency International Web site, www.transparency.org/about_us. Transparency International defines corruption as "*the abuse of entrusted power for private gain.* It hurts everyone whose life, livelihood or happiness depends on the integrity of people in a position of authority" (emphasis in original).

2. Transparency International, *Transparency International Annual Report, 2009* (Berlin: Transparency International–International Secretariat, 2010).

Contemporary Challenge (*continued*)

with a score of 7.5.[3] The fact that Transparency International's deliberately non-partisan political scores and analyses are highly regarded is reflected by the fact that numerous governments, other organizations, and scholars cite their findings as credible. Table 2.1 shows the twenty states perceived as most highly corrupt in the public sector for 2009.

TABLE 2.1: STATES PERCEIVED AS MOST
HIGHLY CORRUPT (PUBLIC SECTOR) IN 2009
*State was in top 20 most corrupt for 2008

1. Somalia*
2. Afghanistan*
3. Myanmar*
4. Sudan*
5. Iraq*
6. Chad*
7. Uzbekistan*
8. Turkmenistan*
9. Iran
10. Haiti*
11. Guinea
12. Equatorial Guinea*
13. Burundi
14. Venezuela*
15. Kyrgyzstan*
16. Guinea-Bissau*
17. Democratic Republic of Congo*
18. Republic of the Congo/Congo-Brazzaville*
19. Angola
20. Tajikstan

Source: ADAPTED from Transparency International Annual Report 2009, Corruption Perceptions Index 2009. *Copyright 2010 Transparency International: the global coalition against corruption. Used with permission. For more information, visit www.transparency.org.*

Clearly, the bottom twenty countries are diverse and range within Africa, Asia, and Latin America and the Caribbean. Yet it is significant to note that among the top-ten countries are three where the United States has been directly involved in conflict and nation building—Afghanistan, Iraq, and Haiti (arguably Somalia, the top perceived corrupt country, could be added to this list, although U.S. efforts there have been much more limited and intermittent). With the exception of Iran and Venezuela, almost all of these countries are quite poor with very low development levels.

---

3. Ibid., 48.

Image 2.1—Mayan women in Guatemala. Photo credit: USAID.

Council shows their wide diversity.[33] As one significant example, Transparency International (TI) is a nongovernmental group of experts that was formed in 1993 specifically to publicize, and to attempt to reduce, corruption within governmental and other sectors. The group's work is potentially very significant for enhancing the good governance that is so central to ensuring human security.

The influence of a group like Transparency International is multiplied even further when it links together with other groups, foundations, and individuals from civil society in the phenomenon of transnational "social movements." These decentralized movements are usually motivated by perceived injustices, ranging from abuse of human rights, corrupt governments, and the prostitution and trafficking of women and children to unfair labor practices of multinational corporations and environmental concerns. As one specific example, indigenous tribal groups in Brazil and Ecuador have received financial, moral, and legal support and advice from many outside groups as they protest and in some cases wage legal proceedings against their ancestral lands being threatened and exploited by developers and oil companies. Perhaps the most prominent example of how globalization has aided in improving human security for individuals, groups, and even nations is represented by the successes of the human rights movement.

The bedrock Universal Declaration of Human Rights (UDHR) was passed by the newly formed United Nations General Assembly in 1948, and again affirmed by the United Nations with these words at a sixtieth anniversary celebration in 2008:

> Many things can be said about the Universal Declaration of Human Rights (UDHR). It is the foundation of international human rights law, the first universal statement on the basic principles of inalienable human rights, and a common standard of

achievement for all peoples and all nations. . . . Drafted by representatives of all regions and legal traditions, the UDHR has stood
the test of time and resisted attacks based on "relativism." The Declaration and its core values, including non-discrimination, equality, fairness and universality, apply to everyone, everywhere and
always.[34]

Over the decades certain states (such as the United States), intergovernmental organizations (such as the Inter-American Commission on
Human Rights), and progressively more and more nongovernmental
groups (such as Amnesty International) and individual activists (such
as Holocaust survivor Elie Wiesel) have established an influential
transnational human rights movement in an attempt to realize the
UDHR goals. For many, the fact that almost all governments now find it
necessary to at least publicly proclaim support for human rights is a signal victory, regardless of the abuses that many of those governments still
carry out. Yet for most human rights advocates, achieving true human
security for all citizens of the world would be the ultimate realization of
human rights. Thus, not only must individual civil and political rights
be protected, but equally such rights as the right to food, shelter, a job, a
peaceful existence, and respect for one's cultural identity must be available to all people.

Nonetheless, even though the UDHR declares the catalog of human
rights to be globally applicable to all people, some governments, national
and religious leaders, and scholars and policy experts continue to disagree
about the universality of certain rights. In fact, the United States has long
prioritized what are often termed the "first generation" of political and
civil rights, which protect the individual from government abuses such
as torture, arbitrary arrest, and limitations on freedom of speech and the
press. These rights are clearly central to democratic governance, always
a central U.S. value. In the past, Americans have been prone to discount
a "second generation" of economic and social rights, such as the "right"
to a job, housing, and medical care—provided by the state, if necessary.
This dichotomy was particularly marked during the cold war era of the
twentieth century when the United States and its "Free World" allies

waged an ideological battle on behalf of democracy and individual liberties, as the communist and socialist world under the Soviet Union and China discounted individual rights and promoted their citizens' enjoyment of greater economic and social benefits. Viewpoints on human rights became even more complicated in the 1970s–1980s as the developing, or "Third World," countries began to press the case for a proposed "third generation" of people's collective, or group, rights to development and protection of cultural and indigenous rights.

Significantly, with the end of the cold war in the 1990s the United States began to publicly acknowledge the importance of economic, social, and cultural factors to sustain and strengthen democratic governance and freedoms. The notion that human rights are actually interdependent with democracy became increasingly accepted. Most recently under the Obama administration there has been an explicit recognition that economic opportunity is a human right, as equitable economic and social development is crucial to effective democracy and its freedoms.[35]

However, while the United States may have broadened its conception of human rights, this does not mean that every country in the world agrees with the conception that all human rights are universal and equal in importance. In fact, an important perspective argues that human rights are "relativistic," that is, human rights are culturally constrained, whether by religion or ethnic or historical traditions. As Callaway and Matthews point out, many developing states believe that the UDHR is really a Western perspective on human rights and that it marginalizes non-Western views, so it cannot be considered universal. In this regard, it should be noted that in 1948 most developing states in Africa and Asia were still colonies and thus were not represented at the United Nations to formulate and sign the declaration, so their criticisms about Western values may have some merit. Certainly, developing countries have expressed some legitimate concerns related to cultural values and the difficulties in importing Western traditions and values without considering all the societal ramifications. Yet one of the problems with arguing that human rights are culturally bound is that this claim can be used by a group holding power as a pretext for denying rights to some peoples and privileging certain groups over others, and in the worst case for justifying ethnic cleans-

Image 2.2—Women meeting to discuss education in Yemen. Photo credit: USAID.

ing and genocide against others. President Obama warned against these tendencies when he visited Ghana in 2009, proclaiming that "we all have many identities—of tribe and ethnicity; of religion and nationality. But defining oneself in opposition to someone who belongs to a different tribe or who worships a different prophet has no place in the 21st century. Africa's diversity should be a source of strength, not a cause for division."[36] Unfortunately, this viewpoint is not necessarily shared by at least some nations and groups, as differences continue to poison relations between various ethnic groups (such as Hutus and Tutsis in Rwanda and Burundi) and religious groups (such as Sunni and Shiite groups in Saudi Arabia and Iraq). Yet nowhere is this tendency to highlight differences more evident, and systematic in nature, than in the case of women.

While most U.S. citizens are familiar with the abuse of Afghan women under the extremist version of Islam practiced by the Taliban, the number of ways in which culture has been used to stymie women's human rights and human security is legion. Discrimination and abuse may be based on national and ethnic values, religious beliefs and norms, or traditional practices, ranging from prohibiting women to work outside the home, inherit property on their own, vote, or run for office, to even female genital mutilation.[37] Probably the most egregious violation of women's rights, however, occurs in conjunction with practices such as human trafficking and the use of sexual violence against women as a deliberate policy in conflict situations. The statistics on the latter are truly staggering. According to the United Nations, "in Rwanda, up to half a million women were raped during the 1994 genocide. The numbers were approximately 60,000 in the Balkans conflicts of the 1990s; in Sierra Leone, the number of incidents of war-related sexual violence among internally displaced women from 1991 to 2001 was approximately 64,000."[38] This problem has continued to expand in the twenty-first century in war-torn areas. During her visit to the Democratic Republic of the Congo in August 2009, Secretary of State Clinton met with representatives of an estimated 200,000 victims of sexual violence in the conflicted country, and later that year she was a key mover of the campaign at the United Nations Security Council to have the use of rape in conflict situations officially declared "a threat to peace and security."[39]

Considering just these few examples of violations of women's human rights, it should not be surprising to find that as early as 1979 the United Nations General Assembly believed it was necessary to adopt the specific Convention on the Elimination of All Forms of Discrimination Against Women. The convention aims to achieve "equality between women and men through ensuring women's equal access to, and equal opportunities in, political and public life. . . . The Convention is the only human rights treaty which affirms the reproductive rights of women and targets culture and tradition as influential forces shaping gender roles and family relations."[40] Clearly, women's access to political and public life is considered essential to effective democratic governance, and there has been some progress toward that goal even in what would generally be considered more traditional societies, where women can often vote. However, it is probably fair to say that cultural practices and expectations concerning a woman's role in the family and society continue to be much more resistant to change. This aspect is of great significance because of increasing evi-

Image 2.3—A nine-year-old girl makes bricks in India. Photo credit: U.S. Department of State.

dence documenting that women are the key to successful development and to overcoming poverty, as it is generally women who ensure food, education, and health care for the children in a family (considered further in the next chapter). Human security cannot be achieved without consistent progress in improving women's rights. Confirming this fact, Secretary of State Clinton has made women's issues an international priority, creating the position of "Ambassador-at-Large for Global Women's Issues" to fully integrate women's rights into U.S. human rights and foreign policy. And at the international level, in 2010 the UN General Assembly unanimously approved the creation of UN Women, a new umbrella organization to consolidate and strengthen the efforts of several smaller, often fragmented UN agencies dealing with women's issues.[41]

It is worth asking at this point, why are these disputes about human rights and cultural issues important for U.S. national security and human security in general? First, it is undeniable that human rights constitute an important international issue that receives consistent media attention in this age of globalization. Perceived abuses of human rights can be detrimental to a country's influence and policy options, as the United States

POLICY SPOTLIGHT

Modern-Day Slavery: Trafficking and Exploitation of Women

While many simply label human trafficking and exploitation as the modern-day equivalent of slavery, the United Nations specifically defines human trafficking as "the recruitment, transportation, transfer, harbouring or receipt of persons, by means of the threat or use of force or other forms of coercion, of abduction, of fraud, of deception . . . for the purpose of exploitation."[1] The major forms of trafficking include forced labor, involuntary domestic servitude, debt bondage among migrant laborers, sex trafficking, bonded labor and forced child labor, and child soldiers. The UN's International Labor Organization cites the following estimated statistics: there are 12.3 million adults and children at any time in forced labor and sexual servitude; there are 1.39 million victims of sex trafficking, both national and transnational; and 56 percent of forced labor victims are women and girls.[2]

Clearly, women are not the only affected persons, but women and girls certainly form the majority of those trafficked and exploited, whether because they are the most susceptible to intimidation and coercion or because so many of the victims are trafficked for sexual exploitation. Globally, trafficking is estimated to have a trade value of some $32 billion a year, and with the global financial crisis beginning in 2008, there have been expectations of increased human trafficking. In 2009 the U.S. State Department singled out the contracting global economy

1. Megan McAdams, "Modern Day Slavery in Mexico and the United States," Council on Hemispheric Affairs report, December 21, 2009, available at www.coha.org/modern-day-slavery-in-mexico-and-the-united-states/.

2. U.S. State Department Bureau of Public Affairs, "Trafficking in Persons: Coercion in a Time of Economic Crisis," *Fact Sheet*, June 16, 2009.

Policy Spotlight (*continued*)

and an increasingly desperate supply of job seekers as ideal conditions for more forced labor and sexual exploitation of women to occur.[3] Analysis of a major trafficking hub in Nairobi, Kenya, in early 2010 seemed to bear this out, as women fleeing conflict and deepening poverty from Somalia, Ethiopia, Eritrea, and Kenya were essentially sold to move on to other countries such as South Africa. Although these women were undoubtedly hoping for a better life, it is more likely that they would be subjected to forced labor and sexual exploitation.[4]

Since at least 2000 the United States has placed emphasis on this multidimensional issue, with the U.S. Congress first mandating reports be published on the topic at that time. As spelled out in the *Trafficking in Persons Report, 2009*, the current U.S. approach "highlights the 'three P's'—prosecution, protection, and prevention. But a victim-centered approach to trafficking also requires attention to the 'three R's'—rescue, rehabilitation, and reintegration. Sharing the best practices in these areas will encourage governments to go beyond the initial rescue of victims and restore to them dignity and the hope of productive lives." Ambassador Luis CdeBaca, director of the Office to Monitor and Combat Trafficking in Persons at the State Department, noted that for 2010 his office would be funding about $20 million worth of programs aimed at law enforcement training, public awareness campaigns, and shelters to protect those rescued from traffickers.[5]

---

3. Abdullahi Jamaa, "Kenya: Slave Trade Booms as Poverty Bites," *Daily Nation on the Web*, allAfrica.com, January 6, 2010, available at http://allafrica.com/stories/printable/201001060958.html; U.S. State Department Bureau of Public Affairs, "Trafficking in Persons."

4. Jamaa, "Kenya."

5. U.S. Department of State, Office to Monitor and Combat Trafficking in Persons, *Trafficking in Persons Report, 2009*, available at www.state.gov.g/tip/rls/tiprpt/2009/123123.htm; Luis CdeBaca, "The Role of the United States in Combating Human Trafficking," presentation at the Center for American Progress, Washington, DC, May 12, 2010, available at www.state.gov/g/tip/rls/rm2010/141728.

found to its cost with well-publicized incidents of inmate abuse at Abu Ghraib Prison in Iraq. And these incidents were particularly harmful to the U.S. image as they seemed to belittle Muslim prisoners in ways contemptuous of their religious traditions. Second, it is difficult to deny the linkage between human rights, peace, and security. When individuals, peoples, and governments feel that their rights are protected, they feel secure and have little inclination to turn to violence and war. In fact, the 2010 U.S. *National Security Strategy* explicitly states that the United States supports governments that respect democracy and human rights because those governments "are ultimately more stable, successful, and secure."[42] Additionally, the United States will face fewer requirements to intervene on a humanitarian basis if rights are not being abused in various regions. Finally, U.S. policy has long assumed that the presence of democracies within the international system promotes U.S. national security, because democracies do not go to war with one another.[43] As institutionalized democracies can exist only if they respect the human rights of their citizens, this provides additional motivation for promoting human rights on a global scale. And while it is tempting to be cynical, Americans have consistently shown concern for supporting human rights and alleviating suffering around the world, whether through official U.S. government agencies or via the widespread network of countless human rights and humanitarian organizations.

CONCLUSION

The fact that human beings identify themselves in a number of ways beyond their citizenship in a particular state is a critically important piece of understanding why so many challenges today are transnational in scope. As this chapter has underscored, the fundamental attachment that we all have to our traditions and cultural identity must be grasped in order to comprehend why globalization can provoke a serious backlash and enhance the possibilities for conflict, terrorism, and human rights abuses. As also explored, these types of human security challenges may be deliberately exploited by extremist groups to further destabilize weak governments or by authoritarian leaders to legitimize the use of repression and violence against opposition or minority groups so as to remain in power. Unfortunately, repressive governments from China to Iran have learned how to monitor and block access to the Internet and other news sources. Too, these global technological advances are leveraged by transnational criminal networks to take advantage of fragile state institutions and further corrupt already struggling governments while threatening the everyday security of citizens. Thus, governments' capacity to abuse their citizens are strengthened at the same time as governments' abilities to protect their citizens are weakened.

On the other hand, the processes of globalization—to include the spread of information and the ease of international communication around the world—can equally lead to positive results. The record of human rights successes over the past sixty years has been possible only through the ability to link an international community of individual citizens and activists, scholars and lawyers, domestic human rights groups, international human rights organizations, foundations, key states, and the United Nations. And it is because of the exponential increase in availability of data that groups like Transparency International have been able to track, analyze, and publicize the pernicious problem of corruption. As the *National Security Strategy* declared in 2010, the United States has "an interest in a just and sustainable international order that can foster collective action to confront common challenges . . . because without such an international order, the forces of instability and disorder will challenge global security."[44] We believe that without such an order, ultimately human security challenges cannot be met nor human security concerns addressed.

To Learn More

In his highly popular book *The World Is Flat: A Brief History of the Twenty-first Century* (New York: Picador/Farrar, Straus, and Giroux, 2007), Pulitzer Prize–winning journalist Thomas L. Friedman stresses the positive technological changes of globalization, arguing that "flattening" of the world is constantly accelerating, equalizing the playing field and empowering more and more individuals in the world to collaborate and succeed.

In *Illicit: How Smugglers, Traffickers, and Copycats Are Highjacking the Global Economy* (New York: Anchor Books/Random House, 2006),

Moisés Naím examines the negative effects of globalization that increasingly enables criminal actors to enrich themselves by breaking the rules and "all the procedures that nations employ to organize commerce, protect their citizens, raise revenues, and enforce moral codes."

For more critical analysis about the often controversial topic of globalization, view the nongovernmental Global Policy Forum's Web site on many aspects of globalization: www.globalpolicy.org/globalization.html.

Visit the World Economic Forum's Web site (www.weforum.org/en/index .htm) to get a sense of an extremely influential business-oriented organization that is truly global in scale and objectives, as they strive "towards a world-class corporate governance system where values are as important a basis as rules. Our motto is 'entrepreneurship in the global public interest.'"

Review the Universal Declaration of Human Rights, adopted by the United Nations General Assembly on December 10, 1948, at www.un .org/en/documents/udhr/.

Contrast the African (Banjul) Charter on Human and People's Rights, adopted by the Organization of African Unity in 1981, to understand how culture and historical traditions may produce different conceptions and priorities in terms of human rights. It is available online through the University of Minnesota's Human Rights Library at www1.umn.edu/humanrts/ instree/z1afchar.htm.

Scan the United Nations' Office of Drugs and Crime Web site at www .unodc.org/ to get a sense of the scope and scale of international and transnational crime, ranging from corruption and drugs to money laundering and human trafficking.

The group Anti-Slavery International calls itself the oldest human rights organization in existence, dating its roots to the Anti-Slavery Society formed by British abolitionists in 1839. Today the group continues to work with other allies to fight slavery worldwide—whether defined as "debt bondage, forced labour, forced marriage, child slavery, human trafficking and descent based slavery." View their projects at www.anti slavery.org/english/default.aspx.

The U.S. Department of State has been publishing annual *Country Reports on Human Rights Practices* since 1999. The reports focus on internationally recognized individual, civil, political, and worker rights. Scan the reports at www.state.gov/g/drl/rls/hrrpt.

For a disturbing chronicle of how globalization has contributed to the carnage of drug-related violence and murder, and the destruction of local government and law enforcement capabilities, read award-winning journalist Charles Bowden's *Murder City: Ciudad Juárez and the Global Economy's New Killing Fields* (New York: Nation Books, 2010).

Rhonda L. Callaway and Elizabeth G. Matthews analyze the important question of whether U.S. foreign assistance really helps to improve human rights around the world or whether it is merely another foreign policy tool, in *Strategic U.S. Foreign Assistance: The Battle Between Human Rights and National Security* (Burlington, VT: Ashgate, 2008).

Notes

1. Friedman, *Lexus and Olive Tree*, 9 (see chap. 1, n. 9).

2. Barack Obama, "Remarks of President Barack Obama: 'Responsibility for Our Common Future' Address to the United Nations General Assembly," September 23, 2009, New York, available at http://usun.state.gov/briefing/statements/2009/september/129519.htm.

3. Gallup, "Americans See Newer Threats on Par with Ongoing Conflicts," April 6, 2010, available at www.gallup.com/poll/117292/Americans-Newer-Threats-Par-Ongoing-Conflicts.aspx.

4. Montgomery McFate defines *culture* as "those norms, values, institutions and modes of thinking in a given society that survive change and remain meaningful to successive generations" ("The Military Utility of Understanding Adversary Culture," *Joint Force Quarterly* 38 [3rd Quarter 2005]: 48n4 [quoting Adda Bozeman, *Strategic Intelligence and Statecraft* (New York: Brassey's, 1992), 57]).

5. RAND News Release, "Effective Police Work, Lack of Muslim Support Limits Danger from Homegrown Jihadists in America," May 5, 2010, available at www.rand.org/news/press/2010/05/05.

6. See the concerns about Somali American youths disappearing from their homes in Minnesota to go fight with al Qaeda elements in Somalia and then potentially return to launch attacks in the United States (Dina Temple Raston, "FBI Sheds Light on Missing Somali-Americans," on *All Things Considered*, March 11, 2009, available at http://www.npr.org/templates/story/story.php?storyId=101751571).

7. Sebastian Rotella, "U.S. Sees Homegrown Muslim Extremism as Rising Threat," Latimes.com, December 7, 2009, available at www.latimes.com/news/nations-and-world-la-na-us-radicalization7-2009dec07.0.2004. See also Scott Shane, "New Incidents Test Immunity to Terrorism on U.S. Soil," *New York Times*, December 12, 2009, available at www.nytimes.com/2009/12/12/us/12assess.html.

8. Barack Obama, *National Security Strategy* (Washington, DC: White House, May 2010), 35; Samuel Huntington, "The Clash of Civilizations?" *Foreign Affairs* 72, no. 3 (1993): 24.

9. For example, Reveron and Murer's detailed studies of numerous conflicts concluded, "The conflicts often 'linked' [by culture] do not represent any global struggle against the West and their connections to one another are spurious at best. There are real economic and political reasons for the conflicts" (Derek S. Reveron and Jeffrey Stevenson Murer, *Flashpoints in the War on Terrorism* [New York: Routledge, 2006], xiv).

10. Friedman also notes that globalization can produce "a powerful backlash from those brutalized or left behind by this new system" (9).

11. Adam Nossiter and Sharon Otterman, "Scores Die as Sect Fights Nigeria Police," *New York Times*, July 29, 2009, available at www.nytimes.com/2009/07/29/world/africa/29nigeria.html; U.S. Department of State, "Secretary's Remarks: On Camera Group Interview with Nashim Zehra of Dunya TV et al.," November 20, 2009, in *Daily Digest Bulletin*, November 21, 2009.

12. Friedman, *Lexus and Olive Tree*, 336.

13. RAND News Release, May 5, 2010.

14. Charlie Savage, "U.S. Indicts 14 Accused of Supporting Terrorist Group in Somalia," *New York Times*, August 5, 2010, available at www.nytimes.com/2010/08/06/us/06terror.html?sq=terrorist_group_somalia&st.

15. Tristan McConnell, "West Warns That Somalia Is Becoming a Haven for International Terrorists," *Times/Timesonline,* December 21, 2009, available at www.timesonline.co.uk/tol/news/world/africa/article6963442.

16. Jerry Z. Muller, "Us and Them: The Enduring Power of Ethnic Nationalism," *Foreign Affairs* 87, no. 2 (2008): 18.

17. Note that at least some of these groups are seeking profits in order to fund an ethnic-based struggle for independence, such as the Wa and Kachin ethnic armies in Myanmar who cultivate and traffic opium for heroin. Others such as the Taliban in Afghanistan have become involved in opium poppies and heroin at least in part to fund their religiously based struggle against the government.

18. United Nations Office on Drugs and Crime, "UNODC and Organized Crime," available at www.unodc.org/unodc/en/organized-crime/index.html?ref =menuside.

19. Thomas Fuller, "U.N. Says Opium Trade Is Expanding in Myanmar," *New York Times*, December 15, 2009, available at www.nytimes.com/2009/12/ 15/world/asia/15drugs.html.

20. Anthony P. Placido, Assistant Administrator for Intelligence, United States Drug Enforcement Administration, Statement Before the House Oversight and Government Reform Subcommittee on National Security and Foreign Affairs, March 3, 2010, "Transnational Drug Enterprises (Part II): Threats to Global Stability and U.S. Policy Responses," available at www.justice.gov/ dea/pubs/cngrtest/ct030310.pdf.

21. "Africa Drug Trade 'Fuels Terror,'" BBC News, December 9, 2009, available at http://news.bbc.co.uk/go/pr/fr/-/2/hi/africa/8402820.stm; Placido, "Transnational Drug Enterprises (Part II)"; William K. Rashbaum, "U.S. Charges 3 Malians in Drug Plot," *New York Times*, December 19, 2009, available at www.nytimes.com/2009/12/19/world/africa/19narco.html; Office of National Drug Control Policy, "Source Countries and Drug Transit Zones: Afghanistan," available at www.ondcp.gov/international/afghanistan.html.

22. Obama, *National Security Strategy*, 49.

23. See Hal Brands, "Third-Generation Gangs and Criminal Insurgency in Latin America," *Small Wars Journal* (2009); and Max Manwaring, *A Contemporary Challenge to State Sovereignty: Gangs and Other Illicit Transnational Criminal Organizations in Central America: El Salvador, Mexico, Jamaica, and Brazil* (Carlisle Barracks, PA: Strategic Studies Institute, 2007).

24. Brands, "Third-Generation Gangs"; Clare Ribando Seelke, "El Salvador: Political, Economic, and Social Conditions and U.S. Relations," *Congressional Research Service Report for Congress*, January 21, 2010.

25. For example, a U.S. State Department report prepared for Congress in 2009 noted that human rights complaints filed against soldiers had increased from 182 in 2006 to 1,230 by 2008 (cited in Ginger Thompson and Marc Lacey, "Mexico Drug Fight Fuels Complaints," *New York Times*, August 19, 2009, available at www.nytimes.com/2009/08/19/world/americas/19mexico .html?).

26. Charles Bowden, *Murder City: Ciudad Juárez and the Global Economy's New Killing Fields* (New York: Nation Books, 2010).

27. Gallup, "Most Americans Concerned About Mexico's Drug Violence," April 3, 2009, available at http://www.gallup.com/poll/117271/Americans-Con cerned-Mexico-Drug-Violence.aspx; Erin Kelly, "Napolitano: Decision Soon on Border Mission," *Air Force Times*, April 21, 2010, available at www.airforce times.com/news/2010/04/gns_napolitano_guard_border_042110/.

28. James C. McKinley Jr., "Fleeing Drug Violence, Mexicans Pour into U.S.," *New York Times*, April 17, 2010, available at www.nytimes.com/2010/04/18/ us/18border.html?; Martin Kaste, "Cartels Fueling Violence in Mexico Take Root in U.S.," National Public Radio, March 26, 2009, available at www.npr .org/templates/story/story.php?storyId=102322570; James C. McKinley Jr., "U.S. Arrests Hundreds in Raids on Drug Cartel," *New York Times*, October 23, 2009, available at www.nytimes.com/2009/10/23/us/23bust.html?.

29. In her visit to Mexico in March 2009, U.S. secretary of state Clinton in sisted that Mexico was not a failed state, but stated that it "faced a 'public safety challenge'" (Mark Landler, "Clinton Reassures Mexico About Its Image," *New York Times*, March 27, 2009, available at www.nytimes.com/2009/03/27/world/ americas/27mexico.html).

30. Tracy Wilkinson, "Calderon Delivers Blunt View of Drug Cartels' Sway in Mexico," *Los Angeles Times*, August 4, 2010, available at www.latimes.com/ news/nationworld/world/la-fg-mexico-calderon-20100805,0,3749476.story.

31. Reuters, "Corruption Deepens Poverty in Afghanistan—U.N. Report," *New York Times*, March 30, 2010, available at wwwnytimes.com/reuters/2010/ 03/30/world/international-uk-afghan-un-rights.html?.

32. Donna Miles, "McChrystal Urges Troops to Serve as Role Models," American Forces Press Service, March 2, 2010, available at www.defense.gov/ news/newsarticle.aspx?id=58150; Assistant Secretary of State Jeffrey D. Feltman and Ambassador Robert F. Godec, Remarks at U.S. House Committee on For eign Affairs, "Yemen on the Brink: Implications for U.S. Policy," February 3, 2010, *U.S. Department of State Daily Digest Bulletin*, February 4, 2010.

33. Obama, *National Security Strategy*, 13; United Nations Department of Economic and Social Affairs, "Consultative Status with ECOSOC and Other Accreditations" Web site, http://esango.un.org/civilsociety/displayConsultative StatusSearch.do?method=search&sessionCheck=false.

34. United Nations Human Rights Web site, www.un.org/events/human-rights/2007/udhr.shtml.

35. Obama, *National Security Strategy*, 5.

36. Rhonda L. Callaway and Elizabeth G. Matthews, *Strategic U.S. Foreign Assistance: The Battle Between Human Rights and National Security* (Burlington, VT: Ashgate, 2008), 17; Barack Obama, "Remarks by the President to the Ghanaian Parliament," July 11, 2009, available at www.whitehouse.gov/the_press_office/Remarks-by-the-President-to-the-Ghanaian-Parliament/.

37. In certain parts of Africa the centuries-old practice of cutting off a young girl's clitoris—female genital mutilation—has been viewed as important to ensure virginity and an appropriate attitude for married women. "According to the UN, about three million girls each year in Africa are at risk of genital mutilation, with more than 91 million girls and women living with the consequences of the procedure. These include bleeding, shock, infections and a higher rate of death for new-born babies" ("Uganda Bans Female Circumcision," BBC News, December 10, 2009, available at http://news.bbc.co.uk/go/pr/fr/-/2/hi/africa/8406940.stm).

38. U.S. Department of State, "United Nations Security Council to Adopt Resolution to Protect Women in Conflict Situations," Press Release, September 30, 2009, available at www.state.gov/r/pa/prs/ps/2009/sept/129997.htm.

39. Howard LaFranchi, "Clinton to Chair Security Council Resolution on Sexual Violence," *Christian Science Monitor*, September 30, 2009, available at www.csmonitor.com/2009/0930/po2s12-usfp.html.

40. United Nations Division for the Advancement of Women, Department of Economic and Social Affairs, "Convention on the Elimination of All Forms of Discrimination Against Women" Web site, www.un.org/womenwatch/daw/cedaw/.

41. U.S. Department of State, "Biography: Melanne Verveer, Ambassador-at-Large for Global Women's Issues," available at www.state.gov/r/pa/ei/biog/122075.htm; Neil MacFarquhar, "A U.N. Agency for Women? Yes! But Those Names . . . ," *New York Times*, July 2, 2010, available at www.nytimes.com/2010/07/03/world/03nations.html.

42. Obama, *National Security Strategy*, 37.

43. Scholarly support for the thesis that democracies do not fight one another—the "democratic peace theory"—has steadily increased. Although at this point scholars may disagree on why this is the case (institutions, norms, and the like), the theory itself is widely accepted among most scholars and, importantly, U.S. policy makers and citizens.

44. Obama, *National Security Strategy*, 40.

3

Economic Security

*The United States has an interest in working with our allies
to help the world's poorest countries grow into productive
and prosperous economies governed by capable,
democratic, and accountable state institutions. We will
ensure a greater and more deliberate focus on a global
development agenda across the United States Government,
from policy analysis through policy implementation. We
are increasing our foreign assistance, expanding our
investments in effective multilateral development
institutions, and leveraging the engagement of others to
share the burden.*

—PRESIDENT BARACK OBAMA,
NATIONAL SECURITY STRATEGY, MAY 2010

Fewer than twenty years separate the decision by the United States to
lead a United Nations–sanctioned humanitarian intervention to assist
starving Somalis because it was the right thing to do and current U.S. intervention efforts to stabilize and develop Afghanistan because national
security interests require it.[1] In fact, perceptions about the potential threat
posed by global poverty—and the importance of equitable development
for global stability and security—have progressed dramatically beyond
the humanitarian ideal of providing international assistance to poor

countries to feed the starving or to assisting people to rebuild after a natural disaster. It is plausible to argue that initially humanitarian and development assistance was given by governments, foundations, and religious institutions for mainly altruistic reasons. However, by the time the United Nations was founded after World War II, the preamble of the United Nations Charter recognized the necessity "to promote social progress and better standards of life in larger freedom" and the need "to employ international machinery for the promotion of the economic and social advancement of all peoples" as a necessary element to avoid another world war. This security-based rationale was soon augmented by a moral rationale that views the right to development as part of a growing catalog of human rights that all people are entitled to solely by virtue of being human beings. As the United Nations Development Programme declared in 2009, "Human development is a development paradigm that . . . is about creating an environment in which people can develop their potential and lead productive, creative lives in accord with their needs and interests. People are the real wealth of nations."[2] This explanation points to a third, specifically economic, rationale for concern over the economic security of people: the belief that the international economic system will be most prosperous if all states and their citizens are able to participate fully in today's globalized economy. For the United States, the economic success generated by developing countries translates into gains from trade and investment with those countries. Additionally, poor developing countries will never be able to repay their huge debts to the rich states if they do not experience some level of development, and this would further weaken the global financial system and the numerous banks that hold those countries' loans.[3] This last point was reinforced for many in light of the painful global recession that made itself felt by the end of 2008.

All three of these rationales are reflected in the U.S. *National Security Strategy* and are seen as key to advancing American security, prosperity, and values. This chapter illustrates the connection between those themes and the multifaceted problem of providing economic security needs for all through equitable and sustainable development. Whereas in the past authoritarian and expansionist regimes were usually considered the greatest threats to human security, today it is weak, poor, undeveloped states. Bad actors can find refuge in these weak or failing states as a base of operations, whether it is al Qaeda terrorists in Afghanistan, Somalia, or Yemen or drug trafficking gangs in many African and Latin American countries. In turn, these actors further destabilize states as they prey upon weak governments and the most vulnerable populations.

To better understand the rationale for the current international consensus on the importance of meeting economic security needs, it is useful to briefly summarize the evolution, and expansion, of the concept of development—including its particular relevance for the United States and within the UN system. Next, development efforts are examined in the context of two key interrelated challenges that must be resolved in order to facilitate not only development but also security and stability in the world—poverty and bad governance in weak and failing states. It is no exaggeration to claim that inequitable development is a bedrock issue that ultimately generates national security issues on its own while it fatally undermines achieving human security.

ECONOMIC SECURITY AND U.S. NATIONAL SECURITY

Historically, the U.S. government and the American people have taken pride in assisting other countries and in delivering humanitarian assistance to those in need, based in large part on the United States' view of itself as a generous society playing a beneficial role in the international community—a shining city on a hill.[4] Significantly, this type of belief has not necessarily been tied to a conviction that foreign or international assistance (also termed official development assistance, or ODA) would increase U.S. security. The specific linkage between international assistance and national security became explicit later in the twentieth century. Just eleven months prior to the United States' entry into World War II in 1941, President Franklin Roosevelt gave a speech to the U.S. Congress, which later came to be termed the "Four Freedoms" speech. In that speech Roosevelt pointed out that "this is no time for any of us to stop thinking about the social and economic problems which are the root cause of the social revolution which is today a supreme factor in the world." He also made it

Image 3.1—Disaster assistance in Bangladesh. Photo credit: USAID.

clear that a more secure world would be founded upon four freedoms, the third of which was "freedom from want—which, translated into world terms, means economic understandings which will secure to every nation a healthy peacetime life for its inhabitants—everywhere in the world."[5]

The relationship between a peaceful world and a prosperous world was further advanced in the immediate aftermath of World War II. Influential statesmen such as George C. Marshall recognized that the U.S. example would be easier to emulate for those nations that were able to achieve a certain level of development, and thus were able to provide both peace and prosperity to their citizens.[6] Foreseeing the appeal that socialism and communism posed to the exhausted and desperate societies of war-devastated Europe after years of conflict, Marshall advocated an expansive foreign aid program in 1947 to help rebuild the continent and restore hope in democracy and capitalism. The resulting Marshall Plan is given much of the credit for enabling Western Europe to develop prosperous economies (aid under the plan would amount to more than $500 billion today as a percentage of U.S. national income, which compares to about $20 billion for international assistance in 2010).[7] Only a few years after the Marshall Plan, the utility of international assistance as a specific tool to enhance U.S. national security became formalized. The Foreign Assistance Act became law in 1961, and the U.S. Agency for International Development (USAID) was created by executive order. USAID's own Web site declares that U.S. international assistance has always supported the two foreign policy objectives of spreading democracy and free trade while helping individual citizens of the developing world.[8]

The rationale for international assistance, based on a combination of U.S. values *and* interests, gained strength as the cold war ended in the 1990s and with it the United States' policy to support governments that were anticommunist but not necessarily democratic or committed to their citizens' needs. In fact, this period coincided with increasingly wide acceptance of the "democratic peace theory." Both scholars and policy makers came to believe that as democracies apparently do not go to war with one another, actively encouraging more democracies in the international system augments U.S. national security. Significantly in terms of development, it was further acknowledged that liberal political democracies could best be achieved, and sustained, where states also developed liberal, free-market economies with a prosperous, educated middle class. This linkage among political democracy, relatively unfettered economic growth and development, and a strong middle class has received strong support in many studies.[9] The rapid expansion of weak, poor, and even failing states like Somalia in the 1990s cemented these beliefs. Without international aid—whether from the United States, the United Nations, or other parties—the citizens of these countries were dying in record numbers or migrating to nearby countries as refugees, increasing regional instability. Short-term humanitarian assistance and even intervention came to be seen as necessary moral and material responses. Yet at the same time, policy makers understood, and many studies underscored, that in the long term only a development approach that addressed poverty in a sustained fashion could make a real difference in these countries.

The necessity for the United States to fully embrace sustained development efforts received renewed impetus in the wake of previously unforeseen threats to national security, especially terrorism. As President George W. Bush pointed out in his administration's 2002 *National Security Strategy*: "The events of September 11, 2001, taught us that weak states, like Afghanistan, can pose as great a danger to our national interests as strong states. Poverty does not make poor people into terrorists and murderers. Yet poverty, weak institutions, and corruption can make weak states vulnerable to terrorist networks and drug cartels within their borders."[10] This point was reinforced by Secretary of State Colin Powell in 2005, when he wrote, "Poverty breeds frustration and resentment, which ideological entrepreneurs can turn into support for—or acquiescence to—terrorism, particularly in those countries in which poverty is coupled with a lack of political rights and basic freedoms." This perspective linking terrorism, lack of development, and poorly governed states has continued to have widespread bipartisan support among U.S. policy makers and is consistently reflected in policies and statements by governmental officials at all levels of the Obama administration. These conclusions were dramatically reinforced with the attempted 2009 Christmas Day bombing of a Northwest Airlines flight to Detroit by a Nigerian student who had apparently been radicalized in Yemen, which ranks as the poorest Arab country and has experienced continuing internal conflict and chaos. Food and nutrition policy scholar Per Pinstrup-Andersen and other experts agree that "widespread poverty, hunger, and inequality contribute to instability at the local, national and international levels and create national security risks for the United States. Failure to deal with these problems will render military efforts ineffective in dealing with the threat of terrorism against the United States and other high-income countries. . . . People without hope and with little or nothing to lose have little stake in the status quo. They are susceptible to terrorist appeals."[11]

Nevertheless, it is important to realize that not all experts posit a direct link among poverty, weak states, and terrorism, with some flatly denying that poverty produces or motivates terrorists.[12] In fact, the typical terrorist that targets the United States is educated and middle class. Further, some studies have shown that the poor may actually have the most antipathy for terrorist groups.[13] Yet almost everyone tends to acknowledge at least an indirect relationship and to agree that failing states—depending on their size and geographic location—do pose immense threats to regional and global stability and security.[14] In response, certain governments and organizations attempt to measure states' relative weakness in order to identify states at risk of collapse. Since 2005 the Fund for Peace organization and *Foreign Policy* magazine have usefully ranked states most-at-risk of failure, based on twelve indicators that are meant to gauge state capabilities and performance.[15] Table 3.1 lists their 2009 assessment of the twenty states most likely to fail.

The fact that fourteen of the countries in this table were also in the top twenty failed states for 2005 gives an indication of the long-term, intractable nature of the challenges bedeviling failing states. This is further reinforced by the assessment that ten of the world's worst humanitarian crises for 2009 involved states on this list, according to the international

TABLE 3.1: TOP 20 MOST-AT-RISK STATES
*Countries have been in the top 20 since 2005.

1. Somalia*	11. Ivory Coast*
2. Zimbabwe*	12. Haiti*
3. Sudan*	13. Burma
4. Chad*	14. Kenya
5. Democratic Republic of Congo*	15. Nigeria
	16. Ethiopia
6. Iraq*	17. North Korea*
7. Afghanistan*	18. Yemen*
8. Central African Republic*	19. Bangladesh*
9. Guinea*	20. East Timor
10. Pakistan	

Sources: *The Fund for Peace and* Foreign Policy *magazine, "Failed States Index, 2009," available at www.fundforpeace.org/web/index.php?option=com_content &task=view&id=99&Itemid=140.*

humanitarian group Doctors Without Borders.[16] Many of the challenges facing these states are dissected in development expert Paul Collier's highly regarded book *The Bottom Billion: Why the Poorest Countries Are Failing and What Can Be Done About It*. Incredibly, Collier places nearly 1 billion people, or one-seventh of the world's population, in fifty-eight countries as being at risk of failure.[17] In light of these sobering assessments, the nearly universal consensus about the importance of development for altruistic, economic, and security reasons should come as no surprise. As early as 1986 members of the United Nations had declared that all humans have a right to development, conceptualized as an all-encompassing process with economic, social, cultural, and political aspects.

THE CHALLENGE OF SUSTAINABLE DEVELOPMENT

Concrete evidence of the importance accorded to achieving human beings' economic security needs is revealed by the fact that the bulk of UN resources today are devoted to supporting economic and social development rather than the more traditional peace and security issues under UN purview.[18] The United Nations Development Programme (founded

Image 3.2—In war-torn Somalia, 8-year-old Najmo continues her education through daily, radio-based distance-learning programs. Photo credit: USAID.

in 1965) "is the world's largest multilateral source of grants for sustainable human development. It coordinates most of the technical assistance provided by the United Nations system."[19] Many other specialized UN agencies have become closely involved in this key area, ranging from the Food and Agriculture Organization and the United Nations International Children's Fund (UNICEF) to regional economic commissions. The diversity of agencies reflects the realization that development consists of many interrelated human security challenges ranging from poverty and human rights to resource scarcity, climate change, and good governance.[20]

Culminating literally decades of efforts—including initial attempts to measure development levels through the Human Development Index,[21] followed by systematic analysis in the UNDP's respected annual *Human Development Reports*—the United Nations organized the 2000 Millennium Summit. At that important meeting 189 heads of state agreed upon a global partnership to achieve eight Millennium Development Goals by 2015 to address the world's main development challenges; world leaders reinforced this commitment again at their 2010 UN summit on the MDGs. The comprehensive approach of the MDGs is an accurate reflection of the consensus that now exists about the interrelated, complex nature of generating development, especially on a sustained basis. The MDGs further reflect a growing belief in the importance of developing capacity among people so they can develop themselves. This critical idea is underscored in the UNDP's current vision of "The Human Development Concept":

> Development is thus about expanding the choices people have to lead lives that they value. And it is thus about much more than economic growth, which is only a means—if a very important one—of enlarging people's choices. Fundamental to enlarging these choices is building human capabilities—the range of things that people can do or be in life. The most basic capabilities for human development are to lead long and healthy lives, to be knowledgeable, to have access to the resources needed for a decent standard of living and to be able to participate in the life of the community.[22]

In perhaps the ultimate expression of development, Nobel Prize–winning economist Amaryta Sen has conceptualized development as freedom, meaning both that human beings require freedom to develop at the same time as development enables freedom.[23] Development thus represents both the ends and the means; even the poorest people need to be actively involved in shaping their development and not viewed as merely recipients of programs designed by others, no matter how well-intentioned. Studies have documented that this type of equitable development is likely to occur under popular (usually equating to democratic) governments.

Both the Bush and the Obama administrations have viewed international aid and assistance as essential for promoting development, democracy, and U.S. security interests. As an element of foreign policy, the primary external development assistance efforts fall under the State Department and specifically the U.S. Agency for International Development. While USAID is nominally an independent U.S. government agency, it receives overall guidance from the secretary of state, who controls its budget. USAID's Web site declares that it supports U.S. "foreign policy interests in

CONTEMPORARY CHALLENGE

Achieving the Millennium Development Goals by 2015

The United Nations' Millennium Development Goals represent a very ambitious global attempt to achieve progress on the following eight goals, which include twenty-one quantifiable targets, measured by sixty indicators.

Goal 1: Eradicate extreme poverty and hunger
Goal 2: Achieve universal primary education
Goal 3: Promote gender equality and empower women
Goal 4: Reduce child mortality
Goal 5: Improve maternal health
Goal 6: Combat HIV/AIDS, malaria, and other diseases
Goal 7: Ensure environmental sustainability
Goal 8: Develop a global partnership for development[1]

By 2010 notable progress had been made across some indicators and in some countries. Yet even with the expressed commitment of UN members to these goals, the overall likelihood of achieving such interrelated and complex targets is very doubtful, as the expanded discussion on poverty below illustrates. Additionally, unfavorable global economic conditions continue to complicate achieving sustained progress. Secretary-General of the United Nations Ban Ki-moon noted with reference to the MDGs in 2009 that "the global economic crisis . . . will throw us off course in a number of key areas, particularly in the developing countries. At worst, it could prevent us from keeping our promises, plunging millions more into poverty and posing a risk of social and political unrest."[2] Nevertheless, the UNSG and the UN community still assess that it is possible to meet many of the MDG goals, even that of halving the number of people globally in poverty. Some critics contend that particular goal is possible only if a "distorted" view of the data is accepted, meaning that one looks primarily at success stories in just a few of the more advanced developing countries with good growth rates such as China, Vietnam, Brazil, and perhaps India. That leaves out the endemic poverty suffered by the majority in sub-Saharan Africa and much of Latin America.[3]

It is worth underscoring that most of these goals are quite challenging, even in better economic times. For example, note that Goal 8's "global partnership" calls for the wealthier developed countries to maintain their development assistance flow, forgive or extend debt repayment for the poor countries, provide more generous market access with reduced or zero tariffs on poorer countries' exports, and assist with making new

---

1. United Nations Development Programme, "Millennium Development Goals, About the MDGs: Basics," available at www.undp.org/mdg/basics.shtml.
2. United Nations, foreword to *The Millennium Development Goals Report, 2009* (New York: United Nations, 2009), available at www.un.org/millenniumgoals/pdf/MDG_Report _2009_ENG.pdf.
3. Thalif Deen, "Is Global Poverty Reduction a Myth?" Inter Press Service News Agency, July 13, 2010, available at http://ipsnews.net/news.asp?idnews=52142.

technologies more easily available.[4] But it is not difficult to understand that domestic concerns and economic crisis can easily sap the political will required, and keeping the MDG promises ultimately depends on the political will on the part of both developed and developing countries. Thus, in his latest report assessing the progress made with only five years remaining to meet the MDG goals, the UN secretary-general specifically noted the problems in achieving Goal 8's global partnership, attributing it mainly to a lack of resources, unmet commitments, and no clear focus or accountability.[5]

While developed countries may be most responsible for the lack of resources and some of the unmet commitments, many would criticize the poorer countries for a lack of commitment, focus, and especially accountability. In other words, as part of their responsibility under the MDGs, developing countries had pledged to do better in governing effectively and openly, having acknowledged that "development rests on the foundations of democratic governance, the rule of law, respect for human rights and peace and security."[6] Yet as a high-ranking U.S. diplomat noted at a United Nations meeting on the MDGs in 2010, the recipients of MDG aid had to do much better at formulating national plans to implement the MDGs effectively, and to do so transparently to ensure accountability. For the United States, key concerns related to measuring development outcomes, the sustainability of development gains, and encouraging innovation and new technologies and methods.[7]

The United States had endorsed the MDGs from the beginning, first under the Clinton administration in 2000 and then under the succeeding Bush and Obama administrations. In fact, for the Bush administration, the situation in Afghanistan in 2001 and the attacks of September 11 graphically demonstrated that under-developed, poor, and ill-governed regions could breed instability and threats, even for major powers. The administration's 2008 "Commitment to the Millennium Development Goals" acknowledged the truth that fragile and failing states "continued to represent the international community's greatest development challenge as well as the most urgent threat to peace and security not only of their own people and their regions, but the rest of the world. These are the countries least likely to achieve the MDGs."[8] If anything, the Bush administration's commitment to international assistance and development only solidified under the Obama administration.

This is critical because without sustained support and attention to these goals they can easily be submerged under the "crisis du jour." As Irish rock star and philanthropist Bono pointed out: "The MDG's are possibly the most visionary deal that most people have never heard of."[9]

---

4. United Nations Development Programme, "Millennium Development Goals, About the MDGs: Goal 8—Develop a Global Partnership for Development," available at www.undp.org/mdg/goal8.shtml.

5. Comfort Ekeleme, "Africa: UN Expresses Concern Over Africa's Slow Pace in Attaining MDGs," *Daily Champion*, allAfrica.com, April 1, 2010, available at http://allafrica.com/stories/printable/201004010255.html.

6. United Nations Development Programme, "Millennium Development Goals, About the MDGs: Basics."

7. Ambassador Rick Barton, "Statement by Ambassador Rick Barton, U.S. Representative on the Economic and Social Council to the United Nations, at Informal Meeting on MDG Summit," April 29, 2010, in *U.S. Department of State Daily Digest Bulletin*, May 3, 2010.

8. U.S. Agency for International Development, *The United States Commitment to the Millennium Development Goals* (Washington, DC: USAID, April 2008), 12, available at www.usaid.gov/about_usaid/mdg/mdgs_0408.pdf.

9. Bono, "M.D.G.'s for Beginners...and Finishers," *The New York Times*, September 18, 2010, available at www.nytimes.com/2010/opinion/19bono.html.

expanding democracy and free markets while improving the lives of the citizens of the developing world" while "spending less than one-half of 1 percent of the federal budget."[24] The fact that USAID points out how little of the U.S. budget it actually spends is not an accident; traditionally, most U.S. citizens believe that their country spends much more on humanitarian and development assistance than it actually does. Furthermore, it is not unusual for the agency to find its policies being driven by politics, with specific restrictions on aid, congressional earmarks, and buy-American provisions. In fact, many experts, former administrators of USAID, and development groups have been disappointed with what they have seen as an increasingly dysfunctional and neglected international assistance system, as reflected in USAID's steady loss of autonomy, resources, staff, and influence.[25]

In fiscal year 2009, a top-level official noted that USAID had given almost $1.9 billion "to 14 UN agencies and international agencies that are working in more than 25 countries. Of that total, the majority went to the World Food Programme, roughly 1.717 billion, and then another 60 million to UNICEF . . . and that assistance goes to many areas . . . agriculture and food security, economic recovery and market systems, humanitarian coordination, and information management."[26] It is worth pointing out that although USAID certainly has the paramount position for U.S. international assistance, the complex nature of development means that many different U.S. government agencies are involved, besides numerous international and nongovernmental agencies and foundations. And, depending on the security environment where development is taking place, the process may involve the presence of the U.S. military to provide security (Afghanistan), training and logistics support for other nations' security forces or UN peacekeepers to establish security and law and order (as in much of Africa), or governmental agencies to deliver and organize humanitarian assistance.

The humanitarian assistance provided by international organizations such as the United Nations, national agencies such as USAID, and many charitable groups may contribute to short-term regional stability and thus enhance security, but this does not address the fundamental challenges of sustainable development. As a recent analysis of past USAID and government foreign assistance concluded, the focus on the short term too often trades off the ability to build sustainable institutions necessary for long-term development.[27] In effect, short-term aid cannot redress endemic poverty or transform weak governments into effective and popular ones. Secretary of State Clinton's major policy address on development at the beginning of 2010 appeared to recognize these shortcomings as she contrasted the distinction between aid and investment, emphasizing that "through investment, we [the United States] seek to break the cycle of dependence that aid can create by helping countries build their own institutions and have their own capacity to deliver essential services."[28] Governments and policy experts increasingly understand that only by building human capacity at both local and national levels can the seemingly intractable problem of poverty be addressed in a meaningful way.

ECONOMIC SECURITY AND THE CHALLENGE OF POVERTY

What is your life like if you are in absolute poverty? For starters, you lack the basic skills and minimum capacities needed to control your own life much less take advantage of globalization. You are most likely illiterate. You might very well be malnourished. You are almost certainly suffering from at least one debilitating disease (such as malaria or HIV/AIDS), which saps your energy and diminishes your productivity. You probably lack assets (such as land and capital) that would enable you to invest in your future. And in many countries, you are at the bottom of the social ladder—a victim of discrimination, ignored by social programs that reach other groups.[29]

While the picture that John Sewell paints of extreme poverty identifies many problem areas, perhaps no statistic related to poverty is more revealing than data detailing hunger and malnutrition. In terms of basic economic security needs, food is clearly the number-one concern. Tragically, according to one economist, the price of food worldwide jumped

THINK AGAIN

International Assistance Does Not Work

Almost all development experts acknowledge the limitations of aid or assistance that is provided (and often directed) by outside donors, ranging from a lack of adequate planning and inappropriate aid or projects for local conditions and traditions to a lack of incorporation of community needs and desires. Yet probably the vast majority of government agencies, foundations, scholars, and policy makers still agree that if employed properly and with adequate conditionality and accountability in place, aid does have positive results on economic growth, development, and the reduction of poverty. This consensus obviously informs the rationale behind the UN MDGs. Yet disagreement about the possibility of growth and development for poor nations via outside assistance was already occurring in the 1950s and 1960s. In 1982 a critical article titled "Foreign Aid Isn't" appeared and criticized the very use of the term *aid* for its unquestionably positive connotation and for the implicit assumption that aid would always benefit the citizens of a country.[1] An increasingly vocal minority in the twenty-first century has continued to level critiques at the whole concept of international aid. In her well-received indictment of aid to Africa, *Dead Aid: Why Aid Is Not Working and How There Is a Better Way for Africa*, economist Dambisa Moyo points out that economically Africa has actually gone backward rather than forward since independence in the 1960s and 1970s, in spite of often massive amounts of aid.[2] In her view aid has effectively held Africa back and should be terminated.

What reasons do Moyo and others give for these critiques? One of the most serious is the charge that bad or weak governance negates the possibility of equitable development, with or without aid. If a government is run by despots and not committed to improving the situation of its population, then essentially resources cannot accomplish anything. The widespread problem of corruption further distorts the intent of any aid programs, even

1. Prakash Loungani, "Foreign Aid Isn't," review of *The White Man's Burden: Why the West's Efforts to Aid the Best Have Done So Much Ill and So Little Good*, by William Easterly, *Cato Journal* (1982): 382–384.

2. Jagdish Bhagwati, "Banned Aid: Why International Assistance Does Not Alleviate Poverty," review of *Dead Aid: Why Aid Is Not Working and How There Is a Better Way for Africa*, by Dambisa Moyo, *Foreign Affairs* (January–February 2010), available at www.foreignaffairs.com/print/65817.

Think Again (*continued*)

when a government does have good intentions but weak institutions. Since many of these fragile states also find themselves in postconflict situations, they may be more focused on the short-term problem of maintaining security and stability of their territory. Too, these are often the states that are threatened by cultural divisions and extremism, whether ethnic or religious in nature. Under these conditions it is extremely important, but also difficult, for any government to allocate assistance fairly to all groups. The examples of Iraq and Afghanistan are instructive here.

Regarding more technical aspects, many weak governments simply cannot absorb large amounts of aid usefully so as to translate it into workable, long-term programs. Indeed, channeling the aid through often rigid, formalized plans and bureaucratic hurdles seems destined to make it ineffective. Conversely, the piecemeal nature of much development aid from many different types of donors may result in duplicative or even conflicting programs in place. Additionally, economists had predicted that countries receiving aid would use sensible policies to encourage their own domestic savings rates, thus reducing aid requirements because eventually they would become self-reliant. But human nature can invalidate economic assumptions; many of these countries realized that once the international community had committed to aid them, donors would continue to do so and that these countries could continue to spend freely and save less. Yet another powerful argument against aid lies in the record of growth and reduction in poverty rates lately achieved by more than a half-billion people in China and India; according to Bhagwati, "The greatest and quickest progress in fighting poverty in history."[3] This is telling since these two countries had received negligible amounts of international assistance (India had received aid, but some years before its growth and poverty rates declined).

Ultimately, one of the most damning critiques of foreign aid may be the fact that it is indeed "foreign" in nature. Moyo is particularly incensed over the fact that non-Africans have been the ones to discuss and direct aid and development strategies for the continent, excluding those African policy makers and public officials who presumably might know something about the topic. Her perspective reflects a growing acknowledgment among all sectors concerned with development that local and community involvement at every level is essential for building the capacity to move out of poverty. This is a conclusion increasingly reiterated by U.S. government agencies in their development programs ranging from Afghanistan to Haiti.

---

3. Ibid.

83 percent between 2005 and 2008, while U.S. government statistics reported that by 2009 food prices remained 40 percent higher than historical
levels.[30] Furthermore, realizing that nearly one-sixth of the world's population was projected to be malnourished (more than 1 billion people)
during 2009 and that, according to the UN's Food and Agriculture Organization, this figure "will represent the highest level of chronically hungry people since 1970" gives one a sense of the scale of the problem.[31] It
also underscores the difficulty of realizing the MDGs in 2015—to half
the number of hungry people. As one illustration, consider the fact that
fully one-quarter of Afghan children die before the age of five primarily
due to hunger and malnourishment, despite the fact that the United States
and the United Nations have spent billions there since the U.S.-led invasion to depose the Taliban in 2001. Or consider that in 2007, almost one
in seven children in sub-Saharan Africa died before his or her fifth birth-
day, with hunger and malnourishment being major contributors.[32]

Although feeding starving and malnourished people is a laudable humanitarian goal, it has real security implications, as the instability in Afghanistan illustrates. The same is true of other desperately poor, unstable
countries like Somalia and Yemen. As noted above, experts may disagree
about whether poverty and inequitable development actually produce
terrorists, but they do tend to agree about the destabilizing effects and
the unrest these factors can trigger. For example, in the wake of food-
related riots in some thirty countries in the spring of 2009, U.S. secretary
of agriculture Tom Vilsack warned of more social instability and uncontrolled migration of people to where there was food unless immediate
steps were taken to dramatically increase agricultural productivity and
food output to reduce hunger.[33]

In one sense it is encouraging to find that international experts associated with the UN's Food and Agriculture Organization tend to agree
that we will have the resources and technical knowledge to increase food
production by 50 percent in 2030 and then by 70 percent in 2050. This is
important because these amounts are necessary to feed the anticipated
world population of 9.1 billion in forty years. However, many experts
argue that in order to effectively address food production, developing
countries—which tend to be very dependent upon agriculture—need

Image 3.3—Market vendors in Sudan. Photo credit: USAID.

much more assistance in improving their domestic agricultural productivity. In other words, the emphasis needs to move even farther away from wealthy countries providing traditional food assistance supplies to long-term technical and related agricultural assistance that enables the hungry to feed themselves. Of course, this assumes that poor countries will continue to own the land necessary to feed their needy people. There is troubling evidence to indicate that a group of countries ranging from Saudi Arabia to India to China, whose own populations are outstretching domestic capabilities to sustain food and water needs, are buying or leasing land in mainly poor countries featuring hungry, malnourished populations. For instance, China has signed an agreement for almost 7 million acres of land in the poor and conflicted Democratic Republic of the Congo to produce palm oil for China's domestic use. Ironically, at the same time, the Congo depends upon the World Food Programme to help feed much of its population.[34]

In yet another complication, food and agriculture experts have warned that the very areas that most need new production in sub-Saharan Africa and South Asia are the same areas featuring severe poverty and difficult growing conditions.[35] For instance, consider that rural South Asia is estimated to have more than half of the world's undernourished children. This type of statistic bears particular significance because of studies demonstrating that "if young children remain malnourished for more than two years, the consequence is stunted growth—and stunted growth is not merely a physical condition . . . their mental potential is impaired as well. Stunted growth is irreversible." It is sobering to realize that according to UN and Afghan government indicators, this condition is already widespread in Afghanistan, an ominous signpost for future progress in that country.[36]

Clearly, hunger, poverty, and agricultural development are inextricably linked. At an even broader level, agriculture is crucial to sustainable development overall within sub-Saharan Africa, accounting for some 20 to 30 percent of gross domestic product and employing 60 to 70 percent of the working population.[37] Unfortunately, whereas in 1980 agriculture worldwide constituted 17 percent of international assistance, that aid later declined to 4 percent in 2000. This occurred in light of the real gains being made in reducing the number of hungry, partly due to increased crop yields through the green revolution's new seeds, fertilizer, and irrigation.[38] Most recently, the trend of steadily rising food prices noted above has brought renewed focus on agricultural assistance from the international community. This may not have come a moment too soon for a desperately poor, failing country like Ethiopia, with a largely agricultural economy, yet where a mere 1.5 percent of U.S. assistance was going to agriculture.[39] In light of this, it may not be surprising that the Obama administration pledged to ask the U.S. Congress to double U.S. agricultural assistance to more than $1 billion for 2010 and to annually increase the U.S. investment, to at least $3.5 billion through 2013. The U.S. government further planned to increase aid over "the full range of issues that affect agricultural development, including increasing agricultural productivity . . . stimulating post-harvest, private-sector growth; supporting the role of women and families in agriculture . . . expanding knowledge and training; increasing trade flows; and supporting good governance and policy reform."[40]

Image 3.4—Open market in Sudan. Photo credit: USAID.

As both the U.S. government and the international community are increasingly recognizing, targeting the role of women in agriculture is particularly crucial for success. The UN Development Fund for Women highlights that "in some regions, women provide 70 percent of agricultural labor, produce more than 90 percent of the food, and yet are nowhere represented in budget deliberations." In fact, at least one report found that only 10 percent of agricultural aid goes to women farmers.[41]

In a much larger sense, incorporating the role of women in every facet of development is vital for countries to make progress out of poverty, considering UN estimates that 70 percent of the world's poor are women.[42] At the same time "women perform 66 percent of the world's work, produce 50 percent of the food, but earn [only] 10 percent of the income and own 1 percent of the property."[43] Girls and women are much less likely to receive education than their male counterparts. Yet already by the 1990s many studies by development economists and respected international organizations and foundations had convincingly demonstrated that educating women had multiplier effects in economic growth for their families

POLICY SPOTLIGHT

The "Miracle" of Microfinance

Increasingly, policy makers and experts are stressing the need for all developmental approaches to incorporate both individual capacity building and local community involvement to achieve progress. Microfinance projects are viewed as an extremely useful tool in this process, as this provides low-income people who normally do not have access to banks with financial assistance such as very small-scale loans that individuals can afford to pay back—unlike traditional moneylenders. Loans are usually made to finance self-employment or a family-run business. Although seed money is normally provided by outside actors, the goal is to create self-sustaining local financial cooperatives where members reinvest at least some of their profits and support one another's endeavors and broaden the types of financial services available. Thus, this type of process is believed to stimulate critically needed local growth, as it educates individuals and empowers them (especially women in their communities) and presumably increases solidarity among community members. Most microfinance ventures today are explicitly targeted at women, because they form the majority poor, they have proved to be a reliable credit risk, and, as noted above, women tend to use their earnings to improve life for their families.[1] Documenting the expansion of microfinance, in 2010 Maria Otero, U.S. undersecretary for democracy and global affairs, reported that "an estimated 150 million people worldwide are now served by microfinance [services]."[2]

In testimony to the transnational impact that just one individual can have, Bangladeshi economist Muhammad Yunus is credited with both creating the microfinance concept in the 1970s and then proving its worth through the highly successful Grameen Bank that he originally started in Bangladesh. Yunus and the Grameen Bank were awarded the Nobel Peace Prize in 2006 in recognition of the success, and promise, of the transnational micro-

---

1. Hillary Rodham Clinton, "Remarks on Development in the 21st Century," presentation at the Center for Global Development, Washington, DC, January 6, 2010, available at www.state.gov/secretary/rm/2010/01/134838.htm.

2. Undersecretary of State for Democracy and Global Affairs Maria Otero, "Women Setting the Economic Policy Agenda," presentation at the National Press Club, Washington, DC, June 3, 2010, available at www.state.gov/g/142891.htm.

credit movement in arguably removing millions of people from extreme poverty. The concept has spread widely throughout the world and receives support from many governments and international organizations like the United Nations Development Programme. As just one example of its application, the UNDP reported on the success of one of its microloan programs in Burkina Faso targeted at women that in 2010 had created five new credit unions and supported several others, all in remote areas where normally poor and illiterate people had no access to financial services.[3] Women were using the microloans to support small businesses. Although each woman had her own business, they were grouped together in a "solidarity-based" credit union, meaning that if one woman defaulted on her loan, the others would continue to back her and the credit union. And, further substantiating the studies above arguing that it is crucial to invest in women to overcome the cycle of poverty, one of the women profiled was using the profits from her business to keep her four daughters in school, something that had not been possible during her own childhood.

The microfinance concept is also supported by at least several thousand large and small nongovernmental organizations, including the Rural Development Institute, which helps women get title to their lands because it believes this is essential to address poverty and hunger. On the other hand, FINCA International, with services in twenty-one countries, is committed to small business loans and to "village banking" that provides its clients (women represent 70 percent) with not only loans but also insurance and savings plans.[4]

Yet in spite of all the promise and seeming results, the microfinance concept is not without its critics, who believe that the concept needs further careful validation. In particular, concerns are raised about the size of interest rates, which can be very high, and whether the very neediest are being reached with financial services or whether those already possessing some income are the main beneficiaries of credit.

---

3. United Nations Development Programme Newsroom, "Poverty Reduction: Women Entrepreneurs in Burkina Faso," available at http://content.undp.org/go/newsroom/2010/may/burkina-faso-le-pnud-soutient-la-cration-de-microentreprises-par-les-femmes-.en?categoryID=349425.

4. Rural Development Institute, "Global Center for Women's Land Rights," available at www.rdiland.org/OURWORK/OurWork_GlobalCenter.html; FINCA, "What Is Microfinance? What Is Village Banking?" available at www.finca.org/site/c.erKPI 2PCIoE/b.2604299/k.FFD9/What_is_Microfinance_What_is_Village_Banking.htm.

and communities. Educated women demonstrably provide better nutrition, health care, and education to their families, while overall women have been found to devote more of their small earnings to food, clothing, and education for their children.[44] In light of this, not only international organizations but also major corporations like Goldman Sachs have been promoting education and resources for women, as these investments "have the greatest positive correlation to enhancing a country's general prosperity and poverty alleviation."[45] These types of conclusions are reflected at the most basic community level in the growing practice of providing women with very small loans ("microfinance") to start their own businesses, and to join together to provide community banking services. These findings are also reflected in government-sponsored programs such as the Bolsa Familia (Family Stipend) program in Brazil, where families (essentially mothers) are paid a small stipend each month to keep their children in school and ensure that they receive periodic health checks. Almost all observers credit this program with at least some of the success in Brazil's decreasing its extreme poverty levels in the twenty-first century.

Yet in spite of all the projects and all the credible data, incorporating women fully into many countries' economies and development plans faces obstacles, including the political and cultural constraints noted in the previous chapter that may restrict women to the home and family and muffle their political voice. This is reflected in the comparative data from the 2009 Global Gender Gap Index compiled by the World Economic Forum, an independent organization of experts.[46] As the forum emphasizes, the data are meant to measure the gaps between men's and women's access to resources and opportunities in each country and not the levels of those actual factors, so it is independent of a country's level of development. Thus, a poorer, less-developed country could score higher than a wealthy country if the poorer country had less of a gap between men's and women's access to resources and opportunities. The World Economics Forum's yearly index also keys gender equality rather than the empowerment of women per se. Significantly, the forum makes the further point that it has consistently found a strong correlation between the yearly Global Gender Gap Index and its yearly Global Competitiveness Index, thus confirming the correlation between gender equality and the ability of states to progress economically.[47]

This short overview of some key aspects of the poverty challenge illustrates the complexity of just one sector critical to development concerns. It would easily require a book to fully analyze development and economic security in all its aspects.

Complicating the picture even further is that so many of the poorest developing countries are also prone to civil conflict, as Paul Collier has demonstrated. Among the four factors that Collier identifies as being central to extreme poverty for the bottom billion is bad governance. The relationship among bad governance, extreme poverty, and hunger is reinforced by Amaryta Sen, who notes that "no substantial famine has ever occurred in a democratic country—no matter how poor. . . . This is because famines are extremely easy to prevent if the government tries to prevent them, and a government in a multiparty democracy with elections and free media has strong political incentives to undertake famine prevention."[48] This raises the question of how an effective, popular government that promotes development can best be established, a question that continues to be debated by policy makers, scholars, and activists around the world.

THE CHALLENGE OF GOOD GOVERNANCE

As noted above, the United States has long believed that not only is democracy good for the United States, but it also enhances U.S. security to have other democratic states in the international system. The belief that democratic governments are also best situated to support economic progress and development is more and more prevalent. As the *National Security Strategy* declared in 2010: "The United States must support democracy, human rights, and development together as they are mutually reinforcing. . . . [W]e are harnessing our bilateral and multilateral capabilities to help nascent democracies deliver services that respond to the needs and preferences of their citizens, since democracies without development rarely survive." Indeed, the United Nations has also embraced democracy as an essential enabler to realize the Millennium Development Goals. Although democracy is acknowledged to be valuable for all people in and of itself, the UNDP believes that democracy also aids development and the MDGs because it allows for any conflicts to be resolved politically and peacefully; it respects the freely expressed priorities of citizens, and it ensures accountability and responsiveness on the part of elected leaders.[49]

Yet whereas in the past elections alone were held to be the sole marker of whether a government was democratic, today democratic governance is widely acknowledged to require transparency, accountability, and the rule of law—elements of what is often termed good governance. These latter requirements are crucial because, just as almost all states now want to claim that they respect human rights, they also want to claim that they are "democracies," often based solely on holding elections, no matter how circumscribed. But as Paul Collier has convincingly argued in *War, Guns, and Votes: Democracy in Dangerous Places*, the superficial-type elections held by many of the countries in the poorest states have "'increased political violence instead of reducing it.' Without rules, traditions, and checks and balances to protect minorities, distribute resources fairly, and subject officials to the law, these governments lack the accountability and legitimacy to discourage rebellion." Furthermore, Collier demonstrates that when elections are fraudulently won, these democracies-in-name-only promote bad governance, because the types of policies required for these leaders to remain in power and reward their followers are not the same ones that would lead to good governance. Larry Diamond, a renowned scholar of democracy, terms these nominally electoral democracies predatory states, which epitomize bad governance, as in these states a government's purpose is not to provide public goods for its citizens but to enrich the ruling officials and their cronies with the wealth of the nation. Not only is this type of governance inimical to political democracy, but it also negates the possibility of sustainable economic growth, both because of the pervasive problem of corruption noted earlier and because it deliberately excludes the majority of the population from incorporation into the state's economy. Furthermore, for legal experts Gary Haugen and Victor Boutros, without fair, effective justice systems, "half a century of development work" is in jeopardy because there is no method to prevent corrupt governmental officials from keeping, or diverting, development aid away from the poor.[50] Thus, they argue that international assistance must focus more on improving the rule of law.

Scholar Robert Rotberg has long studied the interrelated problems of weak and failing states and good governance in developing states, especially in Africa. Together with colleague Rachel Gisselquist and others at Harvard University he devised the original Ibrahim Index of African Governance (2007 and 2008), designed to provide an annual comparative estimate of good governance performance among African states. In order to do this, Rotberg measures the degree to which governments deliver to their citizens essential public goods, which are grouped into five categories: "Safety and Security; Rule of Law, Transparency, and Corruption; Participation and Human Rights; Sustainable Economic Opportunity; and Human Development."[51] Countries receive both overall ratings and ratings by category, based upon well over one hundred indicators. These categories reflect the predominant perspective among many specialists that democratic—meaning good—governance and development are inextricably bound together. In sum, good governance consists of much more than political aspects.

Since the 2009 rankings represent data at a certain point, there are clearly some dramatic changes in governance and society that are not reflected, such as military coups that dislodged democratically elected government (Guinea and Mauritania), internal and interethnic conflict (Kenya), or virtual economic collapse (Zimbabwe). But overall Rotberg concludes that many aspects of governance are quite slow to change. This is not a surprising finding and reinforces the data and conclusions depicted above on corrupt states (Chapter 2), where change occurs very slowly. It is also significant to note that fully half of the states perceived most corrupt in 2009 (Table 2.1) are also on the 2009 ranking of poorly governed states (Table 3.2), and fully half of the states most-at-risk of failing in 2009 (Table 3.1) are also reflected on Table 3.2. Conceivably, there would be even more correlations if all the lists were confined to only African countries.

TABLE 3.2. AFRICAN STATES RANKED AS MOST
POORLY GOVERNED IN 2009

1. Somalia	11. Republic of the Congo/
2. Sudan	Congo-Brazzaville
3. Chad	12. Swaziland
4. Democratic Republic of	13. Equatorial Guinea
the Congo	14. Liberia
5. Ivory Coast/Côte d'Ivoire	15. Burundi
6. Central African Republic	16. Nigeria
7. Eritrea	17. Ethiopia
8. Angola	18. Guinea-Bissau
9. Zimbabwe	19. Sierra Leone
10. Guinea	20. Togo

Source: Rotberg and Gisselquist, Strengthening African Governance.

In spite of what might be considered rather pessimistic trends, it is worth noting that Robert Rotberg still believes that African governance is improving overall. Not only are multiparty elections more common, but there is increasing African consensus that governments exist to serve their peoples and everyday citizens are actively demanding good governance.[52] Too, just as a military coup can easily derail good governance, a freely elected leader like Ellen Johnson Sirleaf in Liberia can make important policy changes with public support. Similarly, while Larry Diamond is fairly pessimistic in his assessment of the prospects for good governance, he does believe that globalization can improve trends by helping to make information available and to connect grassroots movements and civic organizations within civil society. Even in desperately poor societies of Africa, the use of the Internet and cell phones has been exploding. All of this allows ordinary citizens to rise up to demand accountability and better governance—aided by actors from Transparency International and Freedom House to Human Rights Watch and the U.S. government.[53] The U.S. National Security Strategy explicitly recognizes the importance of this phenomenon when it states that "we are closely working with citizens, communities, and political and civil society leaders to strengthen key institutions of democratic accountability—free and fair electoral processes, strong legislatures, civilian control of militaries, honest police forces, independent and fair judiciaries, a free and independent press, a vibrant private sector, and a robust civil society."[54]

CONCLUSION

Achieving sustainable economic security, especially for "the bottom billion," is a herculean task. Even well-intentioned experts, governments, and nongovernmental organizations continue to disagree about the root causes of and optimal paths for achieving development, precisely because the concept is inherently multifaceted and complex. In recognition of this, the U.S. government has come to increasingly accept the conclusion that there is no easy, "formulaic" development model. Each country and each region must be analyzed and assessed carefully with tailored approaches devised.[55] Although this may lead to more successful outcomes, it also increases the time and the expense. Considering the billions of dollars spent by the United States in the past ten years just in Afghanistan, Pakistan, and Iraq, and the uncertain results achieved, it is not surprising to find many skeptics.

Unfortunately, as the previous chapter demonstrated, sustainable human development and security can seem near impossible to achieve not only because of poverty and bad governance but also because of such seemingly intractable issues as cultural extremism, human rights abuses, and terrorist and criminal networks that may become powerful enough to threaten weak, ineffective governments. The desperately poor, conflict- and terrorist-ridden state of Yemen appears to be just the latest casualty featuring all these complex challenges. Where does the international community begin to address the confluence of problems there? And there are more issues threatening human security, as the next four chapters illustrate. Challenges such as those posed by climate change and environmental issues, increasing human activities and competition on the oceans, public health threats such as pandemics, and the ever-accelerating use of cyberspace with all of its risks and rewards will produce consequences that we cannot begin to foresee.

To Learn More

Review the many reports and resources available at the United Nations Development Programme Web site, www.undp.org. The UNDP "is the UN's global development network, an organization advocating for change and connecting countries to knowledge, experience and resources to help people build a better life."

Scan the U.S. State Department's USAID Web site (www.usaid.gov/) for a sense of the breadth and depth of U.S. government programs aimed at assisting development in the world, often in conjunction with other governments and nongovernmental organizations.

Examine the U.S. State Department's Web site on global hunger and food security (www.state.gov/s/globalfoodsecurity/) to view current facts on world hunger, U.S. principles and initiatives aimed at this critical problem, and a world map depicting the size of countries based on the number of undernourished in those countries.

Visit "The Failed States Index" (developed by the *Foreign Policy* journal and the Fund for Peace) to see further details on those states that are currently assessed to be failed or failing and the reasons for failure (www.foreignpolicy.com/articles/2009/06/22/the_2009_failed_states_index).

To examine more closely the many debates about international assistance, see the range of opinions expressed from a coalition of policy experts, practitioners, advocates and organizations via the Modern Foreign Assistance Network at http://modernizingforeignassistance.net/.

In *The End of Poverty: Economic Possibilities for Our Time* (New York: Penguin Press, 2006) prominent economist Jeffrey Sachs offers a generally optimistic portrait of the possibilities of economic growth, along with specific recommendations for how to move the world out of extreme poverty by 2025.

For a devastating critique of current international assistance efforts, read economist Dambisa Moyo's *Dead Aid: Why Aid Is Not Working and How There Is a Better Way for Africa* (New York: Farrar, Straus, and Giroux, 2009).

To understand how one nongovernmental organization from the poor nation of Bangladesh has effectively spread the microfinance concept globally and assisted millions of people, read Ian Smillie's *Freedom from Want: The Remarkable Success Story of BRAC, the Global Grassroots Organization That's Winning the Fight Against Poverty* (Sterling, VA: Kumarian Press, 2009).

Consider the various options for the future of development found in "Patterns of Potential Human Progress," the Pardee Center for International Futures, the University of Denver (www.ifs.du.edu/documents/).

Nicholas D. Kristoff and Sheryl WuDunn's *Half the Sky: Turning Oppression into Opportunity for Women Worldwide* (New York: Alfred A. Knopf, 2009) has been acclaimed for its frank stories of the indignities and atrocities suffered by women around the world, balanced by testimonials to the power of individual women and activists who strive to improve the lives of women and their communities.

Notes

1. In December 1992 the United States initiated Operation Restore Hope under UN sanction as an armed humanitarian intervention action to ensure that food supplies got to millions of starving Somalis caught in a long-term civil-conflict situation.

2. United Nations, Charter of the United Nations, "Preamble," available at www.un.org/en/documents/charter/intro.shtml; United Nations Development Programme, "The Human Development Concept," *Human Development Reports*, available at http://hdr.undp.org/en/humandev/.

3. Vincent Ferraro, "Globalizing Weakness: Is Global Poverty a Threat to the Interests of States?" in *Should Global Poverty Be Considered a U.S. National Security Issue?* commentaries from Woodrow Wilson Center for International Scholars, August 8, 2003, available at www.wilsoncenter.org/index.cfm?fuse action=news.item&news_id=34999.

4. President Ronald Reagan was particularly well known for using early colonial leader John Winthrop's imagery of a city on a hill to depict the United States. For example, Reagan quoted the following in his "Shining City upon a Hill" speech of January 25, 1974: "Standing on the tiny deck of the *Arabella* in 1630 off the Massachusetts coast, John Winthrop said, 'We will be as a city upon a hill. The eyes of all people are upon us, so that if we deal falsely with our God in this work we have undertaken and so cause Him to withdraw His present help from us, we shall be made a story and a byword throughout the world'" (www.originofnations.org/books,%20papers/quotes%20etc/Reagan_ The%20Shining%20City%20Upon%20A%20Hill%20speech.htm).

2
2222222

5. Franklin D. Roosevelt, "Annual Message to Congress" (the "Four Freedoms" speech), January 6, 1941, Franklin D. Roosevelt Presidential Library and Museum, available at http://docs.fdrlibrary.marist.edu/4free.html.

6. General George C. Marshall was a truly remarkable American, achieving military success as a five-star army general who served as chief of staff to President Franklin D. Roosevelt during World War II and then civilian policy-making success as both secretary of defense and secretary of state.

7. Hillary Rodham Clinton, "Secretary Clinton's Remarks at Luncheon Honoring Former Secretary of State George C. Marshall," October 16, 2009, available at www.state.gov/secretary/rm/2009a/10/130645.htm. Note that the increasingly hostile Soviet Union and its new allies in Eastern Europe refused the aid.

8. USAID, "About USAID: This Is USAID," available at www.usaid.gov/about_usaid/.

9. Jeffrey D. Sachs specifically notes that research has "shown strongly that the probability of a country being democratic rises significantly with its per capita income level" ("The Strategic Significance of Global Inequality," in *Should Global Poverty Be Considered a U.S. National Security Issue?*).

10. George W. Bush, *The National Security Strategy of the United States of America* (Washington, DC: White House, September 2002), v. Yet President Bush also noted that "including all the world's poor in an expanding circle of development—and opportunity—is a moral imperative and one of the top priorities of U.S. international policy" (21).

11. Colin L. Powell, "No Country Left Behind," *Foreign Policy* (January–February 2005): 30; Steven Erlanger, "Yemen's Chaos Aids the Evolution of a Qaeda Cell," *New York Times*, January 3, 2010, available at www.nytimes.com/2010/01/03/world/middleeast/03yemen.html; Per Pinstrup-Andersen, "Eradicating Poverty and Hunger as a National Security Issue for the United States," in *Should Global Poverty Be Considered a U.S. National Security Issue?*

12. Carol Lancaster, "Poverty, Terrorism, and National Security," in *Should Global Poverty Be Considered a U.S. National Security Issue?* For some similar views, see Ferraro, "Globalizing Weakness."

13. Eli Berman, Joseph H. Felter, and Jacob N. Shapiro, "Constructive COIN: How Development Can Fight Radicals," SNAPSHOT, *Foreign Affairs*, June 1,

2010, available at www.foreignaffairs.com/articles/66432/eli-berman-joseph-h
-felter-and-jacob-n-shapiro/constructive-coin.

14. "The Failed States Index," *Foreign Policy*, available at www.foreignpolicy
.com/articles/2009/06/22/the_2009_failed_states_index.

15. The Fund for Peace and *Foreign Policy* magazine, "Failed States Index,
2009," available at www.fundforpeace.org/web/index.php?option=com_content
&task=view&id=99&Itemid=140. While many accept the legitimacy of the categories of failed and failing states, and consider this index to be useful, there are
critics such as Saskia Sassen and Razi Ahmed who question its utility, particularly
with reference to Pakistan, in "What Is State Failure?" *Dissent*, July 21, 2010, available at www.dissentmagazine.org/online.php?id=369.

16. "Aid Group Lists Top 10 Worst Humanitarian Crises," *Reuters AlertNet*,
December 21, 2009, available at www.alertnet.org/thenews/newsdesk/N2117
6428.htm.

17. See chap. 1, n. 14.

18. United Nations, *Basic Facts About the United Nations* (New York: United
Nations Department of Public Information, 1998), 125. Reflecting the growing
importance of economic issues, the membership of the Economic and Social
Council, one of the five major organs of the United Nations, was expanded
twice, from eighteen to twenty-seven in 1965 and to fifty-four in 1973. See United
Nations, Charter, "Introductory Note," available at www.un.org/en/documents/
charter/intro.shtml.

19. United Nations, *Basic Facts About the United Nations*, 35.

20. United Nations Development Programme, *Human Development Reports*
Web site, "*Human Development Reports, 2010*, Twentieth Anniversary Edition:
A New Human Development Deal," available at http://hdr.undp.org/en/reports/
global/hdr2010/.

21. The HDI was first created in 1975 and later refined. It was an attempt to
more accurately portray a composite picture of the development levels of countries and regions based on combining achievements in the three basic indicators of life expectancy, educational attainment, and income. Yet it was quickly
realized that even this composite index needed to be disaggregated for regions
and ethnic and gender groups within a country and to be supplemented by
other data and considerations. See United Nations Development Programme,

Human Development Reports: The Human Development Index, available at http://hdr.undp.org/en/statistics/indices/hdi/.

22. United Nations Development Programme, "The Human Development Concept," *Human Development Reports*, available at http://hdr.undp.org/en/humandev/.

23. Amartya Sen, *Development as Freedom* (New York: Alfred A. Knopf, 1999), 53.

24. USAID, "About USAID: This Is USAID."

25. J. Brian Atwood, M. Peter McPherson, and Andrew Natsios, "Arrested Development: Making Foreign Aid a More Effective Tool," *Foreign Affairs* 87, no. 6 (2008): 126.

26. USAID, "Briefing by Assistant Secretary for Population, Refugees, and Migration Eric Schwartz and USAID Acting Administrator for Africa Earl Gast," September 24, 2009, in *U.S. Department of State Daily Digest Bulletin*, September 25, 2009.

27. Atwood, McPherson, and Natsios, "Arrested Development," 127.

28. Hillary Rodham Clinton, "Secretary's Remarks: Remarks at the Peterson Institute for International Economics," January 6, 2010, in *U.S. Department of State Daily Digest Bulletin*, January 7, 2010.

29. John Sewell, "The Realpolitik of Poverty," in *Should Global Poverty Be Considered a U.S. National Security Issue?*

30. Paul Collier, "The Politics of Hunger: How Illusion and Greed Fan the Food Crisis," *Foreign Affairs* 87, no. 6 (2008): 67; White House, Office of the Press Secretary, "Food Security: Investing in Agricultural Development to Reduce Hunger and Poverty," July 10, 2009, available at www.america.gov/st/text-trans-english/2009/July/20090711121105ptellivremos0.862179.html.

31. Food and Agriculture Organization of the United Nations and the World Food Programme, *The State of Food Insecurity in the World: Economic Crises— Impacts and Lessons Learned* (Rome: Food and Agriculture Organization of the United Nations, 2009), 11.

32. Alfred de Montesquiou, "UN Fights Hunger in Afghanistan," Associated Press, December 20, 2009, available at www.google.com/hostednews/ap/article/ALeqM5iPkvpYyC5; United Nations, *The Millennium Development Goals Report, 2009* (New York: United Nations, 2009), 25, available at www.un.org/millenniumgoals/pdf/MDG_Report_2009_ENG.pdf.

33. Javier Blas, "U.S. Urges Food Output Boost to Avert Unrest," *Financial Times*, April 19, 2009, available at www.ft.com/cms/s.

34. Lester R. Brown, "The Emerging Politics of Food Scarcity," Book Bytes, Earth Policy Institute, July 14, 2010, available at www.earth-policy.org/index .php?/book_bytes/2010/pb4ch01_ss3.

35. Neil MacFarquhar, "Experts Worry as Population and Hunger Grow," *New York Times*, October 22, 2009, available at www.nytimes.com/2009/10/22/ world/22food.html.

36. UN Office for the Coordination of Humanitarian Affairs, "Asia-Pacific: Hunger a Growing Threat to Region," February 20, 2009, available at www.irin news.org/PrintReport.aspx?ReportId=83037; Collier, "Politics of Hunger," 70; Montesquiou, "UN Fights Hunger in Afghanistan."

37. Hillary Rodham Clinton, "Secretary's Remarks: Remarks at the 8th Forum of the African Growth and Opportunity Act," August 5, 2009, in *U.S. Department of State Daily Digest Bulletin*, August 6, 2009.

38. MacFarquhar, "Experts Worry."

39. Atwood, McPherson, and Natsios, "Arrested Development," 128. And according to the UN Food and Agriculture Organization, although amounts of foreign direct investment in agriculture in 2009 had been increasing, this still amounted to less than 1 percent of the world's total foreign direct investment (cited in Svetlana Kovalyova, "Food Majors Triple Investment in Ending Hunger," Reuters, November 12, 2009, available at www.reuters.com/article/ Id/US125810118599._CH_.2400/.

40. White House, Office of the Press Secretary, "Food Security."

41. United Nations Development Fund for Women (UNIFEM), "Facts and Figures on Women, Poverty, and Economics," available at www.unifem.org/ gender_issues/women_poverty_economics/facts_figures.php; "Women Farmers Key in Fight Against Hunger," Reuters, April 21, 2010, available at www.alertnet.org/thenews/newsdesk/LDE63K0SY.htm.

42. United Nations Development Fund for Women (UNIFEM), "Women, Poverty and Economics," available at www.unifem.org/gender_issues/women _poverty_economics/.

43. UNIFEM, "Facts and Figures on Women."

44. Isobel Coleman, "The Better Half: Helping Women Help the World," *Foreign Affairs* (January–February 2010), available at www.foreignaffairs.com/

print/65880; Melanne Verveer, U.S. Ambassador-at-Large for Global Women's Issues, "Women as Partners in Progress and Prosperity," Keynote Address at the Pathways to Prosperity in the Americas Women's Entrepreneurs' Conference, October 8, 2009, available at www.state.gov/s/gwi/rls/rem/2009/130681 .htm.

45. Verveer, U.S. Ambassador-at-Large for Global Women's Issues, "Women as Partners."

46. World Economic Forum, "The Global Gender Gap Index 2009 Rankings," available at www.weforum.org/pdf/gendergap/rankings2009.pdf.

47. Ricardo Hausmann, Laura D. Tyson, and Saadia Zahidi, *The Global Gender Gap Report, 2009* (Geneva: World Economic Forum, 2009).

48. Sen, *Development as Freedom*, 51–52.

49. Obama, *National Security Strategy*, 37–38 (see chap. 2, n. 8); United Nations Development Programme, "Democratic Governance," available at www.undp.org/governance/.

50. Kenneth Roth, "Ballots and Bullets," review of *War, Guns, and Votes: Democracy in Dangerous Places*, by Paul Collier, *New York Times*, March 22, 2009, available at www.nytimes.com/2009/03/22/books/review/Roth-t.html; Larry Diamond, "The Democratic Rollback: The Resurgence of the Predatory State," *Foreign Affairs* 87, no. 2 (2008): 42–43; Gary Haugen and Victor Boutros, "And Justice for All: Enforcing Human Rights for the World's Poor," *Foreign Affairs* 89, no. 3 (2010): 56. Incredibly, Haugen and Boutros cite a World Bank study that found that perhaps 85 percent of aid never reaches its intended targets.

51. Robert I. Rotberg and Rachel M. Gisselquist, *Strengthening African Governance: Index of African Governance Results and Rankings, 2009* (Cambridge, MA: Program on Intrastate Conflict and Conflict Resolution, Kennedy School of Government, Harvard University, and World Peace Foundation, October 2009), available at www.nber.org/iag/2009/iag2009.pdf.

52. Robert Rotberg, "An African Scorecard." *International Herald Tribune*, December 5, 2008, available at www.iht.com/articles/2008/12/05/opinion/ edrotberg.php.

53. Diamond, "Democratic Rollback," 47.

54. Obama, *National Security Strategy*, 37.

55. Clinton, "Secretary's Remarks: Remarks at the Peterson Institute."

4

Environmental Security

We come here in Copenhagen because climate change poses a grave and growing danger to our people. All of you would not be here unless you—like me—were convinced that this danger is real. This is not fiction, it is science. Unchecked, climate change will pose unacceptable risks to our security, our economies, and our planet.

—PRESIDENT BARACK OBAMA,
"REMARKS BY THE PRESIDENT AT THE MORNING
PLENARY SESSION OF THE UNITED NATIONS CLIMATE
CHANGE CONFERENCE," DECEMBER 18, 2009

There is strong and growing worldwide consensus that climate change is real and will have profound effects on international security. According to the UN's expert scientists of the Intergovernmental Panel on Climate Change, "By the end of the century, sea levels may rise twice as much as was predicted two years ago . . . [which] means that the lives of some 600 million people living on low-lying islands, as well as those living in Southeast Asia's populous delta areas, will be put at serious risk." The implications of relocating literally millions of human beings in areas threatened by climate change are staggering, and people are already internally relocating from low-lying areas in Bangladesh and the Philippines. For some island countries, like Kiribati and the Maldives, abandoning low-lying areas is not an option, as their entire countries may become uninhabitable by midcentury. Clearly, "ecomigration" is a growing trend, one triggered not only by rising seas but also by desertification and a lack of fresh water in areas like the African Sahel region bordering the Sahara.[1] Environmental conditions do create social and economic stress that can lead to conflict, disease, and the other threats to human security described in this book.

Whereas the United States may have the resources to at least mitigate the effects of climate change within North America, developing countries and their populations do not. Wealthy countries like Australia can build desalinization plants to increase their drinking water supply, but very poor countries like Yemen cannot. Further, climate change threatens the U.S. foreign policy goals of promoting development, good governance, and sustainable agriculture and reducing conflict in developing countries. In the absence of effective governments, illegally armed groups thrive, generating terrorism, piracy, and organized crime. UN secretary-general Ban Ki-moon highlighted the importance of the environment for the entire world community as it relates to conflict:

> The environment and natural resources are crucial in consolidating peace within and between war-torn societies. . . . Lasting peace in Darfur will depend in part on resolving the underlying competition for water and fertile land. And there can be no durable peace in Afghanistan if the natural resources that sustain livelihoods and ecosystems are destroyed. The United Nations attaches great importance to ensuring that action on the environment is part of our approach to peace. Protecting the environment can help countries create employment opportunities, promote development and avoid a relapse into armed conflict.[2]

Consistent with Ban Ki-moon's observation, the U.S. military already regularly responds to natural disasters and other environmental tragedies such as the tragic Haitian earthquake in 2010. This is based on American political culture and values that support a policy of international engagement, humanitarian assistance, and the capacity to deliver food and water wherever needed. Recognition of the importance of human security for global prosperity and stability provides an additional strategic political rationale for managing environmental security. R. K. Pachauri, chairman of the Intergovernmental Panel on Climate Change, made this connection clear during his 2007 Nobel Peace Prize acceptance speech: "Peace can be defined as security and the secure access to resources that are essential for living. A disruption in such access could prove disruptive of peace. In this regard, climate change will have several implications, as numerous adverse impacts are expected for some populations in terms of: access to clean water, access to sufficient food, stable health conditions, ecosystem resources, and security of settlements."[3]

Before further exploring the national security implications of environmental security, it is first important to define its scope.

DEFINING ENVIRONMENTAL SECURITY

Concerns about the environment are not new. The greenhouse effect, ozone-depleting chlorofluorocarbons, and carbon emissions have been discussed for decades. More than a generation ago scholars and scientists were publishing research studies that demonstrated a link between environmental scarcities and growing conflict between societies. For example, by the early nineties Thomas Homer-Dixon and his colleagues provided empirical evidence to show that shortages of agricultural land, forests, water, and fish were already contributing to violent conflict, and they posited that this phenomenon would increase in coming years with a larger world population, unequal resource distribution, and the potential of global warming.[4] But notably it is not just scientists who express environmental concerns, as "green" activists and organizations have given rise to a significant social movement advocating environmental causes in North America, Europe, and Japan—even prior to the impact of globalization. The Sierra Club was founded as early as 1892, Greenpeace was founded in 1971, and Earth First! was founded in 1979. Nevertheless, an important political change has occurred between 2000 and 2010 with respect to environmental issues. Where once environmental groups were marginalized and portrayed as fringe groups, environmentalists are now considered part of the political mainstream, and Green Party candidates regularly compete for, and win, public office in Europe and other regions. The tree-hugger epithet has given way to an entire green culture that permeates government, business, and society. As a symbol of power, the gas-guzzling Hummer has been replaced by the hybrid Prius. In short, being green is in vogue.

Clearly, protecting the environment is an important end in and of itself, but human needs often take priority over conservation. This leads to wildlife habitat being destroyed for agriculture, forests being clear-cut for fuel, and rivers being dammed for hydroelectric power and irrigation. The latter process is particularly prone to cause conflict as many countries in different parts of the world dispute upriver countries' practices that cause stress on countries downstream. For example, Vietnam, Laos, and Cambodia blame China for diverting too much of the shared Mekong River, which provides water for about 60 million people. Or within countries governments can intentionally undermine human security of certain populations dependent on water, as evidenced by Iraq's draining of marshes in southern Iraq in the early 1990s in order to weaken the Shiite population there. (Even within the United States, disputes occur; for example, the states of Georgia, Florida, and Alabama continue to quarrel about fair use of the waters from the shared Chattahoochee River.) Outside of these manmade regional and domestic projects, there are global challenges to environmental security marked by the phenomenon of climate change.

Given the generally slow pace of climate change, its negative effects are somewhat obscured from human perception. Yet to see dramatic evidence of climate change, one can compare images of the Arctic to notice the ice melt, the disappearance of snow on Mount Kilimanjaro, or the expansion of deserts in Africa. Each image provides a ready reference that the climate changes. These changes collectively reduce the amount of fresh water available for drinking and irrigation for food production, negatively impact plant and animal species, and increase societal pressures among already vulnerable populations. For example, in Africa, by 2020, between 75 and 250 million people are projected to be exposed to water stress, reducing vital agricultural production.[5] Already, millions of Africans suffer from food shortages that lead to regular famines. This undermines

Image 4.1—Mount Kilimanjaro in 1993. Photo credit: NASA.

Image 4.2—Mount Kilimanjaro in 2000. Photo credit: NASA.

food security, which is "the right of everyone to have access to safe and nutritious food, consistent with the right to adequate food and the fundamental right of everyone to be free from hunger."[6] As an earlier chapter noted, food is a precondition for escaping extreme poverty and for improving development, stability, and security, a factor that is already painfully clear in struggling countries in East Africa, Southeast Asia, and Central America.

CLIMATE CHANGE, SCIENCE, AND POLICY

In the twentieth century, scientists began to more clearly understand how and why the earth's climate changes, and to share their findings. Initially, scientific influence was largely limited to interested environmental groups; however, certain U.S. policy makers such as former vice president Al Gore championed the cause. In Gore's 1992 book *Earth in the Balance*, Gore argued, "Global warming is also a strategic threat. The concentration of carbon dioxide and other heat-absorbing molecules . . . [poses] a worldwide threat to the earth's ability to regulate the amount of heat from the sun retained in the atmosphere. . . . [H]uman civilization is now the dominant cause of change in the global environment. Yet we resist the truth."[7] Gore's argument was consistent with views outside of the U.S. government and evident in the expansion of international programs designed to protect the environment in various ways.

The United Nations' concerted interest began in 1972 when the United Nations Environment Programme was created in Stockholm, Sweden. UNEP's mandate is to coordinate the development of environmental policy consensus and to bring important environmental issues to the attention of governments and the international community for action. Among these issues are ozone depletion, biodiversity, and climate change. Significantly, the organization is explicitly linked to economic development concerns, as evidenced by the majority of developing states that sit on its governing council and its headquarters being situated in Nairobi, Kenya. In fact, UNEP is guided by the idea of sustainable development, which Chapter 3 noted is development that meets the needs of the present without compromising the ability of future generations to meet their own

Image 4.3—As the Arctic melts, polar bears like these can become threatened. Photo credit: Alphonso Braggs, U.S. Navy.

needs. Sustainable development suggests that harvesting timber, creating grazing areas for cattle, and preserving wild species must not, and need not, be in conflict. Instead, through careful planning, loggers, ranchers, and environmentalists can work together to promote development and protect the environment. Gro Harlem Brundtland, who served as a UN special envoy on climate change, maintains that the "environment is where we all live; and development is what we all do in attempting to improve our lot within that abode. The two are inseparable."[8] An environmental area that has gained increased attention and is viewed as out of balance is human economic activity and climate.

The notion that the climate does change is not inherently controversial; for example, the conclusion that the last ice age ended 10,000 years ago is widely accepted. However, the current controversy rests on disagreement about the pace, cause, and impact of climate change. Regarding the speed, the prevailing scientific theory predicts gradual temperature change will produce a 0.2-degree Celsius rise in surface temperatures every decade.[9] Although this is slow, it is already observable in the Arctic and glacial parts of the world. For instance, some evidence suggests that all of the glaciers in Montana's Glacier National Park will be gone by 2030.

Given the generational pace of climate change, optimists see science and society keeping up with inevitable environmental change. Just as humans adapted to the ice age, optimists argue that we will adapt to climate change again through technology and human migration. People will relocate from low-lying areas to higher ground, new crops will be developed for a new climate, and new types of energy will reduce the use of fossil fuels. At the same time, geoengineering will draw excess carbon dioxide from the atmosphere or reflect excess light back into space. It is argued that some countries like the United States and Canada may actually benefit from climate change as the growing season is extended. Longer growing seasons will enable increased food production and food exports. In short, for optimists time is an ally in coping with climate change.

An alternative, more pessimistic theory regarding the pace predicts that abrupt climate change will occur, as made notorious by the film *The Day After Tomorrow*. According to the film's scenario, climate change produces cooler temperatures that trigger an ice age, forcing the mass movement of people from the Northern Hemisphere to more tropical climes. As depicted in the film, the greatly accelerated pace of climate change was clearly rooted in fiction, but some scientists believe abrupt climate change will begin with gradual glacial melting that may already be happening. The process would alter the ocean's salinity, which slows the warming ocean currents. This could occur over years instead of decades and would produce colder temperatures instead of warmer ones. The prediction of colder temperatures is counterintuitive to expectations of a warming planet, but Peter Schwartz and Doug Randall have considered the global and national security implications of this possibility:

> Large population movements in this scenario are inevitable. Learning how to manage those populations, border tensions that arise and the resulting refugees will be critical. New forms of security agreements dealing specifically with energy, food and water will also be needed. In short, while the US itself will be relatively

better off and with more adaptive capacity, it will find itself in a world where Europe will be struggling internally, large numbers of refugees washing up on its shores and Asia in serious crisis over food and water. Disruption and conflict will be endemic features of life.[10]

Recall that this is the type of scenario that Homer-Dixon and his colleagues projected might occur in their work dating back to the early 1990s.

It is significant that developing countries with huge populations like China and India are quite likely to be negatively impacted by climate change. These countries are already stressed by water scarcity and fail to produce enough food for their populations.

CLIMATE CHANGE AND SECURITY

Although the public's awareness of climate change has increased and environmental movements have become mainstream, a direct linkage between climate change and national security has not been universally accepted. This should not be surprising, as climate change is less obvious than an influenza pandemic and much slower than zombie-computer denial-of-service attacks. Instead, climate change is viewed as a contributing factor that can worsen already existing problems. For example, the director of national intelligence testified in 2009, "Climate change, energy, global health, and environmental security are often intertwined, and while not traditionally viewed as 'threats' to U.S. national security, they will affect Americans in major ways." As the climate changes, we may be faced with increasing food and water shortages and damage to property, especially in vulnerable coastal or other locations, and the spread of disease may be facilitated. Of course, deforestation, carbon emissions, ozone depletion, and other forms of pollution directly impact human security by threatening quality of life, impacting the pace of development, and stressing many societies. The director of national intelligence warned that "the greatest danger may arise from the convergence and interaction of many stresses simultaneously. Such a complex and unprecedented syndrome of problems could cause outright state failure, or weaken important pivotal states counted on to act as anchors of regional stability."[11] As discussed in an earlier chapter, state failure has captured the attention of strategic thinkers since the early 1990s, and climate change is now credited as at least a contributing factor to weak states, if not one of the underlying conditions.

THINK AGAIN

Disputing the Science Behind Climate Change

In spite of the growing, majority scientific consensus regarding climate change and high-level political support for programs to reduce carbon dioxide emissions around the world, the concept of climate change continues to be attacked. The skepticism ranges along a spectrum, from former Greenpeace activist Bjorn Lomborg, who challenges the most pessimistic assessments of a decaying earth but still sees the need for improvement in how humans interact with the environment, to others who believe that there is no basis to believe human activity is impacting the world's climate detrimentally and that climatic change is a natural, cyclical occurrence. In the United States, perhaps the most significant skeptic of climate change is Senator James Inhofe (R-OK), who has been leading the campaign against policy that would limit carbon emissions. In 2003 he attracted some support when he declared on the U.S. Senate floor that the notion of global warming was "the greatest hoax ever perpetrated on the American people." He has continued to back up that claim by pointing to instances where certain scientists and popular authors such as Dr. Michael Crichton have disputed the majority consensus view expressed by the expert scientists of the UN's Intergovernmental Panel on Climate Change and the University of East Anglia's Climatic Research Unit. Senator Inhofe received additional support when he released a report in 2010 that addressed a controversy caused by e-mails and documents released from the University of East Anglia's Climatic Research Unit. (The e-mails suggested that scientific counterevidence against climate change was intentionally stifled and that the scientists were politically motivated to make a case for global warming being

Think Again (*continued*)

induced by human activity. However, a number of expert panels such as the independent East Angla review team found no evidence that the scientists had deliberately manipulated data, or that climate change was a farce).[1] In an opinion piece in *U.S. News and World Report*, the senator wrote:

> Call it the global warming crackup, an unfolding process of contradictory claims about glaciers, weather, and scientists asserting a consensus when none exists. Global warming alarmists can't make up their minds because the entire basis for their energy rationing project has collapsed into a mess of errors, exaggerations, and deceit.
>
> My minority report shows the world's leading climate scientists acting like political scientists, with an agenda disconnected from the principles of good science. And it shows that there is no consensus—except agreement there are significant gaps in what scientists know about the climate system. It's time for the [Obama] administration to recognize this. Its endangerment finding rests on bad science. It should throw out that finding and abandon greenhouse gas regulation under the Clean Air Act—a policy that will mean fewer jobs, higher taxes, and economic decline.[2]

The impact of climate change skeptics does seem to affect Americans' thinking, although there is more support for the concept in other countries. Some polls have suggested that even a majority of U.S. citizens believe climate change is overrated. This is clearly a contentious political issue that will not be resolved anytime soon.

---

1. James M. Inhofe, "Climate Change Update: Senate Floor Statement," January 4, 2005, available at http://inhofe.senate.gov/pressreleases/climate update.htm; United States Senate Committee on Environment and Public Works Minority Staff, "United States Senate Report: 'Consensus' Exposed: The CRU Controversy," February 2010, available at www.epw.senate .gov/inhofe; Sir Muir Russell, "The Independent Climate Change E-mails Review," July 2010, available at www.cce-review.org/.

2. James Inhofe, "Inhofe: Climategate Shows There's No Global Warming Consensus," *U.S. News and World Report*, March 23, 2010, available at http://politics.usnews.com/opinion/articles/2010/03/23/inhofe-climate gate-shows-theres-no-global-warming-consensus.html.

UN leaders share these concerns. Former secretary-general Kofi Annan wrote, "Environmental degradation has the potential to destabilize already conflict-prone regions, especially when compounded by in-equitable access or politicization of access to scarce resources. I urge Member States to renew their efforts to agree on ways that allow all of us to live sustainably within the planet's means." The current UN secretary-general, Ban Ki-moon, agreed that "when resources are scarce—whether energy, water or arable land—our fragile ecosystems become strained, as do the coping mechanisms of groups and individuals. This can lead to a breakdown of established codes of conduct, and even outright conflict."[12] With this in mind, the secretary-general envisioned specific threatening scenarios that should stimulate action to reduce the effects of climate change:

- The adverse effects of changing weather patterns, such as floods and droughts, and related economic costs, including compensation for lost land, could risk polarizing society and marginalizing communities. This, in turn, could weaken the institutional capacity of the State to resolve conflict through peaceful and democratic means, to ensure social cohesion, and to safeguard human rights.
- Extreme weather events and natural disasters, such as floods and drought, increase the risk of humanitarian emergencies, and thus the risk of instability and dislocation.
- Migration driven by factors such as climate change could deepen tensions and conflicts, particularly in regions with large numbers of internally displaced persons and refugees.
- Scarce resources, especially water and food, could help transform peaceful competition into violence.
- Limited or threatened access to energy is already known to be a powerful driver of conflict. Our changing planet risk[s] making it more so.[13]

The importance of environmental security is also influencing strategic military thinking in the United States. As the U.S. government continues to use the military in ways to prevent conflict, the military identifies climate change as one of the underlying causes of contemporary strife. Former U.S. commander of naval forces in Europe Adm. T. Joseph Lopez captures the connection between climate change and instability: "More poverty, more forced migrations, higher unemployment. Those conditions are ripe for extremists and terrorists."[14] The group National Security and the Threat of Climate Change (composed of distinguished retired military officers) sees it as essential for the military to prepare for natural disasters, pandemic disease events, and other climate change–induced tragedies warranting a response from the United States. They expect that humanitarian assistance, disaster relief, and stability operations will be persistent features of future military operations.

Because of this, the Pentagon now considers gradual warming and abrupt climate changes as important factors leading to economic malaise, border collapse, and global conflict. As the 2008 U.S. *National Defense Strategy* declares, "As we plan, we must take account of the implications of demographic trends, particularly population growth in much of the developing world and the population deficit in much of the developed world. The interaction of these changes with existing and future resource, environmental, and climate pressures may generate new security challenges."[15] Along these lines, "the U.S. should commit to global partnerships that help less developed nations build the capacity and resiliency to better manage climate impacts."[16] At an operational level, this is already occurring, according to former commander of the Thirteenth Air Force Lt. Gen. Lloyd S. "Chip" Utterback: "More often than not out there in the Pacific we deal with disasters. If there is not an earthquake, there is certainly a volcano erupting. There are landslides in the Philippines, floods in Vietnam and Burma. India and Bangladesh deal with flooding, cyclones, and typhoons."[17]

At the same time the U.S. military responds to environment-induced tragedies, it is also attempting to become more environmentally responsible. This is an important change, since the military historically treated the environment rather cavalierly as a battle space, testing site, or dumping

POLICY SPOTLIGHT

Ecomigration

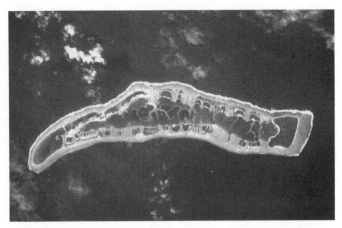

Image 4.4—Uninhabited Millennium Island is one of thirty-two atolls constituting the Republic of Kiribati in the South Pacific that are at risk from rising sea levels. Photo credit: NASA.

Based on expert Intergovernmental Panel on Climate Change projections, sea levels are expected to rise between 0.8 and 2.0 meters by the year 2100. This will have devastating effects on low-lying areas around the world, including Bangladesh, the Netherlands, and the United States' Gulf Coast. Additionally, sea-level rise will literally wash away some existing countries, including Tuvalu, Kiribati, the Marshall Islands, Fiji, and the Maldives. The president of the Maldives has been particularly active in raising awareness of his country's plight. The most

ground. The navy, for example, has committed to deriving 50 percent of its energy needs from alternative sources by 2020.[18] A part of this effort is showcasing a "green fleet" by 2016. A hundred years earlier, it was the navy's "Great White Fleet" that was billed as a hallmark of U.S. power through its global combat capability. Though it will be composed of nu-

Policy Spotlight (*continued*)

spectacular event was holding his cabinet meeting underwater wearing scuba gear.

Located in the Indian Ocean, the highest point in the Maldives is just 2.0 meters, or 6.5 feet, above sea level, but 80 percent of the islands are below 1.0 meter, or 3.0 feet. Because of this, the government has not been waiting to act until sea levels rise. The president has been searching for a new homeland for the 370,000 Maldivians facing ecodisplacement. Sri Lanka, India, and Australia are potential new homelands, but complex negotiations are just beginning. At least in the modern era, this may be the first instance of a country relocating from its geographic territory. Although the logistics of relocating 370,000 people from the Maldives may be daunting, if we multiply this by the number of states potentially affected, the implications are truly staggering. Many in the U.S. Gulf Coast region experienced some sense of the complexity and cost of this type of scenario as they faced the prospect of having to relocate permanently from coastal areas due to the implications of the 2010 British Petroleum oil spill.

In preparation for the seemingly inevitable sea-level rise, the Maldives and other low-lying countries have formed the Alliance of Small Island States (AOSIS) to serve as an ad hoc lobby and negotiating voice for small-island developing states within the UN system. With at least forty-two members located around the world, the group works to raise awareness of climate change and lobbies for strict controls on the world's temperature. In September 2009, AOSIS issued a declaration that, among many things, called for "urgent, ambitious and decisive action to significantly reduce emissions of all green house gases . . . [and] increased levels of financial and technological resources" for its members. But small states dependent on donors for financial assistance are too limited in what they can accomplish. Thus, at the 2009 Copenhagen climate change summit, these countries pushed for, and received, the promise of access to an international fund to mitigate the impact of climate change.

clear ships, hybrid electric surface ships, and biofuel-consuming aircraft, this proposed green fleet is meant to show the world a completely different face of U.S. military power. The message seems to be that a country can be powerful and environmentally conscious, contrary to claims made by detractors.

The less obvious and unexpected role of climate change and national security is its place in Great Power competition. Well-known British strategist Colin Gray sees climate change as one potential source of conflict between states in the future, and scholar Michael Klare sees resource competition as a critical factor that could lead to future wars. Per these

CONTEMPORARY CHALLENGE

Resource Competition and Internal Conflict

In 2009 the Uppsala Conflict Data Program tracked zero interstate conflicts, twenty-nine intrastate conflicts (e.g., Sudan), and five internationalized internal conflicts (e.g., Congo) that are occurring in just twenty-five countries.[1] Many of these internal conflicts involve subnational groups vying for political influence and economic resources, particularly where the distribution of resources is skewed. And as populations are stressed the potential for instability and conflict clearly grows, especially where groups may already be at odds due to ethnic, racial, or religious differences. Homer-Dixon's analysis of cases from more than twenty years ago found strong support for the finding that the movement of large groups of population due to environmental factors was likely to cause conflicts between groups with different identities, such as ethnic differences.[2] More recently, the International Institute for Sustainable Development found that after the 2007–2008 drought in Syria, residents abandoned 160 villages and relocated to other areas. Clearly the movement of people and their ensuing resource competition will feed differences that can lead to or sustain conflict. Among these differences may be instances where traditional societies have already shown re-

---

1. Uppsala codes "internationalized internal armed conflict" as conflict "between the government of a state and one or more internal opposition group(s) without intervention from other states" (Uppsala Conflict Data Program, Centre for the Study of Civil Wars, International Peace Research Institute, *UCDP/PRIO Armed Conflict Dataset Codebook* [Oslo: Uppsala Conflict Data Program, 2008]).

2. Homer-Dixon, "Environmental Scarcities and Violent Conflict."

perspectives, the United States and China would clash over hydrocarbon resources in the Arctic, Africa, or South America. Of course these assessments are speculative, and there is no way to predict that climate change may produce resource rivalry among states that will lead to war. In fact, when it comes to the Arctic, ongoing discussions among the United

---

Contemporary Challenge (*continued*)

sistance to perceived Western modes of development and modernity, such as in Southwest Asia, the Middle East, and certain parts of Africa.

Increasing conditions of environmental insecurity also seem likely to fuel resource wars over such necessities as water, especially in view of the fact that the world population is now projected to exceed 9 billion people by 2050—perhaps twice as many as earlier predicted. The growing global awareness of the importance of water is reflected in the fact that, for the first time ever, in July 2010 the UN General Assembly declared the right to water (and sanitation) to be a basic human right in a nonbinding vote. Yet at the same time a comprehensive 2009 UN water resources study estimates that by 2030, "nearly half of the world's population will be living in areas of high water stress." Although water scarcity is potentially a threat to human security, Steve Lonergan of the United Nations Environment Programme has argued that "fighting over water makes very little sense economically or politically . . . [but] water has been used as a strategic goal or target, as part of military activities." Indeed, Wendy Barnaby is optimistic overall, noting that "countries do not go to war over water, they solve their water shortages through trade and international agreements."[3] Clearly, this issue is open for debate, but it seems most likely that wars over water will occur where other stressors between peoples are already present, such as in the Middle East. Access to water, especially for agricultural purposes, is a major factor contributing to the seemingly intractable conflict between Israel, Jordan, and the Palestinian people.

---

3. Andrew C. Revkin, "U.N.: Young and Old Boom on the Road to 9 Billion," *New York Times*, March 11, 2009, available at http://dotearth .blogs.nytimes.com/2009/03/11/un-young-old-boom-on-road-to9-billion; Martin Mittelstaedt, "UN Warns of Widespread Water Shortages," *Globe and Mail*, March 12, 2009, available at www.theglobeandmail.com/ servelt/story/RTGAM.20090311.wwater0312/BNStory; Steve Lonergan, "Water and War," available at www.unep.org/ourplanet/imgversn/ 154/lonergan.html; Wendy Barnaby, "Do Nations Go to War over Water?" *Nature*, March 19, 2009.

States, Russia, Canada, and European countries suggest that diplomacy will be the dominant tool. The same, however, cannot be said for conflict within states where resource competition often leads to internal conflict, as numerous case studies by scholars have shown.

ADDRESSING CLIMATE CHANGE

The warnings about environmental security are increasingly ominous and have prompted calls for action, but a backlash also exists concerning the causes, severity, and implications of climate change. In particular, climate change has quickly become a contentious economic, and therefore political, issue. This dates back to the framework adopted at the 1997 climate change summit in Kyoto, Japan, where countries committed to limiting their carbon emissions. As carbon emissions are believed to be a key factor in climate change, it was agreed that carbon emissions must be reduced. Unsurprisingly, the most developed countries have tended to produce the most carbon emissions, because their use is highly correlated to economic activity. The Kyoto Protocol originated in the 1992 United Nations Framework Convention on Climate Change signed in Rio de Janeiro, and it declares in Article 2: "The ultimate objective [is the] stabilization of greenhouse gas concentrations in the atmosphere at a level that would prevent dangerous anthropogenic interference with the climate system. Such a level should be achieved within a time-frame sufficient to allow ecosystems to adapt naturally to climate change, to ensure that food production is not threatened and to enable economic development to proceed in a sustainable manner."

In principle, the United States initially accepted the goals of climate change treaties such as Kyoto, but domestic concerns and an ingrained belief in the value of the free market system have conflicted with implementation. For example, the United States tends to favor providing business incentives to reduce carbon emissions, while European governments tend to regulate businesses more heavily. Indicative of this difference is the fact that the U.S. Senate refused to ratify the Kyoto treaty (though President Clinton signed it), and President George W. Bush then withdrew consent for the treaty. For the Bush administration, climate change was primarily an economic issue and was shrouded in scientific uncertainty. However, by the end of the Bush administration's second term in 2008, its leading officials had accepted the science of climate change. Yet the administration characteristically pursued its own domestic policy to reduce emissions outside the international framework established in Kyoto. For many critics of the United States' unilateral tendencies in the twenty-first century, climate change represented just one more issue dividing the United States from the consensus of international opinion.

Regardless of official Washington's opposition to the climate change treaty, the pace of the transnational environmental movement did not slow appreciably. In fact, the Nobel Prize Committee awarded its Peace Prize to former vice president Al Gore and the Intergovernmental Panel on Climate Change in 2007. The committee cited their joint efforts "to build up and disseminate greater knowledge about man-made climate change, and to lay the foundations for the measures that are needed to counteract such change." In his acceptance speech, Gore said, "We, the human species, are confronting a planetary emergency—a threat to the survival of our civilization that is gathering ominous and destructive potential." And this conclusion has obvious global appeal. South African bishop Desmond Tutu, a 1984 Nobel Peace Prize Laureate himself, put it in spiritual terms: "To ignore the challenge of global warming may be criminal. It certainly is disobeying God. It is sin. The future of our fragile, beautiful planet is in our hands. We are stewards of God's creation."[19] These ideas were captured in an Oscar-winning film, *An Inconvenient Truth*, which featured Al Gore and greatly increased public awareness of climate change.

Twelve years after Kyoto, carbon emissions were still the prominent theme at a follow-on global climate change summit in Copenhagen, Denmark. On the eve of the 2009 climate change summit, policy specialist Michael Levi argued that carbon emissions "must be cut deeply in the coming decades if the world is to control the risks of dangerous climate change." If not, experts Jessica Wallack and Veerabhadran Ramanathan predict, "the earth's temperature stands to careen out of control."[20] The conclusion seemed inescapable to most: For countries to control climate change, they must reduce their carbon emissions.

During the Copenhagen climate change summit, countries focused on carbon emissions from the world's major polluters, including China, the United States, Europe, and India. Debate centered on the size of the cap to emissions, the baseline year for determining it, and the achievability of the cap. Yet in spite of preparatory work and growing public concern about climate change, there remained an unbridgeable chasm between developed and developing countries. Under the earlier Kyoto framework, developed countries had agreed to measure carbon emissions using 1990 as a baseline year, with countries that reduced carbon emissions being allowed to sell their "surplus pollution" on the open market as credits to other countries that could not meet their reduction goals. This new business of trading carbon credits is valued in the billions of dollars, though the European Union's system has had mixed success to date. With so much at stake, the baseline year has proved to be critical to discussions, as it favors certain economies. Because the baseline was set as 1990, it reflected Soviet-era industrial activity, which collapsed in 1992. Since Soviet economic policies were not environmentally friendly, the successor countries in central and eastern Europe now have higher-than-normal carbon emissions quotas relative to the size of their respective economies. Yet with inflated carbon emissions quotas, declining population, and corresponding economic activity, Europe has much to gain from continuing to use the 1990 baseline. Likewise, since China was not a major economy in 1990 when the Kyoto framework was adopted, it is exempt from emissions caps altogether and is situated in a favorable position.

Logically, as one would expect, the countries that produced high carbon emissions in 1990 or were exempted from caps, like Europe and China, favor adhering to the Kyoto framework and its baseline. Many of these countries have surplus carbon credits to sell for billions of dollars when using this measure. However, the United States objects to the 1990 baseline and sees 2005 as a more realistic year for emissions. In support of this change, the United States notes that using 2005 standards, Europe's cuts amount to just 13 percent relative to 17 percent of the United States' cuts. Additionally, China is particularly concerned with the method of determining carbon emissions. Since it is the most populous country and the largest carbon emitter in the world, it does not favor the 1990 or 2005 benchmark, but instead favors a per capita index or carbon in-

FIGURE 4.1 WORLD'S LARGEST CO$_2$ EMITTERS, 2007

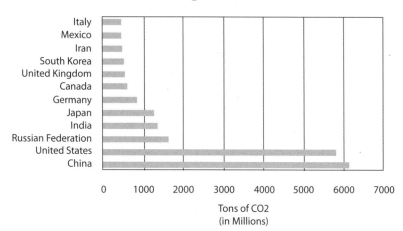

Source: International Energy Agency, CO$_2$ Emissions from Fuel Combustion High-lights 2009, available at www.iea.org/co2highlights/pp.44-46.

tensity measure. Using this method would place China toward the bottom of polluting countries instead of at the top. It should not be surprising to find that when it comes to carbon emissions, the overall amount seems to matter most in terms of environmental impact, not how the number is calculated (see Figure 4.1).

At the start of the Copenhagen summit in 2009, developing countries seemed more willing to reduce emissions than at Kyoto in 1997, but they expected economic assistance from developed countries to reach these objectives. In retrospect, the expectation for the United States to subsidize China's green energy movement was probably unrealistic, and that proved to be the case. Not only was the United States still recovering from an economic recession itself, but China also regularly lends the U.S. government hundreds of billions of dollars. This raised the obvious and politically contentious question as to why the United States should then assist China. President Obama was blunt on this issue and raised the expectation that China, Brazil, and India "make some changes, as well—not of the same pace, not in the same way, but they're going to have to do something to assure that whatever carbon [developed countries are] taking out of the environment is not just simply dumped in by other parties."[21] China was not pleased with the U.S. stance, however, and sent a markedly low-level delegation to attend such a high-level meeting, clearly refusing to negotiate.

Although the 2009 summit attempted to address climate change as a *global* concern for all of humanity, it is apparent that *national* concerns about the economic impact of reducing carbon emissions prevented a comprehensive agreement. In Copenhagen, the director of the UN secretary-general's climate change support team, Janos Pasztor, captured the challenges of addressing climate change from the United Nations' global perspective: "This is not a climate-change negotiation. It's about something much more fundamental. It's about economic strength. [Countries] just have to slug it out."[22] Of course, countries are mainly guided by national objectives and policies that seek to balance economic growth and pollution and not long-term global human security concerns. China and India have argued, for instance, that their growth should not be curtailed just because the West's industrial revolution began centuries ago. While the carbon emissions coming from China and India top the world's output, their governments maintain that increased economic activity can actually improve human security. The claims make sense for these developing countries, as economic development is a more pressing concern than climate change. Over the long term, these countries argue, their societies will become stronger through development before the severe effects of climate change are apparent in the latter half of the twenty-first century.

For its part, the Obama administration has attempted to link the economy and climate change in a positive equation. Through clean energy programs like building wind turbines or solar panels, it asserts that the economy and the environment both could be helped. Additionally, geo-engineering solutions are being explored wherein carbon dioxide can be captured from the air and placed into underground reservoirs or giant solar shades can be placed in orbit to reflect sunlight into space. Only time will tell if this approach will prevent the forecast tragedies, but many governments are not waiting to fully appreciate the security concerns of climate change and are preparing accordingly.

CONCLUSION

More so than the many other challenges addressed in this book, environmental security does not discriminate by levels of development and privilege. Instead, all human beings regardless of their citizenship are affected by environmental change. However, as with so many other human security issues, people in developing countries are more vulnerable to environmental change since they lack adequate resources to cope effectively with the problems generated by climate change. In any case, there are no clear dividing lines among states and experts on the cause, pace, and solutions to climate change, as science, economics, and politics are uncomfortably mixed.

As this chapter demonstrates, addressing climate change from a global perspective will continue to be elusive, as national governments seek either to promote development, thereby increasing use of hydrocarbons, or to sustain high levels of human development without compromising economic activity. Given that the most catastrophic effects of climate change will probably not be evident until later this century, incremental policy solutions may keep pace with environmental change. However, this type of approach will increasingly frustrate those countries that attempt to reduce carbon emissions through alternative energy programs but whose efforts are offset by increased carbon emissions from rapidly growing countries in regions like Asia. Likewise, frustration with limited changes will doubtless continue to motivate the expanding green social movement around the world, including its growing linkages to the sustainable development movement.

In the short term, other environmental issues like natural disasters, population density, water scarcity, and desertification will doubtless challenge human security in many parts of the world. And as developed countries like the United States seek to promote development elsewhere, they must inevitably encounter varied environmental challenges that often involve political issues. This already occurs when the United States supports organizations that dig wells, promote sustainable agricultural practices, and assist with environmental projects. Unfortunately, already struggling governments may be further weakened by the accelerating effects of climate change, which will reduce their capacity to take advantage of international assistance, provide basic services expected of modern governments, or improve human security for their populations. For all these reasons, the U.S. government will need to continue to address the potential for underlying environmental conditions that engender conflict and to study climate change scenarios to understand future implications and human security concerns. In turn, all human beings will need to remain sensitive to this issue and to make judgments about how their individual and group actions may impact the environment.

To Learn More

Former Greenpeace activist Bjorn Lomborg explores the extent to which the environment is deteriorating in *Cool It: The Skeptical Environmentalist's Guide to Global Warming* (New York: Vintage, 2008).

The Center for International Earth Science Information Network at Columbia University (www.ciesin.org) works at the intersection of the social, natural, and information sciences and specializes in online data and information management, spatial data integration and training, and interdisciplinary research related to human interactions in the environment.

Marc Levy asks, "Is the environment a national security issue?" in *International Security* 20, no. 2 (2001): 35–62.

Track global climate patterns through the National Oceanographic and Atmospheric Administration at www.ncdc.noaa.gov/oa/climate/globalwarming .html.

Watch an animation of the planet's snow cover at http://earthobservatory .nasa.gov/GlobalMaps/view.php?d1=MOD10C1_M_SNOW.

Examine the principles of the United Nations Framework Convention on Climate Change at http://unfccc.int/essential_background/convention/background/items/1349.php.

Explore the Alliance of Small Island States to see how they perceive climate change and the approaches they take to lobby carbon emitters at www .sidsnet.org/aosis/.

The World Watch Institute is an independent and interdisciplinary nongovernmental research organization, founded in 1974, that "focuses on the 21st-century challenges of climate change, resource degradation, population growth, and poverty by developing and disseminating solid data and innovative strategies for achieving a sustainable society." Scan their many programs, events, and publications online at www.worldwatch.org/.

The Pacific Institute tracks water conflicts over the past 5,000 years. Explore the first water-related conflict between the Mesopotamian city-states of Lagash and Umma at http://worldwater.org/conflictchronology.pdf.

Scan the Web site of the Nobel Peace Prize–winning, UN-created Intergovernmental Panel on Climate Change experts to view their conclusions on global warming: www.ipcc.ch/index.htm.

Review U.S. senator James Inhofe's findings disputing global warming in the United States Senate Committee on Environment and Public Works Minority Staff, "United States Senate Report: 'Consensus' Exposed: The CRU Controversy," February 2010, at www.epw.senate.gov/inhofe.

Notes

1. Macabrey, "Sea Levels May Rise Faster"; Vedantam, "Climate Fears Are Driving 'Ecomigration'" (for both, see chap. 1, n. 32).

2. Ban Ki-moon, "Secretary-General's Message on the International Day for Preventing the Exploitation of the Environment in War and Armed Conflict," November 6, 2008.

3. R. K. Pachauri, "Nobel Peace Prize Lecture," December 10, 2007, available at http://nobelprize.org/nobel_prizes/peace/laureates/2007/ipcc-lecture.html.

4. Thomas F. Homer-Dixon, "Environmental Scarcities and Violent Conflict: Evidence from Cases," in *Theories of World Peace: An "International Security" Reader*, ed. Michael E. Brown et al. (Cambridge: MIT Press, 1998), 501–536.

5. R. K. Pachauri, "Statement at UN Summit on Climate Change," September 22, 2009.

6. Rome Declaration on World Food Security, World Food Summit, Rome, November 13, 1996, available at www.fao.org/docrep/003/w3613e/w3613e00 .HTM. As early as 1948 the foundational Universal Declaration of Human Rights declared the right to food to be a fundamental human right.

7. Al Gore, *Earth in the Balance: Ecology and the Human Spirit* (New York: Houghton Mifflin, 1992), 29–30.

8. United Nations Environment Programme, *Organizational Profile* (Nairobi, Kenya: UNEP HQ, 2009), 11.

9. Intergovernmental Panel on Climate Change, *Climate Change, 2007: Synthesis Report* (Valencia, Spain: Intergovernmental Panel on Climate Change, November 12, 2007).

10. Peter Schwartz and Doug Randall, "An Abrupt Climate Change Scenario and Its Implications for United States National Security," October 2003, available at www.gbn.com/consulting/article_details.php?id=61, 22.

11. Dennis C. Blair, "Annual Threat Assessment of the Intelligence Community for the Senate Select Committee on Intelligence," February 12, 2009, available at www.dni.gov/testimonies/20090212_testimony.pdf.

12. Both quoted in Ban Ki-moon, "Statement at the Security Council Debate on Energy, Security, and Climate," April 17, 2007, available at www.un.org/apps/sg/sgstats.asp?nid=2524.

13. Ibid.

14. T. Joseph Lopez, "Voices of Experience: On Climate Change and the Conditions for Terrorism," in *National Security and the Threat of Climate Change*, by CNA, 17 (see chap. 1, n. 24).

15. Department of Defense, *National Defense Strategy of the United States* (Washington, DC: Department of Defense, June 2008), 5.

16. See http://securityandclimate.cna.org, 7.

17. Quoted in Bryan Bender, "Pentagon Flexes Its Altruism Muscle: Aims to Win Trust with Soft Power," *Boston Globe,* July 28, 2008.

18. Secretary of the Navy Ray Mabus, "Remarks at the Naval Energy Forum," McLean, VA, October 14, 2009, available at www.navy.mil/navydata/ . . . /Mabus/ . . . /SECNAV%20Energy%20Forum%2014%20Oct%2009%20Rel1.pdf.

19. Al Gore, "Nobel Peace Prize Lecture," December 10, 2007; Desmond Tutu quoted in presentation speech by Professor Ole Danbolt Mjøs, chairman of the Norwegian Nobel Committee, Oslo, December 10, 2007.

20. Michael A. Levi, "Copenhagen's Inconvenient Truth: How to Salvage the Climate Conference," *Foreign Affairs* 88, no. 5 (September–October 2009): 92; Jessica Seddon Wallack and Veerabhadran Ramanathan, "The Other Climate Changers," *Foreign Affairs* 88, no. 5 (September–October 2009): 113.

21. Barack Obama, "Remarks by the President During Press Availability in Copenhagen," December 18, 2009.

22. Quoted in Jeffrey Ball, Stephen Power, and Alesandro Torello, "Divisions Persist on Core Questions as Leaders Arrive," *Wall Street Journal,* December 15, 2009.

5

Maritime Security

*The security of the Maritime Domain is a global issue.
The United States, in cooperation with our allies and
friends around the world and our State, local, and private
sector partners, will work to ensure that lawful private and
public activities in the Maritime Domain are protected
against attack and criminal and otherwise unlawful or
hostile exploitation.*

—NATIONAL SECURITY PRESIDENTIAL
DIRECTIVE 41/HOMELAND SECURITY
PRESIDENTIAL DIRECTIVE 13 (2004)

When thinking about security, the oceans are often taken for granted. No country governs them, no corporation controls them, and no military dominates them. Yet, like the air, the oceans are essential for human life in providing food and oxygen. Beyond this, oceans also provide for human economic and social needs. Oceans offer key resources such as minerals to supply the metals industry and energy to fuel cars and heat homes. Further, the oceans are primarily a transportation resource, facilitating the movement of people to improve their human security by emigrating to North America and Europe. And oceans can undermine human security through naturally occurring events like hurricanes and tsunamis.

Given the global nature of trade, oceans are the vital highways of international commerce. Oceans enable Americans to eat fresh fruit from South America in the middle of winter, allow Europeans to drink coffee from East Africa, and enable Asians to drive their cars with oil from the Persian Gulf. Considering the number of imports Americans consume, the international character of the economy is obvious. But unless there is an environmental tragedy such as an oil spill like the 2010 BP event in the Gulf of Mexico, a major natural disaster such as a hurricane, or maritime crime such as piracy that disrupts trade, oceans are often overlooked by policy makers and national security professionals. To better understand concerns about the oceans, this chapter provides a sketch of the global maritime domain, examines salient security issues affecting the oceans, and considers current and future challenges facing policy makers and societies as they attempt to reduce maritime insecurity.

GLOBAL MARITIME DOMAIN

When looking at the earth from space, one fact is obvious: Water is the dominant feature. To be precise, 70 percent of the planet is covered by water, and a significant portion of the earth is covered by frozen water in the Arctic and Antarctica. Water is so prevalent that astronomer and writer Carl Sagan dubbed the earth a pale-blue dot, overlooking the brown landmasses that dominate international affairs. Although Sagan meant to evoke how small the earth is in cosmic terms, his accurate description serves as a reminder of how important water is to the planet— 80 percent of the world's population lives on or near a coast, and 90 percent of international commerce travels by sea. Without healthy and safe oceans and access to water in general, human progress is severely limited. As economist Jeffrey Sachs has argued, "Sea-navigable regions are generally richer than land-locked regions. ... [R]egions easily accessible to sea-based trade almost everywhere have achieved a very high measure of economic development."[1] Historically, great powers have been those with access to the sea, such as the United States, Britain, France, Germany, Holland, Spain, Portugal, and Japan. Countries forecast to be great powers in the twenty-first century also include seafaring nations

Map 5.1—Strait of Hormuz. The Strait of Hormuz is one of the most important global choke points where an estimated 40 percent of the world's seaborne oil travels. Map courtesy of the Library of Congress.

like China, India, and Brazil. By contrast, economist Paul Collier has singled out being landlocked as one of the most important "traps" that characterize the poorest countries of the world.[2]

In assessing the maritime domain, some key features are obvious, such as the oceans, bays, and straits. Less obvious are those features important for security such as choke points and ports. The U.S. government takes an expansive view of the maritime domain and includes in its conception "all areas and things of, on, under, relating to, adjacent to, or bordering on a sea, ocean, or other navigable waterway, including all maritime-related activities, infrastructure, people, cargo, and vessels and other conveyances."[3]

The U.S. definition of the maritime domain is thus all-encompassing, but it is important to point out three distinct zones reflected in the near-universally accepted 1982 United Nations Convention on the Law of the Sea.[4] According to UNCLOS, territorial waters are those under government sovereign control and legally recognized as twelve nautical miles from the low-water mark of a coastal state. This zone is under the exclusive control of the state, but ships of all nations are allowed innocent passage. Beyond twelve nautical miles is the Exclusive Economic Zone, which extends seaward to two hundred nautical miles. Within an EEZ, the coastal state has special rights to use and exploit marine resources for oil exploration, seabed mining, and fishing. The international community still enjoys the rights and freedom of navigation and over flight in the EEZ, as well as the ability to lay submarine telecommunications cables and other non-resource-related uses of the oceans. Beyond two hundred miles is considered international waters, where all coastal and noncoastal states have equal access and enjoy the freedom of the seas and other activities.

Unless one travels by sea, it is difficult to appreciate how large the oceans are and the role they play in separating the continents. On average, it takes about two weeks to cross the Pacific by sea or a week to cross the Atlantic. This distance provides natural barriers to war for those countries favorably situated. The United States, for example, has been relatively im-mune from foreign invasion because of its peaceful neighbors in North America, with the Atlantic Ocean separating the country from Europe's wars and the Pacific Ocean separating it from Asia's conflicts. Even the recent United States–Soviet Union rivalry, which largely defined U.S. for-eign policy in the twentieth century, was predicted to lead to large land battles in Europe and not in North America. To be sure, both countries prepared for great naval battles in the North Atlantic and the Pacific, but land and air warfare tended to dominate planning.

Oceans can also amplify a country's relative power in the world, en-abling competent seafaring countries to have global presence, influence, and disproportionate control of territory, people, and commerce. His-torically, countries such as the United Kingdom, Portugal, and Oman created networks of ports and trading posts throughout the world that enriched their societies through trade and plunder. At its height, it was said the sun never set on the British Empire due to its control of territory on every inhabited continent. This would not have been possible without the Royal Navy. The remnants of British and European exploration and colonization are evident in the languages spoken in South America, Asia, and Africa. European languages both form the basis for many cultures in the world and facilitate communication within regions. Along these lines, Madagascar adopted English in 2007 as one of its official languages alongside French and the local Malagasy, not to speak to Americans necessarily but to facilitate interactions with countries in East Africa such as Kenya.

Today, oceans are still essential for economic development. Witness China's rapid economic development through large-scale exports that is made possible by containerized shipping and sea transport. In addition to accounting for an amazing 90 percent of international commerce, trade by sea also includes 50 percent of oil movement. Additionally, about 65 percent of the world's oil reserves and 35 percent of the world's gas reserves are located in the oceans. The prevalence of sea-based hydrocarbons satisfies demands to fuel economic activity, but also causes friction among states that compete for these resources. Finally, intercontinental information flows are enabled by the sea, with 95 percent of communications traveling via submarine fiber-optic cables that connect the continents. Thus, it is not surprising that economic development and a country's prosperity are often linked to its proximity to the sea.

Significantly, countries that control the land adjacent to where oceans meet often sit astride key trade routes (see Table 5.1). Known as choke points, these narrow straits or canals are considered vital to maritime trade. The Panama Canal, the Suez Canal, the Strait of Gibraltar, the Strait of Malacca and Singapore, and the Strait of Hormuz are among the most significant choke points in the world. Singapore's creation and accelerated development were based on its geographic location along one of the most heavily trafficked waterways in the world. Every day, more than two hundred ships transit the Strait of Malacca, making Singapore an important transshipment point for global trade. (Malacca is the shortest sea route between Persian Gulf oil and gas suppliers and the Asian markets, which amounts to about 15 million barrels of oil per day.) Or consider the Bab el Mandeb, which connects the Indian Ocean to the Mediterranean Sea via the Red Sea and is a critical route, bringing more than 3 million barrels of oil a day from the Persian Gulf to Europe.[5] Additionally, as the Arctic ice melts, new trade routes and choke points are expected to open in the High North, which has consequences for countries along the Arctic (Canada, United States, Russia, Denmark, and Norway) and those countries that rely on current trade routes for development such as Panama,

TABLE 5.1. KEY MARITIME CHOKE POINTS AROUND THE WORLD

EUROPE	MIDDLE EAST	AFRICA	SOUTHEAST ASIA	CARIBBEAN
Strait of Gibraltar	Suez Canal	Mozambique Channel	Strait of Malacca	Panama Canal
Strait of Dover	Strait of Hormuz	Bab el Mandeb	Lombok Strait	Straits of Florida
Kiel Canal			Luzon Strait	Windward and Mona Passages

Kenya, and Yemen. It appears that shorter maritime routes between Europe and Asia that sixteenth-century European explorers searched for may be a reality in the twenty-first century as the Arctic Ocean becomes navigable.

CHALLENGES TO MARITIME SECURITY

There is increasing awareness of the shared dangers complicating maritime security. In 2008 the United Nations General Assembly declared that as of 2009, June 8 would be celebrated as World Oceans Day. Secretary-General Ban Ki-moon issued a press release on that day, commenting that "human activities are taking a terrible toll on the world's oceans and seas. Vulnerable marine ecosystems, such as corals, and important fisheries are being damaged by over-exploitation, illegal, unreported and unregulated fishing, destructive fishing practices, invasive alien species and marine pollution, especially from land-based sources."[6] Intergovernmental institutions such as the International Maritime Organization attempt to unify international efforts to improve maritime safety and security. Conventions such as the Safety of Life at Sea (1974) and the associated International Ship and Port Facility Security Code (2002) seek to prevent security incidents on ships and in ports. Programs such as the Container Security Initiative place U.S. Customs inspectors in international ports to screen cargo. And international naval coalitions with countries as diverse as Russia, South Korea, and Denmark are sending warships to combat piracy in East Africa.[7]

At the same time that governments are sending their navies to conduct non-war-fighting missions, nongovernmental proenvironmental groups seek to reduce maritime insecurity, too. For example, Greenpeace and the International Crisis Group identify overfishing as a root cause of piracy and call for better regulation of the world's fishing fleets. And the Sea Shepherd Conservation Society regularly intervenes in whaling activities, which reduced Japan's whale harvest by 50 percent in 2010. Other groups like Friends of the Earth and the Basel Action Network attempt to limit maritime pollution by targeting destructive ship-disposal practices that escape state regulation or provide fuel for cash-strapped militaries to increase patrols of ecologically important areas. The World Wildlife Fund, for example, supports Mozambique's navy through fuel subsidies to reduce poaching.

The changed nature of security is bringing together nontraditional partners. Because navies provide necessary presence and logistical capabilities, their governments and various nongovernmental groups are coming together to address the specific sources of maritime insecurity, which include illegal, unreported, and underreported fishing; piracy; illicit trafficking of people, drugs, and weapons; and maritime pollution.

ILLEGAL, UNREPORTED, AND UNDERREPORTED FISHING

Fish provide more than 2.9 billion people with at least 15 percent of their average per capita animal protein intake. Yet illegal, unreported, and underreported (IUU) fishing devastates fish stocks and undermines developing countries' food supplies. In 2007 United Nations General Assembly Resolution 62/177 deplored the fact that "illegal, unreported, and underreported [fishing] constitutes a serious threat to fish stocks and marine habitats and ecosystems, to the detriment of sustainable fisheries as well as the food security and the economies of many states, particularly developing states." The United Nations Food and Agriculture Organization declared that IUU fishing constitutes a serious threat to: (1) fisheries,

Image 5.1—This illegal swordfish catch was seized in West Africa. Photo credit: U.S. Coast Guard.

especially those of high-value varieties that are already overfished (e.g., cod, tuna, redfish, and swordfish); (2) marine habitats, including vulnerable marine ecosystems; and (3) food security and the economies of developing countries.[8] Numerous UN resolutions encourage states to take effective measures to deter illegal activities that undermine fisheries' conservation and management practices.[9] Given the importance of fish protein, the scope of the problem is global, but it has had a disproportionate effect on developing countries that do not have alternate food sources, the income to afford food imports, or the maritime forces to reduce IUU fishing.

For example, case studies conducted in nine African countries show estimates of total financial losses in their Exclusive Economic Zones to illegal fishing reaching an estimated US$335 million per year.[10] When considering all of sub-Saharan Africa, the total estimated EEZ losses are estimated to be a staggering $937 million per year.[11] This represents major income considering how poor almost all these countries are. Losses to struggling societies have an immediate economic impact, but future fish stocks are jeopardized, too. At the current rate of overfishing, forecasters predict that the ecological systems that support the fish population will collapse by 2045, thus negating the primary protein sources for African coastal nations.[12] Consequently, the United Nations Food and Agriculture Organization has been brokering a global treaty to combat IUU fishing. Since boats involved in illegal activities must bring their catch ashore, enforcement in ports is seen as the best solution. To support this, the United States and other countries are using their navies to assist developing countries to build capacity for fisheries management to include monitoring their EEZs, patrolling territorial waters, and securing their port facilities.[13]

PIRACY

The other side of the illegal fishing coin in East Africa is piracy. That is, fishermen made redundant by illegal overfishing have used their seamanship skills and knowledge of the seas to partner with criminal groups to hijack ships in the Indian Ocean and Gulf of Aden.[14] Though largely a nuisance to developed countries since the nineteenth century, piracy has once again captured international attention and concern. In 2008 ship hijackings of a Ukrainian ship loaded with armored battle tanks and a Saudi supertanker laden with 2 million barrels of oil valued at more than $100 million pushed piracy into the headlines. Yet the world has actually lived with piracy for millennia (even Roman ruler Julius Caesar was once a victim). Pirates entered American history in the eighteenth century when President Thomas Jefferson condemned the practice. His condemnation extended to the European countries that paid tribute or ransoms to the Barbary states of North Africa that sponsored piracy. When American commerce was threatened, both President Jefferson and President James Madison sent the U.S. Navy and Marine Corps to North Africa to stop the pirate attacks and were mainly successful through military intervention. Three centuries later, however, there are important differences, as merchant fleets are mainly private, piracy is not state sponsored, and threats to sea-lanes are now thought of as a global threat rather than a national one. Further, navies have had very little influence in reducing piracy in the twenty-first century.

The International Maritime Bureau defines piracy and armed robbery as "an act of boarding or attempting to board any ship with apparent intent to commit theft or any other crime and with apparent intent or capability to use force in the furtherance of that act."[15] Up until 1994 reports of piracy and armed robbery against ships were relatively equally distributed around the world. As global trade increased throughout the 1990s, piracy increased in key shipping lanes in the South China Sea, the Strait of Malacca, and the Indian Ocean. Since 2004 there have been about 275 annual attacks worldwide but over 400 by 2009 (see Figure 5.1). Recently, pirate waters have shifted away from Southeast Asia to both coasts of Africa. In West Africa piracy is primarily armed robbery at sea that occurs close to shore. In cases like these, criminals board ships at anchor in the middle of the night and steal valuables from the crew or ship. But in the eastern Horn of Africa, piracy is hijacking that occurs hundreds of miles from the coast. The objective is to hold ships and crews for ransom.

Somali pirates, operating in relatively small numbers, gain control of a vessel and then direct that vessel to Somali waters until ransoms are paid. Acts of piracy ranging from crimes of opportunity against anchored vessels in the Gulf of Guinea and the Nigerian Delta to ship seizures orchestrated by organized gangs in the Gulf of Aden and Somali waters can earn anywhere from a few thousand dollars in stolen booty to millions of dollars in ransom paid to recover a merchant ship and its crew. Thus, a pirated vessel can produce exceptional income for the generally poor perpetrators of piracy. The reemergence of piracy not only poses a threat to the local land-based economies of African states where piracy exists, but also negatively impacts the global maritime economy with observable costly effects on trade routes. These costs include extra fuel to avoid known pirate activity, additional insurance coverage, and embarking private security teams as an extra precaution.

As piracy developed in East Africa, pirates garnered world attention because their activities affected the waters of the Red Sea and the Gulf of Aden, which are a strategic link between Europe and Asia. The area is an essential oil transport route with 30 percent of the world's oil passing through the Gulf of Aden. Although pirates do not routinely target the larger tankers transiting the area, pirates had become increasingly bold by 2010. A significant attack against a large tanker in the Gulf of Aden

Image 5.2—Dhows like these are used by fishermen and pirates alike. Photo credit: Andre N. McIntyre, U.S. Navy.

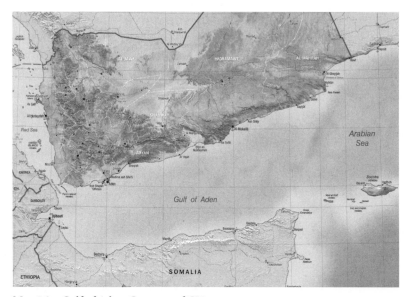

Map 5.2—Gulf of Aden. Courtesy of CIA.

FIGURE 5.1: RISING MARITIME PIRACY ATTACKS

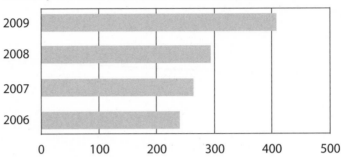

Source: ICC Commercial Services, "2009 Worldwide Piracy Figures Surpass 400," January 14, 2010, available at www.icc-ccs.org/images/stories/News/ Large_Images/piracy_graph.png.

could cause delays or closure of the traffic through the Bab el Mandeb strait, preventing Persian Gulf tankers from reaching the Suez Canal. This would lead to greater energy costs and a disruption to European energy supplies.[16]

Piracy not only affects the commercial shipping industry but also directly affects efforts of the UN World Food Programme, which delivers 90 percent of the food to Somalia by sea.[17] In fact, the first U.S.-flagged ship that was almost hijacked in 2009 was carrying food aid to alleviate starvation in Somalia.[18] Although East Africans generally show greater concern about illegal fishing than about piracy, international relief efforts to those societies are directly threatened by piracy. To ensure food aid does reach populations in East Africa, naval coalitions are conducting convoy operations. As one would expect, the pirates avoid areas patrolled by naval coalitions and have extended their range into the Indian Ocean. Several attacks in 2010 were closer to the Indian coastline than they were to the Somali coastline.

Since pirates operate on the sea and hijack seagoing vessels on the world's oceans, it is easy to see piracy as a maritime issue. Yet pirates operate from land and thrive in parts of the world where there are security deficits that allow illegally armed groups (pirates included) to operate. Most experts agree that the problems of Somali piracy begin ashore. Martin Murphy explains that the seven basic factors that enable maritime

CONTEMPORARY CHALLENGE

Piracy in the Gulf of Aden

Relatively rare, piracy in the Gulf of Aden increased dramatically from just 7 incidents in 2004 to 217 incidents in 2009. In contrast to piracy in Southeast Asia or in West Africa, piracy in the Gulf of Aden is linked to hijacking and kidnapping. In 2009 it is estimated that pirates collected at least $100 million in ransoms for their victims. Most of the pirates come from Somalia, which has not had a stable government for thirty years and continues to be wracked by civil war. With this type of security deficit, illegal armed groups are relatively free to exploit the maritime domain and act as smugglers and pirates.

Although there are limits to naval actions, policy makers have created naval coalitions and deployed warships to the region to protect ships in convoys, respond to ships in distress, and deter piracy. Unfortunately, navies cannot stop piracy. First, there are not enough ships in the world's navies to adequately patrol oceans. The lack of shipbuilding over the past twenty years has left a seapower deficit in the world that pirates, drug smugglers, and human traffickers exploit. Second, international coordination is challenging. There are at least three discrete task forces conducting maritime patrols in the region and additional unilateral efforts by China, India, and Russia. Third, there is no single method to deter the pirates. Transnational actors, like pirates, do not care if the United States is a superpower, that NATO is the most developed military alliance in the world, or that China and India have global ambitions. Piracy is business, and navies are just one more obstacle to avoid. Finally, piracy begins ashore. To date, international efforts neglect (for obvious reasons) addressing conditions in Somalia that encourage and support piracy. When the United States attempted to alleviate famine in Somalia in 1992–1993, it eventually found itself caught between many warring Somali clans, which was memorialized in Mark Bowden's tragic story of *Blackhawk Down*. This experience still resonates for the United States and many other countries who might otherwise intervene to restore order and help this archetypal failed state develop economic opportunities that might discourage piracy.

piracy are elements of sanctuary.[19] Large ungoverned areas, poor governance, the inability of governments to adequately patrol their territorial
waters or defend sea ports, and the violence and chaos existing in large
portions of the Horn of Africa offer pirates (and other criminal or terrorist organizations) this sanctuary of protection and freedom of operations. Addressing piracy therefore requires bringing security, stability,
and development to countries like Somalia, as outlined in previous chapters. However, given the decades-long civil war there, this is proving to
be a significant challenge for Somalis, even with the assistance of the international community. Numerous international attempts since the early
1990s have failed to bring stability to Somalia, yet dealing with symptoms
of the problem continues to be unsatisfactory. U.S. efforts to improve security in ungoverned spaces that provide sanctuary for illegally armed
groups like pirates are captured in the government's twenty-first-century
naval strategy: "Creating and maintaining maritime security is required
to mitigate the threats of piracy, terrorism, weapons proliferation, and
other illegal activities. Countering these 'irregular and transnational
threats' will enhance global security, secure freedom of navigation for the
benefit of all nations, and protect our homeland. This Strategy also
pledges that the United States will assist the international community in
policing the 'global common' and suppressing common threats."[20]

DRUG TRAFFICKING

Illegal fishing and piracy only recaptured international attention in 2008,
but illicit trafficking of drugs by sea has provoked a maritime security response for decades.[21] Criminal groups increasingly benefit from maritime
insecurity by exploiting trade routes to traffic drugs, people, and weapons,
as referenced in an earlier chapter. They thrive in the vastness of the
oceans and relative lack of maritime domain awareness or response capabilities within the developing world. Heroin produced in Afghanistan
reaches Europe by sea. Cocaine produced in Colombia reaches Europe
and the United States by sea. And methamphetamines produced in Asia
reach Africa by sea.

Noncommercial maritime vessels, such as go-fast (cigarette boats with
large outboard motors) and fishing boats, are the principal conveyances

THINK AGAIN

Pirates Are Not Criminals

It may be surprising to find that not everyone sees pirates as the scourge of humanity. Some view them as being forced into this way of life due to political and economic misfortune, and others even see pirates as heroes fighting back against illegal dumping and illegal fishing. Perhaps the most prominent person dissenting from a negative view of pirates is Libya's president, Mu'ammar Gadhafi, who likened them to a navy merely protecting Somali waters. He told the United Nations General Assembly in 2009:

> I am telling you the Somalis are not pirates. The pirates are ourselves because we exploited all the fishing grounds. We undermined their livelihood. We undermined their economies and their regional waters. All the ships of the world, whether from Libya, India, Japan or America exploited Somali waters and we are the aggressors. After the Somali state collapsed we came to pick up the remnants. The Somalis had to defend their marine wealth, which is their food and the food of their children. Then they transformed themselves into pirates to defend themselves. They are not pirates. They only defend their livelihood. And now you are handling it in the wrong way. You are saying let us send warships to strike the Somalis. No. Warships should go to strike the pirates who undermined the Somali wealth and resources. You have to strike the foreign fishing boats.[1]

Gadhafi's defense of pirates has gained little traction, but Africans tend to avoid seeing pirates as a security challenge. This stems from the land-oriented focus of African militaries, an indirect link between maritime commerce and African development, and a romantic view of pirates who secure million-dollar ransoms for foreign ships and foreign crews. For many desperately poor Africans, there may even be a hint of admiration in the fact that such humble individuals can outfox the wealthy and relatively privileged of the world.

---

1. Mu'ammar Gadhafi's speech to the United Nations General Assembly, November 23, 2009, provided and translated courtesy of the Jamahiriya News Agency (Jana), available at www.btinternet.com/~davidbeaumont/msf/gadafi .htm.

Image 5.3—USS *McInerney* tows a captured semisubmersible vehicle carrying seven tons of cocaine. The seized vessel has the capability to travel from Ecuador to California. Photo credit: Justin Cooper, U.S. Navy.

used by traffickers to move cocaine shipments through the eastern Pacific. Go-fast boats and private aircraft are the most common cocaine transport methods used by traffickers in the western Caribbean, which is an important transshipment corridor. The result is that Mexican and Colombian drug trafficking organizations generate, remove, and launder between $18 billion and $39 billion in wholesale drug proceeds annually.[22] These groups use the profits to equip themselves with the latest weapons, which are often more advanced than their national governments' forces. For example, Colombian drug trafficking organizations increasingly use semisubmersible vehicles to evade detection. Resembling small submarines, an estimated sixty semisubmersibles may have shipped more than 330 metric tons of cocaine, or other illicit and dangerous materials, in 2009.[23] The traffickers' increasing sophistication has warranted a military response to detect and interdict these vessels, as police forces lack the capacity to detect submarine-like vehicles.

POLICY SPOTLIGHT

Drug Trafficking

One consequence of drug trafficking is the destabilizing impact on countries located between producing and consuming countries. Countries of Central America, the Caribbean, and West Africa are particularly vulnerable to traffickers, who exploit long, unguarded coastlines and limited law enforcement capabilities. In 2009 the Department of State identified the following countries as major drug transit countries: the Bahamas, Bolivia, Brazil, the Dominican Republic, Guatemala, Haiti, Jamaica, Mexico, Nigeria, Pakistan, Panama, Paraguay, Peru, and Venezuela.[1] In these countries, traffickers seek out local partners in gangs who provide fuel and supplies in exchange for drugs and weapons. In many cases, small countries lack the security institutions to deal effectively with the problems that drug traffickers bring to their islands and coastal areas. In larger countries, systemic corruption may impair a concerted institutional response. The consequences are evident everywhere in increased domestic drug consumption and related violence.

In Mexico, for example, more than 8,000 people were killed in drug-related violence in 2009. In general, while drug trafficking organizations target rivals as they commit brutal killings like decapitation, they also target civilians and officials from the law enforcement and judicial systems. The scale of violence exceeds Mexico's law enforcement capabilities, so military units are now employed against drug trafficking cartels. As one example, in December 2009, it took more than two hundred marines in a two-hour gun battle to confront drug kingpin Arturo Beltran Leyva. And in the small Caribbean island of Jamaica, authorities launched a monthlong campaign that resulted in more than seventy-three civilians being killed in June 2010 before Christopher Coke, alleged drug boss of the most powerful Jamaican drug-smuggling gang, was captured.[2]

---

1. U.S. Department of State Bureau of International Narcotics and Law Enforcement Affairs, *2009 International Narcotics Control Strategy Report*, February 27, 2009, available at www.state.gov/p/in/rls/nrcrpt/2009/vol1/116522.htm.

2. Raspert Turner and Chris Kraul, "Alleged Jamaican Drug Lord Is Captured," *Los Angeles Times*, June 22, 2010, available at http://articles.latimes.com/2010/jun/22/world/la-fg-jamaica-arrest-20100623.

Since the 1980s maritime forces have attempted to reduce illicit trafficking by sea. In the twenty-first century, these governmental efforts increased, as traffickers used better techniques to get the drugs to market
in the United States and Europe. Building on a 1990s Clinton-era initiative, the Bush administration declared the Caribbean to be America's
third border in 2004, which was widely applauded in the hemisphere. At
the time, the Caribbean Community (also known as CARICOM) "recognize[d] our interdependence and the importance of close cooperation
to combat new and emerging transnational threats that endanger the very
fabric of our societies. By virtue of their small size, geographic configu-
ration and lack of technical and financial resources, Caribbean States are
particularly vulnerable and susceptible to these risks and threats. This is
especially true for illicit trafficking in persons, drugs, and firearms, terrorism and other transnational criminal activities."[24] The Third Border
Initiative is intended to focus U.S.-Caribbean engagement through targeted programs that comprise both new and ongoing activities designed
to enhance cooperation in the diplomatic, security, economic, environmental, health, and education arenas. This includes programs to detect
and interdict drug traffickers.

For the U.S. military in general, and U.S. Southern Command in particular, the global illicit drug trade is a significant transnational security
threat that undermines democratic governments, terrorizes populations,
impedes economic development, and hinders regional stability.[25] Executive director Antonio Maria Costa of the UN Office of Drug Control and
Crime warned that "states in the Caribbean, Central America and West
Africa, as well as the border regions of Mexico, are caught in the crossfire
between the world's biggest coca producers, the Andean countries, and
the biggest consumers, North America and Europe."[26] This formulation
labels Caribbean countries as victimized bystanders to a Yankee-only
drug problem,[27] but the Department of State has recognized that this view
is changing:

> Instead, too often, there was a perception that without demand,
> supply would end, and that transit countries need not worry about
> addiction among their domestic populations. We now know that

the lure of such incredible profits, as the drug traffic generates, makes this a trade that circumvents such a simple formula. Those who want to supply drugs make it their business to encourage demand by paying transit state residents in drugs instead of money and manipulating prices to get and keep addicts. Drug abuse and addiction is widespread in most transit countries; at least to some extent, drug supply creates its own demand. We all face a thinking, well-financed enemy and we must all, every legitimate nation-state and international authority, work together to thwart this network.[28]

The international challenge of combating drug trafficking is slowly moving the Latin American and Caribbean region beyond resentment about the United States' interventionist past in the hemisphere. Indeed, there is a shared insecurity enabling cooperation on mutual challenges. But this has not been easy. Drug traffickers successfully exploit weak security institutions around the world and in this hemisphere, taking advantage of political tension created by U.S. drug policy. Additional gains made in controlling illicit trafficking from Colombia's Caribbean coast are increasingly offset by drug trafficking occurring from Colombia's Pacific coast or its neighbor Venezuela. The challenge for the United States remains how to build renewed relationships without overwhelming these countries with U.S. military and law enforcement efforts. With the exception of the forces of the huge country of Brazil, the U.S. Marine Corps is bigger than every military in the Western Hemisphere.

MARITIME DISPUTES

The preceding discussion highlighted how subnational and transnational actors are exploiting the maritime domain, which has facilitated international cooperation among countries that seek to reduce illicit trafficking and piracy. At the same time, other maritime issues inspire competition among countries and societies. Among these issues are disputes over inhabited and uninhabited islands. For example, in 1982 the United Kingdom and Argentina fought a war over islands in the South Atlantic located three hundred miles from South America and seven hundred miles from Antarctica, islands that are about the size of Connecticut. The dispute stems from competing claims of what the British call the Falklands and the Argentines call the Malvinas. Both claims are rooted in centuries-old colonial claims made by the British and the Argentine government.

The outcome of the 1982 war that claimed about 1,000 lives proved disastrous for the Argentine military government, which later collapsed, and successful for the British, who retained control of the islands, where 3,200 people live. Relations between Argentina and the United Kingdom normalized in the 1990s, but with the prospect of new hydrocarbon resources discovered near the South Atlantic islands, the Argentine government challenged the United Kingdom's claims again in 2007. Venezuelan president Hugo Chávez has seized upon the issue to promote South American unity. In February 2010 he told Queen Elizabeth II, "The time for empires are over, haven't you noticed? Return the Malvinas to the Argentine people. Things have changed. We are no longer in 1982. If conflict breaks out, be sure Argentina will not be alone like it was back then."[29] In spite of Chávez's statement, both countries lack the military capabilities they once had, and the British seem to have international law on their side. The British first claimed the islands in the sixteenth century, 70 percent of the islands' inhabitants claim British ancestry, and the islands are a self-governing British territory. Nevertheless, the colonial nature of the dispute stemming from early European exploration, the rich natural resources there that include fishing stocks and wildlife, and the potential for new hydrocarbon finds make the Falklands-Malvinas a contentious maritime dispute.

In Asia there are numerous similar competing claims over the largely uninhabited Spratly Island chain, which are dispersed over a six-hundred–mile area in the South China Sea. To date, China, Taiwan, Vietnam, the Philippines, and Malaysia have overlapping claims. Brunei also established a fishing zone in the Spratly Island chain, but has made no formal claim as of this writing. The islands are little more than exposed reefs, rock outcroppings, and atolls that are barely above sea level and with a total area of about four square kilometers. In spite of this small size, the seabed there contains important hydrocarbon deposits that five countries seek to claim and develop. Because of historic rivalries (e.g., China and Vietnam) and political differences among the countries (e.g., China and Taiwan), the Spratly Islands are often characterized as a potential military flash point. In spite of this, no significant military action has occurred. Instead, national oil companies from China, Vietnam, and the Philippines signed a joint accord in 2005 to further seismic exploration of the Spratly Island chain. Economic incentives seem likely to ameliorate tensions and facilitate cooperative dispute resolution.

In addition to the Spratly Island chain involving a number of significant countries, Japan is embroiled in several island disputes, too. Japan's northern territories composed of the islands of Etorofu, Kunashiri, and Shikotan and the Habomai group are administered by Russia, which calls them the Southern Kuril Islands. The islands were occupied by the Soviet Union in 1945 and remain a roadblock to the formal end of World War II hostilities between Japan and Russia. Additionally, Japan and South Korea jointly claim the Liancourt Rocks (Take-shima/Dokdo), which have been occupied by South Korea since 1954. Finally, China and Taiwan dispute Japan's claims to the Senkaku-shoto (Diaoyu Tai) islands and Japan's economic claims in the East China Sea. Disputes like these serve as reminders of lingering political challenges, but also show how underwater hydrocarbon exploration can create tension among governments.

Given the uncertain impact of China's rise on international affairs, maritime disputes like those in the South China Sea also offer a window into Beijing's decision making. So far, China seems to rely on international law to further its claims (though there are clear cases of maritime harassment). Law professor Xinjun Zhang of Tsinghua University writes:

> On balance, international law has come to be seen as a more important and necessary means for China to achieve its foreign policy ends, even though obstacles and uncertainty persist. Moreover, China's turn to international law has been uneven, and unsurprisingly so. International law is more likely to be an appealing instrument for China where the other party to a dispute is a near-peer in political, economic and military power (as is the

case, for example, with Japan), or where the other parties are significantly less powerful than China (as is the case, for example, with
the ASEAN [Association of Southeast Asian Nations] countries).[30]

The implications of this are clear. International law can be an effective
way to peacefully resolve maritime disputes, but perhaps only when the
parties have sufficient military capabilities to make war too costly.

This idea could be extended when considering the thawing Arctic
Ocean. Some analysts have compared the Arctic as the new "great game"
to the British and Russian empires' competing for influence in central
Asia in the nineteenth century. For example, maritime expert and scholar
Scott Borgerson testified to Congress in 2009,

> When taking a pan-Arctic view there are also a number of nagging
> sovereignty disputes. Every single bilateral relationship where Arc-
> tic countries share a physical border, except one, Norway and Den-
> mark, has at least one significant point of disagreement. Like
> previous assumptions that the icecap is melting more slowly than
> it actually is, it would be a mistake to assume that all these poten-
> tial flashpoints will remain sleeping dogs. The combination of new
> shipping routes, trillions of dollars in possible oil and gas re-
> sources, and a poorly defined picture of state ownership make for
> a toxic brew.[31]

In fact, Russia's 2009 national security strategy warned that within a
decade, nations could be at war over the Arctic as countries vie for important new maritime trade routes and new economic opportunities for
hydrocarbon exploration.

The Arctic Ocean has always played a critical role in national security.
For the past fifty years, the Arctic enhanced nuclear deterrence for both
the United States and the Soviet Union (and now Russia), since submarines
could hide there free from air surveillance. While nuclear stockpiles are
being reduced, ballistic missile submarines remain potent tools in the
American and Russian nuclear deterrent posture, but their stealth is
threatened by Arctic melt. Submarine activities are certain to continue, but

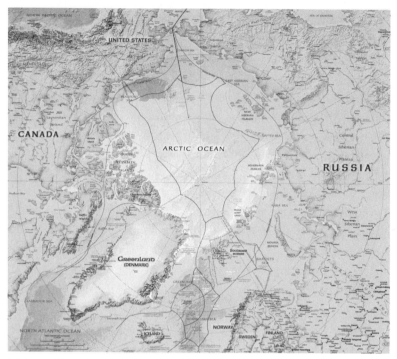

Map 5.3—The Arctic. Courtesy of the CIA.

the melting Arctic also changes the roles that surface navies play. Former U.S. Navy oceanographer Rear Adm. David Gove says the Arctic region "is primarily a maritime domain and the U.S. Navy of the future must be prepared to protect sea lines of communication supporting maritime commerce and other national interests—including national security—there."[32]

As the Arctic melts, new trade routes connecting the Atlantic to the Pacific across the North Pole may be a reality in the future, albeit for a few weeks during the summer. The expected shipping channel will reduce the transit between Europe and Asia by 10,000 miles. Looking east, German merchant ships proved in 2009 that they could transit from Europe to Asia via a Northeast Passage. By doing so, shipping companies can bypass the contentious waters of East Africa (with its piracy threat) and Southeast Asia and save money on fuel and crew days at sea. With anticipated commercial shipping traffic, the navies of Canada, the United States, Norway, Denmark, and Russia expect to map the Arctic sea-lanes, provide search and rescue, and protect their sovereignty claims there. The challenge of ownership is already proving to be contentious.

In August 2007 Russia planted its flag on the seafloor at the geographic North Pole. It did so under the United Nations Convention on the Law of the Sea by arguing that the underwater Lomonosov Ridge and North Pole are extensions of its landmass.[33] The titanium Russian flag is largely symbolic; however, both Canada and Denmark (through Greenland) have counterclaimed the underwater features as extensions of their territories. In 2010 Canada staged its own underwater claim using a remotely piloted submersible vehicle, which it is using to map its claims. The twenty-one-country Commission on the Limits of the Continental Shelf is currently reviewing the claims, but the United States is not represented since it has not ratified UNCLOS. James Kraska argues that "the only way the Arctic nations can effectively manage the risks of increased activity, protect against asymmetric threats and maintain safety and regional order is to cooperate with one another."[34] Thus, the United States needs to increase its diplomatic activities and ratify the UNCLOS treaty.

CONCLUSION

Although oceans have always been an essential part of human social and commercial activity, there is an increased urgency to protect them. Illegal fishing, overfishing, and illegal dumping threaten a significant food source for many countries. When it comes to the United States, the 2010 BP oil-well disaster in the Gulf of Mexico underscores how connected the seas are to life on land. Further, the accident emphasizes that governments, including the United States, currently lack adequate prevention, regulation, and accident response capabilities to safeguard the maritime security of the U.S. Gulf Coast.

The maritime security deficit allows criminal organizations, transnational actors, and pirates to exploit the maritime domain. Given the oceans' size and the complexity of the security environment, no single country can provide security against all threats (not even a superpower's navy). Rear Adm. Jeffrey Lemmons put this in a strategic context: "Now we have a maritime strategy that speaks about the tenets of a strong maritime nation, the things that a maritime nation needs to be able to do [including] forward presence and providing maritime security in partnership with other nations to support and sustain the maritime economy."[35] With an emphasis on partnership to fill security gaps, programs that strengthen the maritime capabilities of countries are likely to continue for the foreseeable future. At the same time, competing claims on islands, the Arctic, and underwater resources will continue to challenge governments to resolve disputes peacefully. Fortunately, there appear to be more incentives to cooperate than to contest claims through war. Yet this does not mean that individuals and nongovernmental groups, including the influential environmental movement, will not continue to test the limits of maritime security.

To Learn More

Get the latest update on global piracy incidents at the International Maritime Bureau Piracy Reporting Centre: www.icc-ccs.org/.

Read the weekly worldwide threats to shipping report prepared by the U.S. Office of Naval Intelligence: www.nga.mil/portal/site/maritime/?epi_menu ItemID=3e37041ec7a4546e36890127d32020a0&epi_menuID=e106a3b5e50edc e1fec24fd73927a759&epi_baseMenuID=e106a3b5e50edce1fec24fd73927a759.

Visit the headquarters of the commander, Fifth Fleet, the U.S. admiral responsible for antipiracy operations in the Gulf of Aden, at www.cusnc.navy.mil/.

Peter Lehr in *Violence at Sea* (New York: Routledge, 2007) offers an overview of maritime piracy, examining threats that piracy poses to global security and commerce, as well as measures and policies to mitigate the threat.

Peter Chalk in *The Maritime Dimension of International Security: Terrorism, Piracy, and Challenges for the United States* (Washington, DC: RAND Corporation, 2008) examines the challenges for U.S. policy to bring security to the maritime domain.

Martin N. Murphy in *Small Boats, Weak States, Dirty Money: Piracy and Maritime Terrorism in the Modern World* (New York: Columbia University Press, 2009) offers a detailed analysis of modern piracy and the challenges associated with creating maritime security.

Follow journalist John Burns on his personal voyage to understand pirates in *Dangerous Waters: Modern Piracy and Terror on the High Seas* (New York: Dutton, 2002).

Read the latest Department of State report on major drug-transit or major illicit drug-producing countries at www.state.gov/p/inl/rls/index.htm.

James Kraska examines the prospect for conflict in the Arctic in "Northern Exposures," *American Interest Online*, May–June 2010, available at www.the-american-interest.com/article-bd.cfm?piece=810.

Notes

1. Jeffrey D. Sachs, "Tropical Underdevelopment," CID Working Paper no. 57, December 2000, 1.

2. Collier, *Bottom Billion* (see chap. 1, n. 14).

3. White House, *National Strategy for Maritime Security* (Washington, DC: White House, September 2005).

4. The United States signed UNCLOS and abides by it, but the Senate has not yet ratified it. Initial concerns about seabed mining prevented ratification, but it remains in limbo due to concerns about how treaties impact U.S. sovereignty. This occurs in spite of ratification support from President Bush, President Obama, a majority of the U.S. Senate, and the Pentagon.

5. Energy Information Agency, "World Oil Transit Chokepoints Energy Data," January 2008, available at www.eia.doe.gov/cabs/World_Oil_Transit_Chokepoints/Full.html.

6. UN Secretary-General Ban Ki-moon, "The Secretary-General Message on World Ocean Day," United Nations Press Release, June 8, 2009, available at www.un.org/Depts/los/reference_files/worldoceansday.htm.

7. See, for example, James Kraska, "Coalition Strategy and the Pirates of the Gulf of Aden and the Red Sea," *Comparative Strategy* 28, no. 3 (2009): 197–216.

8. Food and Agriculture Administration of the United Nations, *The State of World Fisheries and Aquaculture* (New York: UN Press, 2008).

9. United Nations General Assembly, Resolution 62177: Sustainable Fisheries, Including Through the 1995 Agreement for the Implementation of the Provisions of the United Nations Convention on the Law of the Sea of 10 December 1982 Relating to the Conservation and Management of Straddling Fish

Stocks and Highly Migratory Fish Stocks, and Related Instruments, February 28, 2008.

10. MRAG, "Illegal, Unreported, and Unregulated Fishing," Policy Brief 8, 2005, p. 6, fig. 2, available at www.mrag.co.uk/Documents/PolicyBrief8_IUU .pdf. MRAG conducted yearlong case studies for ten countries, nine of which were African countries: Guinea, Somalia, Angola, Mozambique, Sierra Leone, Seychelles, Liberia, Kenya, and Namibia. Papua New Guinea was estimated at US$40 million and subtracted from the total US$375 million estimate.

11. Ibid., p. 8, table 3. The estimate from sub-Saharan EEZs is based on MRAG research estimating total losses for the region.

12. Kip Ward, *United States Africa Command, 2009 Posture Statement* (Stuttgart: Africa Command, 2009).

13. A long-term solution is viewed as reducing global fishing fleets, especially those that are artificially high due to government subsidies. With reduced capacity, IUU fishing is estimated to decline.

14. United Nations Convention on the Law of the Sea, *Oceans and Law of the Sea Division for Ocean Affairs and the Law of the Sea* (2001), available at www.un.org/Depts/los/convention_agreements/texts/unclos/part7.htm. Article 100: "All states shall cooperate to the fullest possible extent to repress piracy." Article 101: "Piracy consists of illegal acts or voluntary participation in acts of violence, detention or depredation committed for private ends by the crew or passengers of a private ship or aircraft on the high seas against another ship or aircraft outside the jurisdiction of any State." Article 102: "Piracy by warship, government ship or government aircraft whose crew has mutinied and as defined in article 101." Article 103: "Definition of a Pirate ship. Any ship or aircraft intending to use dominant control to commit acts referred to in article 101." Article 104: "Pirate vessels may retail their State flag." Article 105: "Any State may seize a pirate ship, ship taken by piracy or under the control of pirates to arrest persons and seize property." Article 106: "The seizing State is liable for a pirate ship or aircraft taken without adequate grounds." Article 107: "Seizure may only be carried out by warships or military craft or ships clearly marked and authorized for government service."

15. ICC International Maritime Bureau, www.icc-ccs.org.

16. Energy Information Administration, www.eia.doe.gov/cabs/World_Oil _Transit_Chokepoints/Bab_el-Mandab.html.

17. Peter Smerdon, "Canadian Reprieve for Naval Escorts to Somalia," World Food Programme News, September 26, 2008, www.wfp.org/english/ ?ModuleID=137&Key=2949.

18. The temporary seizure of the *M/V Maersk Alabama* represented a first in the recent increase in ship hijackings in the vicinity of Somalia. See Derek Reveron, "Game Changer in Somalia? Not Yet," *New Atlanticist*, April 8, 2009, available at www.acus.org/new_atlanticist/game-changer-somalia-not-yet.

19. Martin Murphy, "Piracy and the Exploitation of Sanctuary," in *Armed Groups: Studies in National Security, Counterterrorism, and Counterinsurgency*, edited by Jeffrey H. Norwitz (Newport, RI: U.S. Naval War College, 2008), 160.

20. Department of the Navy, "A Cooperative Strategy for 21st Century Seapower" (Washington, D.C.: Department of the Navy, October 2007), available at www.navy.mil/maritime/maritimestrategy.pdf.

21. Ethan A. Nadelmann, *Cops Across Borders: The Internationalization of U.S. Criminal Law Enforcement* (University Park: Pennsylvania State University Press, 1993).

22. Office of National Drug Control Policy, *National Drug Threat Summary* (Washington, DC: Office of National Drug Control Policy, 2009), available at www.usdoj.gov/ndic/pubs31/31379/index.htm.

23. James Stavridis, *U.S. Southern Command 2009 Posture Statement* (Miami: SOUTHCOM, 2009).

24. "U.S./CARICOM/Dominican Republic Statement on Third Border Initiative," January 14, 2004, www.america.gov/st/washfile-english/2004/January/ 20040114144116nesnom0.569256.html#ixzz0AZrjgdVl.

25. Stavridis, *U.S. Southern Command 2009 Posture Statement*.

26. Quoted in UN Office of Drugs and Crime, *Annual Report, 2009* (New York: United Nations, 2009), 11, available at www.unodc.org/unodc/data-and-analysis/WDR.html.

27. Horace A. Bartilow and Kihong Eom, "Busting Drugs While Paying with Crime," *Foreign Policy Analysis* 5, no. 2 (2009): 93–116.

28. Department of State, *International Narcotics Control Strategy Report* (Washington, DC: Department of State, 2008), available at www.state.gov/p/ inl/rls/nrcrpt/2008/vol1/html/100772.htm.

29. Hugo Chávez quoted in Tom Leonard, "Hugo Chavez Demands Queen Return Falkland Islands to Argentina," *Telegraph,* February 22, 2010, available at www.telegraph.co.uk/news/worldnews/southamerica/falklandislands/7293985/ Hugo-Chavez-demands-Queen-return-Falkland-Islands-to-Argentina.html.

30. Xinjun Zhang, "China's 'Peaceful Rise,' 'Harmonious' Foreign Relations, and Legal Confrontation—and Lessons from the Sino-Japanese Dispute over the East China Sea," *Foreign Policy Research Institute E-Notes* (April 16, 2010).

31. Scott Borgerson, "Prepared Testimony on U.S. National Security Interests in the Arctic Before the House Committee on Foreign Affairs," March 25, 2009, available at www.cfr.org/publication/18922/prepared_testimony_on_us_national _security_interests_in_the_arctic_before_the_house_committee_on_foreign _affairs.html?breadcrumb=%2Fbios%2F13363%2Fscott_g_borgerson.

32. David Gove, "Arctic Melt: Reopening a Naval Frontier," *U.S. Naval Institute Proceedings* (February 2009).

33. Signed in 1982, UNCLOS "lays down a comprehensive regime of law and order in the world's oceans and seas establishing rules governing all uses of the oceans and their resources. It enshrines the notion that all problems of ocean space are closely interrelated and need to be addressed as a whole" (www .un.org/Depts/los/convention_agreements/convention_overview_convention .htm).

34. James Kraska, "Northern Exposures," *American Interest Online,* May–June 2010, available at www.the-american-interest.com/article.bd.cfm?piece =810.

35. Zachary M. Peterson, "Navy Creates New Offices to Better Align with Maritime Strategy: International Partnerships, MDA Eyed," *Inside the Navy,* March 23, 2009.

6

Health Security

Events which threaten the health of the people of this nation could very easily compromise our national security. Whether it's a pandemic or a premeditated chemical attack, our public health system must be prepared to respond to protect the interests of the American people. In order to be prepared to both respond to an incident and to recover, we need a strong national health system with individuals and families ready to handle the health effects of a disaster.

—HEALTH AND HUMAN SERVICES SECRETARY
KATHLEEN SEBELIUS, 2009

Two oceans have kept the United States relatively immune from foreign invasion. And through the midterm, no country has either the strategic rationale or the military capabilities to attack the United States. Yet homeland security preoccupies strategic thinking. Terrorism, especially the nuclear type, is often assumed to pose an existential threat to the United States, yet the combination of homeland security vigilance and terrorist ineptitude has kept the United States relatively safe since 2001. However, the United States is not completely immune from harm, sometimes from the most unexpected sources.

Unseen microbes, bacteria, and viruses threaten Americans, and their prevalence is increasing. Robert Cook notes, "Humanity has become vulnerable to cross-species illnesses, thanks to modern advances such as the rapid transportation of both goods and people, increasing population density around the globe, and a growing dependence on intensified livestock production for food." Further, more bacteria have become antibiotic resistant, which complicates treatment. Infectious disease is still the number-one killer of humans. Globally, millions die from tuberculosis, HIV/AIDS, and malaria, not to mention the more exotic and highly publicized Ebola hemorrhagic fever. In the United States, tens of thousands die each year from seasonal flu, and more than 1 million suffer from HIV/AIDS. There is also concern that terrorists could weaponize diseases and launch biological attacks such as the 2001 anthrax attacks. Fortunately, there have been no successor attacks, and naturally occurring diseases pose a greater threat to human security in the United States and elsewhere. Former director of national intelligence Dennis Blair testified to this point: "The most pressing transnational health challenge for the United States is still the potential for emergence of a severe pandemic, with the primary candidate being a highly lethal influenza virus."[1]

Since disease knows no boundaries, the United States is vulnerable to chronic and infectious diseases prevalent in many parts of the world. In recent years, epidemiologists have raised concerns about pandemic influenza. Commonly known as the "bird flu," H5N1 influenza first captured the world's attention in 1997. The impact of H5N1 has been largely limited, but in 2009 another strain of flu demonstrated just how easily influenza crosses borders and impacts all segments of a population. The initial outbreak of the influenza virus H1N1, formerly known as "swine flu," began in early spring in Mexico; by June the infections were so widespread that the World Health Organization (WHO) declared it a pandemic. Before the first wave of the outbreak was over, it had shuttered Mexico's economy, infected Colombia's president, and caused hundreds of millions of infections worldwide. In the fall of 2009 President Barack Obama declared a national emergency to ensure that the government had the necessary authorities to prepare for and react to winter infections.

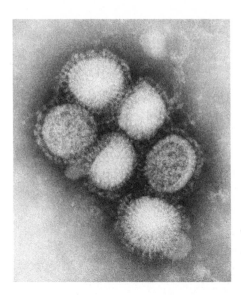

Image 6.1—Negative-stain EM image of the 2009 H1N1 influenza virus. Photo credit: C. S. Goldsmith and A. Balish, Centers for Disease Control and Prevention.

In addition to the immediate costs infections have on individuals, disease outbreaks have serious social costs, too. Globally, HIV/AIDS kills millions each year and has devastated numerous African countries, undermining efforts to achieve the United Nations Millennium Development Goals and more productive societies. The interconnections created by globalization apply equally to health security. Diseases long since conquered in the West, such as tuberculosis, malaria, and polio, are now making a comeback, as international travel, migrating birds, and immigration expose Americans to once-vanquished diseases that are lingering or reemerging in developing countries. Before examining trends in key diseases, the chapter first examines how public health became a question of national security. Possibilities for improving health security around the globe are also considered.

HEALTH AND SECURITY

Fifteen years ago, military planners and policy makers were unlikely to link public health and national security. Instead, health issues were deemed decidedly domestic issues and at odds with traditional foreign

policy concerns centered on potential peer competitors, nuclear proliferation, or rogue states. However, after the emergence of avian influenza
in Asia in 1997, national security professionals began to reconsider infectious disease as a potential matter for national security. Hypothetical
scenarios illustrated that disease could shut down international air traffic
as governments make an effort to limit the scale of a pandemic. Interest
heightened again during the 2003 severe acute respiratory syndrome
(SARS) outbreak that infected 8,000 and killed 800 globally.

Though these separate outbreaks were unrelated and relatively small,
the potential for a regional and even global pandemic is very real. The
last three pandemics of the twentieth century killed more than 43 million
people. Although medical treatments have improved since the early
1900s, diseases continue to mutate, which challenges pharmaceutical research and development of new medicines. Consequently, infectious diseases have the potential to spread rapidly and cause mass casualties,
especially with our highly mobile societies. In its 2007 report on future
security challenges, the U.S. military noted that "a pandemic in North
America would be protracted and pervasive, causing substantial societal
impact and persistent economic losses in almost every state."[2] In addition
to overwhelming hospitals and clinics, commerce would slow as people
were quarantined (voluntarily or not), and civil disturbances could overwhelm law enforcement as people's demands increased. The military
compares a modern pandemic to the fourteenth-century plague, or
"Black Death," which killed about one-third of Europe's population. Because of this, there are fears that future pandemics are capable of producing widespread death, social disorder, and civil disturbances.

Besides the possibility of pandemic influenza in the United States, national security professionals consistently view public health as a security
issue in developing countries in sub-Saharan Africa. For example, in his
1996 National Security Strategy, President Clinton highlighted disease
and its impact on development: "New diseases, such as AIDS, and other
epidemics which can be spread through environmental degradation,
threaten to overwhelm the health facilities of developing countries, disrupt societies and stop economic growth."[3] In many cases, a disease like
HIV/AIDS poses a triple tax on poor, developing societies, which must

care for the infected, absorb the productivity loss when sick people withdraw from the workforce, and care for the orphans created when millions of parents die every year. Further, these orphans become vulnerable to modern slavery either as domestic, industrial, and sex workers or as child soldiers who can readily take part in Africa's internal wars.

Although there are strong humanitarian reasons to be concerned about disease in developing countries, by the end of the twentieth century it was the wide-reaching threat of the effects of disease that became the focus of concern. International travel and migratory birds raised awareness of diseases like West Nile disease and avian influenza. Accordingly, the United States began to articulate strategies that addressed disease as a material threat to Americans, one that is a threat to all Americans' human security. The 1999 *National Security Strategy* noted, "Diseases and health risks can no longer be viewed solely as a domestic concern."[4] Instead, health is a legitimate matter of national security.

By recognizing health as a national security issue, the United States affirmed its status as a superpower with global interests because of the potential for disease threats everywhere on the planet. In President Clinton's 1998 *National Security Strategy* he noted: "Problems that once seemed quite distant—such as resource depletion, rapid population growth, environmental damage, *new infectious diseases* and uncontrolled refugee migration—have important implications for American security."[5] Proximity to a threat has now become irrelevant, as the United States identifies potential threats in every country that lacks strong public health sectors.

President Bush continued the tendency to view disease as a national security challenge in the twenty-first century and stated, "We will also continue to lead the world in efforts to reduce the terrible toll of HIV/AIDS and other infectious diseases." He funded international health programs at unprecedented levels and issued Homeland Security Presidential Directive 21. Among other things, this directive defined a catastrophic health event as "any natural or manmade incident, including terrorism, that results in a number of ill or injured persons sufficient to overwhelm the capabilities of immediate local and regional emergency response and health care systems." White House concerns for health security continued under the Obama administration in 2009, but emphasized the global rather than the national perspective, along with the interconnection of many troubling issues. President Obama told the UN General Assembly, "Far too many people in far too many places live through the daily crises that challenge our humanity—the despair of an empty stomach; the thirst brought on by dwindling water supplies; the injustice of a child dying from a treatable disease; or a mother losing her life as she gives birth."[6] Consequently, U.S. health assistance programs now exist in almost every country of the developing world. These efforts are primarily funded through the international assistance account budget of the Department of State, but the Department of Health and Human Services provides important technical information. In 2009 a *National Health Security Strategy* was released that outlined ten objectives, including working with global partners to enhance national, continental, and global health security.

Concerns about public health are not simply a Trojan horse for U.S. expansionism or hegemony, as some critics may warn. Rather, the tendency to view disease as a national security threat is now common to the foreign policies of virtually all developed countries. These nations recognize that along with the benefits of globalization, there are increased vulnerabilities as well. For example, the Netherlands has defined its national security challenges through diverse threats such as SARS, bird flu, floods, and terrorism, acknowledging that through increased interdependencies, what once were relatively minor threats can lead to societal disruption. Similar sentiments are conveyed in the United Kingdom's national security policy, which sees pandemics as a part of threats and risks that "are driven by a diverse and interconnected set of underlying factors, including climate change, competition for energy, poverty and poor governance, demographic changes and globalization." The European Union reflects these views and includes pandemics as one of several global challenges facing Europe. In this regard, the European Centre for Disease Prevention and Control noted, "Pandemics do not recognise national borders. They affect not only public health but also societies and economies throughout the EU and the world." Finally, the influential World Economic Forum includes pandemics as one of the most important risks to global stability.[7] Transnational disease has the potential to slow commerce and equally development by interfering with the international movement of goods and people.

Concerns about disease are manifested in international assistance programs that prioritize human security concerns over traditional security issues. These are based on the UN Millennium Development Goals (covered in an earlier chapter), which include reducing child mortality, improving maternal health, and combating HIV/AIDS, malaria, and other diseases. In support of these health goals, the United States established a $15 billion HIV/AIDS program known as PEPFAR (President's Emergency Program for AIDS Relief) and a $1.2 billion antimalaria program. In 2009 Europe launched a €300 million program that targets malaria, tuberculosis, and AIDS.

Ideas and concerns about health security transcend the political sphere and in recent years have become integral to national security strategic thinking. The National Intelligence Council of experts inspired or affirmed this view when it linked pandemic disease to conflict: "If a pandemic disease emerges by 2025, internal and cross-border tension and conflict will become more likely as nations struggle—with degraded capabilities—to control the movement of populations seeking to avoid infection or maintain access to resources." No longer just a fringe national security concern, pandemic disease is now included as a major issue along with terrorism, rogue states, and peer competition over energy. The 2008 *National Defense Strategy* explained the rationale for these concerns: "The United States, our allies, and our partners face a spectrum of challenges, including violent transnational extremist networks, hostile states armed with weapons of mass destruction, rising regional powers, emerging space and cyber threats, natural and *pandemic* disasters, and a growing competition for resources."[8]

So important is concern about a future pandemic that the secretary of defense designated responsibility for global pandemic monitoring to U.S. Northern Command, which is primarily responsible for homeland defense, including missile defense. Operating in conjunction with the National Response Plan, Northern Command anticipates natural and man-made disasters to prevent and mitigate crises. Under its charter, Northern Command has responsibility for planning and responding to pandemic influenza. This includes preventive measures and reactive operations if quarantine or civil disturbances exceed state governments' capacities.

While the military's role in homeland defense is still developing, the international nature of disease elevates the issue to the interstate and even global level. For example, the United States and China have signed an agreement to strengthen cooperation to increase capacity for detecting, responding to, and controlling an influenza pandemic.[9] Although China is often portrayed as a potential military rival to the United States, the common challenge of health security can ameliorate relations and induce cooperation, whether between governments or among relevant nonstate actors.

The strategic implications of a pandemic are many. First, disease retards and ultimately prevents development. Considering that reducing global poverty is a key U.S. and UN goal, disease is one of many challenges to overcome. Second, pandemic disease can potentially produce mass casualties greater than traditional warfare. For example, the 1918 influenza outbreak killed more than twice the number of Americans who died fighting during World War I. Third, a pandemic seems inevitable. Since disease is naturally occurring, governments are limited in their ability to prevent pandemics. The best governments can hope to do is minimize their impact through greater awareness and vaccination programs. The remainder of the chapter explores these implications by examining pandemics and related health threats to understand their importance for national and human security, along with the challenges to addressing these threats.

DISEASE

There are at least 1,500 microbes that cause human illness, but most attention is focused on influenza, which is a highly adaptive virus that produces respiratory disease in humans and animals such as wild waterfowl, and domesticated pigs and poultry. Michael Osterholm has noted, "Dating back to antiquity, influenza pandemics have posed the greatest threat of a worldwide calamity caused by infectious disease."[10] Influenza is seasonal in temperate climates like the United States and Europe. During a

Health Security and National Security

That public health has become a national security concern is surprising to many and challenges the traditional separations made between domestic and international issues. On the one hand, the key to health security lies in domestic policy to ensure there are adequate vaccine stocks, trained health professionals, and educational campaigns to promote personal hygiene. (For instance, to prevent the flu, the government reminds us to wash hands frequently.) On the other hand, the transnational nature of disease requires high levels of international cooperation and coordination to monitor disease outbreaks and coordinate responses. Rebecca Katz and Daniel Singer argue that this approach is not without some risk:

> While health professionals may welcome the higher profile and greater resources given to their issues, characterizing a health issue as a national priority (and particularly as a security issue) may change the understanding of a health threat, put relatively greater emphasis on the views of those outside the health community and potentially alter the approach to solving the problem. Consequently, care should be taken in deciding which health issues should be given priority on par with national security issues and included explicitly in national foreign policy.[1]

As with all human security issues, finding a balance among the policy experts, medical professionals, organizations that deliver services, and government agencies is key to improving human security. Since issues like health do not fall neatly in the national security realm, coordination among many sectors, along with a division of responsibilities, is key. Nongovernmental organizations seem to have the best understanding of local issues. International groups like Doctors Without Borders, the Gates Foundation, or the Carter Center partner with groups in various countries to maximize delivery of health services and work through complicated cultural issues. For example, some leaders in sub-Saharan Africa deny that HIV/AIDS is caused by a virus and therefore prevent groups from providing care. Local groups may understand how to manage these issues. Likewise, cultural norms may preclude HIV/AIDS preventive measures prescribed by the ABC program of "abstinence, be faithful, and condom use." Groups sensitive to local beliefs may help develop a strategy that can still reduce the incidence of HIV/AIDS. Sadly, in the most unfortunate cases, medical professionals may be restricted from traveling or even killed in cases where they are alleged to be pursuing political or religious agendas, as has occurred with nongovernmental medical experts in Afghanistan.

---

1. Rebecca Katz and Daniel Singer, "Health and Security in Foreign Policy," *Bulletin of the World Health Organization* (March 2007): 85, available at www.who.int/bulletin/volumes/85/3/06-036889.pdf.

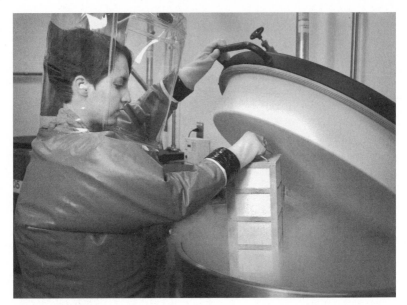

Image 6.2—A CDC scientist inserts a rack of boxes containing biological stocks into the liquid nitrogen freezer for storage. Photo credit: James Gathany, Centers for Disease Control and Prevention.

typical year, "seasonal flu" infects millions, but claims the lives of only tens of thousands each year. However, the greatest danger lies in the virus's ability to mutate and to transmit from animals to humans.

On average, three influenza pandemics per century have been documented since the sixteenth century, occurring at intervals of ten to fifty years. Of those in the twentieth century (1918, 1957, and 1968), the 1918 influenza was the most deadly, killing an estimated 50 million people worldwide. The American death toll for the 1918 pandemic was 675,000 lives, or 6 percent of the U.S. population at that time. Unlike seasonal flu, where mortality is greatest in the very young and the very old, pandemic influenza strains tend to be deadliest for young to middle-age adults. If a large-scale influenza pandemic were to occur in the United States today, it could produce 75 million hospitalizations and up to 1.5 million deaths.[11] And if history is a guide, then hysteria will also generate security concerns such as rioting and other large-scale civil disturbances. Of greatest concern today are two strains of influenza that have already demonstrated a global reach: H5N1 and H1N1.

H5N1 (*hemagglutinin* type 5 and *neuraminidase* type 1) is an influenza variant that is commonly referred to as "bird flu." First appearing in southern China, H5N1 originated in aquatic birds such as ducks and geese and then passed to chickens and other domesticated birds. The virus occasionally passes from bird to human, and people living in developing countries who tend to live close to their livestock are especially vulnerable. Though transmission from bird to human is relatively rare, it is a very serious event. Once in the lung cells of a mammalian host, the virus can "reassort," or mix genes with already existing human influenza strains. Once adapted, this newly reassorted influenza can more easily transmit from human to human. An influenza variant with components from a previously nonhuman strain is considered a "novel" influenza, and as such it poses a unique threat. First, the virulence of such an influenza strain is unknown, and potentially more deadly. Second, there would be no human resistance to such a variant, as humans have not had exposure to it before. These reassortments, when highly contagious, are the beginnings of what could become a pandemic.

It is not possible to predict how or when a virus will mutate in such a way that it poses a threat to humans, but once it does, the results can be deadly. When the H5N1 virus infects domestic poultry, 100 percent of chickens are killed within forty-eight hours. It is unclear how humans would react, but prediction models suggest many casualties. This is based both on the nature of the virus and on inadequate emergency health care facilities. Dr. Steven Phillips and Rear Adm. George R. Worthington have argued that "on any given day, the emergency rooms of most U.S. hospitals are at or near capacity, and it is unrealistic to expect them to respond effectively to sudden large-scale needs."[12] In an effort for the health care system to become more efficient, a substantial number of hospital closures occurred over the past two decades. Largely driven by business concerns of profitability or sustainability in public hospitals, this has created a vulnerability, since overcapacity is a virtue when it comes to a public health crisis. Adding to these concerns in the developed world, the poorer regions of the world are characterized by a lack of medical capacity to meet even routine health needs.

In 2009 a novel influenza captured the world's attention when what became known as "swine flu," or H1N1 (*hemagglutinin* type 1 and *neuraminidase* type 1), emerged in La Gloria, Mexico. In February 2009 five-year-old Édgar Enrique Hernández suffered from a flu virus that had mutated from pigs. Édgar recovered, but the mutated virus gave rise to a global pandemic. Just five months after the first case, there were 300,000 laboratory-confirmed cases, 4,000 deaths, and infections in 191 countries

TABLE 6.1: 2009 H1N1 CASES, HOSPITALIZATIONS, AND DEATHS IN THE UNITED STATES

	MID-LEVEL RANGE	ESTIMATED RANGE
CASES		
0–17 years	~16 million	~12 million to ~23 million
18–64 years	~27 million	~19 million to ~38 million
65 years and older	~4 million	~3 million to ~6 million
Cases Total	~47 million	~34 million to ~67 million
HOSPITALIZATIONS		
0–17 years	~71,000	~51,000 to ~101,000
18–64 years	~121,000	~87,000 to ~172,000
65 years and older	~21,000	~15,000 to ~29,000
Hospitalizations Total	~213,000	~154,000 to ~303,000
DEATHS		
0–17 years	~1,090	~790 to ~1,550
18–64 years	~7,450	~5,360 to ~10,570
65 years and older	~1,280	~920 to ~1,810
Deaths Total	~9,820	~7,070 to ~13,930

Note: Cases have been rounded to the nearest million. Hospitalizations have been rounded to the nearest thousand. Deaths have been rounded to the nearest ten.

Source: "CDC Estimates of 2009 H1N1 Influenza Cases, Hospitalizations, and Deaths in the United States, April–November 14, 2009," December 10, 2009, available at www.cdc.gov/h1n1flu/estimates/April_December_12.htm.

CONTEMPORARY CHALLENGE

Declaring an H1N1 Pandemic

The World Health Organization is the directing and coordinating body for public health issues within the UN system, and thus the truly global health organization. With an annual budget of more than $4 billion, WHO provides global guidance on public health challenges, shapes the medical research agenda, sets norms and standards for disease monitoring, provides countries technical support, and builds sustainable medical capacity. Included in its charter is the responsibility to assess health trends. WHO produces annual reports on global public health and has the authority to declare pandemics.

Within weeks of the first reported case of H1N1, WHO declared a "public health emergency of international concern," on April 26, 2009. On June 11 of that year, WHO declared a phase 6 pandemic, which is the highest phase, when widespread human infection is greatest. According to WHO director-general Dr. Margaret Chan, "Influenza pandemics, whether moderate or severe, are remarkable events because of the almost universal susceptibility of the world's population to infection."[1]

The decision to declare phase 6 was rather controversial and caused some confusion and panic. Prevention advice was largely limited to counseling the public to improve personal hygiene such as hand washing, but it also resulted in vaccine development. Additionally, WHO had to take into account related economic and social concerns; thus, a key piece of WHO messaging was focused on dissociating the virus name from "swine flu." The virus name gave rise to mass pig slaughters that were detrimental to many societies, so WHO was at pains to publicize that there is no risk of infection from consuming well-cooked pork and pork products. This incident reflects the fact that WHO has no enforcement power and must work with diverse governments and groups around the world to improve public health.

---

1. World Health Organization, "World Now at the Start of 2009 Influenza Pandemic," Statement to the Press by Dr. Margaret Chan, Director-General of the World Health Organization, June 11, 2009, available at www .who.int/mediacentre/news/statements/2009/h1n1_pandemic_phase6 _20090611/en/index.html.

and territories. At the end of 2009, up to 67 million Americans were infected.[13] Given the pace of infections, the World Health Organization declared a pandemic, and many governments increased their preparedness measures.

Given the relative speed with which influenza can mutate and infect humans, it has been given priority by the U.S. national security establishment. In 2005, for example, the federal government developed a *National Strategy for Pandemic Influenza* and later created www.flu.gov to inform and prepare Americans. Under the national strategy, the Department of State is the lead federal agency for international influenza issues. The government has raised the profile of influenza to something historically bigger than seasonal flu, but admits that primary responsibility lies with individuals, as with so many human security issues. Yet the strategy does rest on three pillars and addresses the full spectrum of events that link a farmyard overseas to a living room in America. Although the circumstances that connect these environments are very different, the strategic principles remain relevant. The pillars of the strategy are:

- Preparedness and Communication: activities that should be undertaken before a pandemic to ensure preparedness, and the communication of roles and responsibilities to all levels of government, segments of society, and individuals.
- Surveillance and Detection: domestic and international systems that provide continuous "situational awareness" to ensure the earliest warning possible to protect the population.
- Response and Containment: Actions to limit the spread of the outbreak and to mitigate the health, social, and economic impacts of a pandemic.[14]

The national pandemic strategy has survived two presidential administrations and the H1N1 pandemic. However, the U.S. government has not been able to generate a civil defense–type mentality with pandemics yet, but it keeps trying. Conventional wisdom sees the government's role as limited to providing information and sponsoring vaccine development.

In contrast to traditional security concerns, the human security concern of influenza shifts security from the nation-state to the individual. Key to the government's efforts is to empower individuals to be responsible for their own health. On one hand, this is consistent with American political culture that resists the federal government providing security

POLICY SPOTLIGHT

Preparing for a Global Pandemic

There are lessons to be learned from past outbreaks in order to inform preparations for future ones. In 2002–2003, a corona virus caused severe acute respiratory syndrome, which was responsible for 774 dead and 8,100 hospitalizations worldwide. SARS spread to twenty-seven countries within months, from Asia to Toronto by means of a Canadian tourist. Within weeks, the outbreak spread from Toronto within Ontario, and was hastened by the hospitals' lack of preparation for infectious disease. Tellingly, 45 percent of those infected were health care workers. Toronto's economy was hobbled by both the outbreak and the ensuing travel advisory issued by the World Health Organization.[1]

Canada's experience with SARS is instructive and has implications for air travel. Monitoring passengers on board airplanes is now routine, and airports in Asia employ special heat-sensing technology to detect travelers with fevers. Some countries, like China, are particularly aggressive and routinely quarantine passengers who exhibit flulike symptoms. This creates an obvious tension between an individual's civil liberties and governments' efforts to control pandemics; as with disease, fear of pandemics drives policy. In any case, these measures can easily fail, as it is even more difficult to detect certain viruses in their initial stage than it is to detect explosives or weapons of mass destruction among airline passengers.

1. World Health Organization, "Severe Acute Respiratory Syndrome (SARS): Status of the Outbreak and Lessons for the Immediate Future," May 20, 2003, available at www.who.int/csr/media/sars_wha.pdf.

FIGURE 6.1: 2010 GLOBAL DISEASE-FIGHTING PROGRAMS

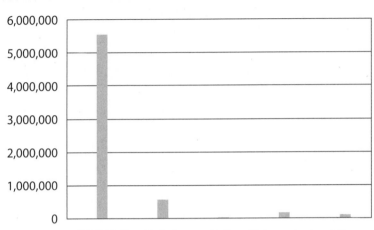

Source: Adapted from U.S. Agency for International Development, Congressional Budget Justification Foreign Assistance Summary Tables, Fiscal Year 2010, *available at www.usaid.gov/policy/budget/cbj2010/.*

within the United States. On the other hand, hand washing may not be a confidence-instilling defense! Furthermore, the scope of pandemics can quickly overwhelm state and local governments, with the potential to quickly destabilize society. To date, the relationship among the various government actors and society is largely being tested through practice events, and the true test cannot occur until a pandemic begins to take hold in the United States. Yet even with these limitations, the United States is still much more prepared to cope, and capable of doing so, with a pandemic than are the many poor societies of the world.

HIV/AIDS

Whereas the influenza virus is considered potentially the deadliest across all demographic groups, HIV/AIDS already claims millions of lives each year around the globe. Unlike influenza, the human immunodeficiency virus (HIV) is transmitted through behavior that results in the sharing of infected bodily fluids. HIV is a retrovirus that infects cells of the human

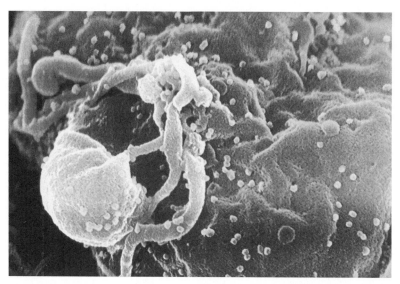

Image 6.3—Scanning electron micrograph of HIV-1 budding from cultured lymphocyte. Photo credit: Cynthia Goldsmith, Centers for Disease Control and Prevention.

immune system, destroying or impairing cellular function. The most advanced stage of HIV infection is acquired immunodeficiency syndrome, or AIDS. It can take ten to fifteen years for an HIV-infected person to develop AIDS, a process that can be slowed by antiretroviral drugs. Like influenza, treatment is limited to antiviral drugs, which can slow immune system degeneration and protect an infected person from secondary infections. Yet eventually, as the virus deteriorates a person's immune system, death often comes from a secondary infection such as tuberculosis or influenza.

According to the World Health Organization, approximately 33 million people live with HIV/AIDS. The geographic distribution of those infected with HIV/AIDS is not random. Instead, there are high concentrations of infected in sub-Saharan Africa, with southern African societies being primarily infected. In the West infections are highest among intravenous drug users and homosexuals. But in Africa women are infected at the highest rates. Incredibly, in Botswana nearly 1 in 3 people is infected, while nearly 1 in 5 South Africans has the disease.

Cultural norms in sub-Saharan Africa tend to prevent condom usage, resulting in the faster spread of HIV/AIDS. In 2007 alone, an additional 2.7 million became infected and 2 million died from the disease. Based on current trends, it is expected that by 2025 there will be 50 million HIV-positive people who will predominately live in sub-Saharan Africa.[15] This poses a serious challenge for promoting future economic development and stable, productive societies in many African countries.

To date, there is no cure for HIV/AIDS. The complexity of the virus and limits of medical research have kept researchers focused on vaccine development since 1984. Fortunately, recent work in Southeast Asia is pointing the way to a vaccine, which has shown a 30 percent success rate in vulnerable populations. However, much more work remains to be done, and prevention efforts still dominate policy actions.

The transformation in viewing HIV/AIDS as a national security threat rather than a sexual disease has not been easy. Some religious leaders have viewed HIV/AIDS as the supreme punishment for immoral acts.[16] Yet many experts have recognized that the disease does not discriminate and that absolute infection rates are highest among heterosexual women who may receive it from their spouses. Furthermore, the destabilizing effect on societies in Africa and the observed link between sick and absent parents and child soldiers have helped move the issue to the forefront of international security. Former World Bank president James Wolfensohn captured the challenges of AIDS as a health security issue when he commented, "Many of us used to think of AIDS as a health issue. We were wrong. . . . Nothing we have seen is a greater challenge to the peace and stability of African societies than the epidemic of AIDS. . . . We face a major development crisis, and more than that, a security crisis." In recognition of this fact, in 2000 the United Nations Security Council declared HIV/AIDS to be a threat to international peace and security. The associated UN resolution stressed that the HIV/AIDS pandemic, if unchecked, may pose a risk to stability and security.[17]

Analyst Laurie Garrett has examined the linkage between HIV and security, concluding that "the stability of states with high rates of HIV infection may well be threatened, but more likely through a process of erosion of its elite populations, its political leadership, its college-trained

Image 6.4—Antimosquito tents like these are an effective way to reduce malaria. Photo credit: USAID.

professionals, and its skilled labor forces."[18] There are additional effects on security forces in states with high infection rates. Already, an alarming 25 percent of African military personnel are HIV positive. This not only further debilitates weak states but also subjects civilian populations to infection, given that military personnel are important vectors. In recognition of this fact, HIV testing among deploying peacekeepers is now common to prevent future spread of the disease by soldiers.

MALARIA

In contrast to influenza and HIV/AIDS, malaria is insect borne, making prevention seem easier. Yet it remains one of the most challenging diseases in the world, with 300 to 500 million persons infected annually, producing about 1 million deaths each year. Malaria is a bloodborne infection transmitted by mosquitoes. The parasites destroy red blood cells, which leads to anemia and lung and kidney failure and can result in death. And in contrast to influenza and HIV/AIDS, the vast majority of those killed are children. In fact, 90 percent of fatalities are children under the age of five, a fact that has clear implications for retarding future development in affected countries.[19]

Preventing malaria is not as simple as it might appear. More than half the world's population live in areas where malaria infection is possible. There is generally less risk of infection at altitudes greater than 4,000 feet, but climate is the main determinant. Tropical climates offer ideal conditions for mosquito breeding, and the political instability often prevalent in developing countries complicates control and treatment. This includes parts of South America, sub-Saharan Africa, South Asia, and Southeast Asia. Additionally, it is worth noting that a number of experts believe that the rise of global temperatures may increase the range of such traditionally tropical diseases as malaria and yellow fever into areas such as Europe.[20]

Given the scope of the malaria challenge, governments that prioritize development assistance increasingly include antimalarial programs in an effort to reduce the disease's impact. The U.S. government, for example, has a five-year $1.2 billion program designed to reduce malaria deaths by 50 percent in fifteen countries. This is consistent with economist Jeffrey Sachs's advice that economic development in tropical ecozones would benefit from a concerted international effort to develop health technologies specific to the needs of tropical climates. Logically, a healthy workforce can be a much more productive workforce. As World Bank president Robert Zoellick has observed, "Malaria is not only a disease of poverty; it's also a cause of poverty."[21]

The main U.S. government antimalaria program is the President's Malaria Initiative. PMI is an interagency initiative led by the U.S. Agency for International Development and implemented together with the Centers for Disease Control and Prevention. The U.S. global malaria coordinator, advised by representatives of USAID, the Centers for Disease Control and Prevention and the Department of Health and Human Services, the Department of State, the Department of Defense, the National Security Council, and the Office of Management and Budget, oversees the program. Since prevention is the primary effort, the program focuses on distributing mosquito nets, antimalarial drugs, and insecticide. At the same time, the program also seeks to strengthen partner countries' health services through education, training, and resources. This approach is increasingly important as budget deficits and the challenges of an economic recovery start to negatively impact funding levels.

CONCLUSION

Pandemics have long been a part of human civilization. More recently, the threat of pandemics was crystallized in the three influenza pandemics of the twentieth century that killed tens of millions. The 2009–2010 influenza and HIV/AIDS pandemics coupled with malaria cripple societies, stifle development, and produce millions of deaths every year. When thinking about pandemics and societies like the United States, it is not a question of if but when the next pandemic will produce millions of deaths. Given the potential for an enormous loss of life and socioeconomic instability, pandemics are now included on the national security agenda of many countries.

As this chapter demonstrates, disease seldom discriminates; it impacts both rich and poor societies. This linkage is declared in the 1999 *National Security Strategy*, as the U.S. government seeks "to create a stable, peaceful international security environment—one in which our nation, citizens and interests are not threatened; the health and well-being of our citizens are enhanced by a cleaner global environment and effective strategies to combat infectious disease." This was reiterated in the 2009 *National Health Security Strategy* that emphasizes collaboration from the individual to intergovernmental organizations. Realistically, as Laurie Garrett argues, "In the event of a deadly influenza pandemic, it is doubtful that any of the world's wealthiest nations would be able to meet the needs of their own citizenry—much less those of other countries."[22] Diseases can no longer escape notice since large-scale, quick-moving infections have the ability to upset social stability, even necessitating a military response to support civil authorities. Further, disease undermines the key development goals established by the United Nations and supported by the United States.

Most challenging for the United States is pandemic influenza. As previous discussions make clear, H5N1 and H1N1 cannot be contained by borders or robust prevention. Pandemics, by their very nature, are international in scope and have become a key feature of the national and human security landscape. Fortunately, pandemics do facilitate international cooperation since all people are vulnerable regardless of nationality, ideology, or geography. The United States and China are at the forefront of this struggle and cooperate at bilateral, global, and regional levels to prevent and respond to pandemic influenza. Ironically, whereas traditional security concerns like military modernization can cause friction between great powers, human security concerns such as diseases can create trust. And whereas fear can cause conflict, shared insecurity can generate peace.

The inevitability of pandemics need not lead to complacency or overreaction. Environmental monitoring and prevention measures can reduce the impact of the next pandemic. Although no single vaccine can provide broad-spectrum immunity for future diseases, governments and other groups can manage the impact of the next pandemic, if they remain prepared. The relatively quick response to the 2009 H1N1 pandemic that included vaccine production illustrates how negative effects can be minimized. Yet even though fatalities were limited in 2009–2010, director-general of the World Health Organization Dr. Margaret Chan had earlier warned the world, "Pandemic influenza is . . . looming on the horizon. The threat has by no means receded and we would be very unwise to let down our guard, or slacken our preparedness measures. As with climate change, all countries will be affected, though in a far more rapid and sweeping way."[23] Thus, health security remains a crucial component of ensuring each nation's security and every individual's human security.

To Learn More

John M. Barry details last century's pandemic that claimed tens of millions of lives in *The Great Influenza: The Story of the Deadliest Pandemic in History* (New York: Penguin Books, 2005).

Laurie Garrett examines trends and forecasts in *The Coming Plague: Newly Emerging Diseases in a World Out of Balance* (New York: Penguin Books, 1995).

In *Guns, Germs, and Steel: The Fates of Human Societies* (New York: W. W. Norton, 1999), Jared Diamond considers how disease has shaped human societies.

Track pandemics through the World Health Organization at www.who.int and at the Department of Defense, Global Emerging Infectious Disease Surveillance Program, at www.geis.fhp.osd.mil/GEIS/SurveillanceActivities/Influenza/influenza.asp.

Read the Centers for Disease Control and Prevention advice on protecting yourself from the H1N1 influenza at www.flu.gov.

See the U.S. National Intelligence Council's article "The Global Infectious Disease Threat and Its Implications for the U.S., 2000," available at www.fas.org/irp/threat/nie99-17d.htm.

Scan the United States' first-ever *National Health Security Strategy*, released by Health and Human Services secretary Kathleen Sebelius in December 2009, at www.hhs.gov/aspr/opsp/nhss/nhss0912.pdf.

Given the U.S. military's global presence and the role it plays in strengthening other countries' militaries, health has become a key component of security assistance. Examine how the Department of Defense is assisting allied militaries and uniformed services in the global war against AIDS at www.med.navy.mil/sites/nhrc/dhapp/Pages/default.aspx.

Stefan Elbe outlines the ethical challenges associated with treating health issues as security issues for the journal *International Studies Quarterly*. See "Should HIV/AIDS Be Securitized? The Ethical Dilemmas of Linking HIV/AIDS and Security" (2006).

Notes

1. Robert A. Cook, "The Human-Animal Link," *Foreign Affairs* (July–August 2006): 59; Blair, "Annual Threat Assessment" (see chap. 4, n. 11).

2. Joint Forces Command, *Joint Operating Environment: Trends and Challenges for the Future Joint Force Through 2030* (Norfolk, VA: Joint Forces Command, 2007), 53.

3. White House, *A National Security Strategy for Enlargement and Engagement* (Washington, DC: White House, 1996).

4. White House, *A National Security Strategy for a New Century* (Washington, DC: White House, 1999), 13.

5. White House, *A National Security Strategy for a New Century* (Washington, DC: White House, 1998), 1 (emphasis added).

6. Bush, *National Security Strategy*, ii (see chap. 3, n. 10); Homeland Security Presidential Directive 21 (Washington, DC: White House, October 18, 2007); President Barack Obama, "Remarks by the President to the United Nations General Assembly," September 23, 2009.

7. The Netherlands Ministry of the Interior and Kingdom Relations, *National Security Strategy and Work Programme, 2007–2008* (The Hague: The Hague Center for Strategic Studies, May 2007), available at www.hcss.nl/en/publication/689/Dutch-National-Security-Strategy.html; Prime Minister of the United Kingdom, *National Security Strategy of the United Kingdom: Security in an Interdependent World* (London: Crown, March 2008), 3, available at http://interactive.cabinetoffice.gov.uk/ . . . /security/national_security_strategy.pdf; http://ec.europa.eu/health/ph_threats/com/Influenza/novelflu_en.htm; World Economic Forum, *Global Risks, 2007: A Global Risk Network Report* (Geneva: World Economic Forum, January 2007), available at www.weforum.org/en/media/publications/GlobalRiskReports/index.htm.

8. National Intelligence Council, *Global Trends, 2025: A World Transformed* (Washington, DC: National Intelligence Council, 2009), 95; Department of Defense, *National Defense Strategy*, 1 (emphasis added) (see chap. 4, n. 15).

9. Department of State, "United States–China Joint Initiative on Avian Influenza," November 19, 2005, available at http://2001-2009.state.gov/r/pa/prs/ps/2005/57157.htm.

10. Michael T. Osterholm, "Preparing for the Next Pandemic," *Foreign Affairs* (July–August 2006): 25.

11. Joint Forces Command, *Joint Operating Environment*.

12. Steven J. Phillips and George R. Worthington, "When Disaster Strikes," *Naval Institute Proceedings*, October 2009, 33. See also House Oversight and Government Reform Committee, 111th Congress, "Committee Holds Hearings on the Lack of Hospital Emergency Surge Capacity," May 2008, available at

http://oversight.house.gov/index.php?option=com_content&task=view&id=35
13&Itemid=2.

13. Centers for Disease Control and Prevention, H1N1 Flu General Information Web page, "CDC Estimates of 2009 H1N1 Influenza Cases, Hospitalizations, and Deaths in the United States, April–November 14, 2009," December 10, 2009, available at www.cdc.gov/h1n1flu/estimates/April_December_12.htm.

14. White House, *National Strategy for Pandemic Influenza* (Washington, DC: White House, 2005), 3.

15. National Intelligence Council, *Global Trends, 2025*, 23.

16. For example, Reverend Jerry Falwell reportedly said, "AIDS is the wrath of a just God against homosexuals. To oppose it would be like an Israelite jumping in the Red Sea to save one of Pharaoh's charioteers" (cited in Timothy Noah, "Jerry Fallwell's Hit Parade," Slate.com, May 15, 2007, available at www.slate.com/id/2166220).

17. James Wolfensohn, "Speech Delivered to the UN Security Council," New York, January 10, 2000; United Nations, Security Council Resolution 1308, July 17, 2000.

18. Laurie Garrett, *HIV and National Security: Where Are the Links?* (New York: Council on Foreign Relations, 2005), 10.

19. USAID, *The President's Malaria Initiative: Third Annual Report* (Washington, DC: USAID, 2009).

20. Andrea Swalec, "Climate Already Helping Disease Spread North: Study," Reuters Alertnet, June 10, 2010, available at www.alertnet.org/thenews/news desk/LDE65918G.htm.

21. Robert Zoellick, "World Bank Group President Robert Zoellick's Remarks at the 2008 Millennium Development Goals Malaria Summit," United Nations Headquarters, New York City, September 25, 2008, available at http://siteresources.worldbank.org/ . . . /RBZ_remarks_at_MDG_Forum_2008 -malaria.pdf.

22. White House, *A National Security Strategy for a New Century* (1999), 5; Laurie Garrett, "The Next Pandemic," *Foreign Affairs* (July–August 2006): 17.

23. Quoted in Department of State, *Avian and Pandemic Influenza: The Global Response*, 2008, available at http://2001-2009.state.gov/documents/organization/111559.pdf.

7

Cyber Security

The policy of the United States is to protect against the debilitating disruption of the operation of information systems for critical infrastructures and, thereby, help to protect the people, economy, and national security of the United States. . . . Securing cyberspace is an extraordinarily difficult strategic challenge that requires a coordinated and focused effort from our entire society—the federal government, state and local governments, the private sector, and the American people.

—WHITE HOUSE, *THE NATIONAL STRATEGY TO SECURE CYBERSPACE*, 2003

The preceding chapters focused on human security challenges such as inequitable development, pandemics, water scarcity, and illegal fishing. As this book has made clear, these types of challenges are more common than nation-state war for many people throughout the world. Often, these challenges take place in developing countries far from American shores, but they do pose a threat to U.S. interests and international assistance efforts to reduce poverty, violence, disease, and environmental change. Fortunately for U.S. citizens, authorities in the United States are responsive to nonstate threats and have been able to limit their damage to Americans' human security. However, the same cannot be said of a new class of threats in the cyber world, which affect all human beings. In cyberspace, Americans' privacy is challenged by state and nonstate actors, Americans' livelihoods are challenged by malicious code, and Americans' freedoms are challenged by efforts to stop malevolent activity. This chapter considers these challenges in the nonphysical world since all Americans enjoy the benefits of living in the information age—music downloads, cell phones, and cash from ATMs.

Within just the past decade, people everywhere have become as dependent on the virtual world for their daily activities as they are dependent on the physical world for human activities. Consider the implications for yourself when the network is down, cell phone calls are dropped, or a virus crashes your hard drive. In many cases, daily routines are broken, frustrations rise, and work stops. There are clear benefits to information technology, which we now embrace as essential to our lives, our economy, and ultimately our national security. Information technology connects people in unique ways. Global fiber-optic networks have also enabled communication in an unprecedented manner, propelling the emergence of India as the world's "back office," allowing companies to move offshore, and giving consumers access to a variety of data from around the planet.

The International Telecommunications Union of the United Nations found that nearly one-quarter of the world's 6.7 billion people use the Internet, while more than half of the world's population have mobile phone access.[1] This interconnection of the world's population within and across societies holds tremendous implications for economic growth and development, particularly for impoverished areas. It also gives countries the potential to overcome the challenges of being landlocked or geographically isolated from the developed core countries in North America, Europe, and North Asia. Yet, at the same time, this interconnection has the potential to trigger a culturally based backlash in traditional societies against perceived attempts to impose an alien culture and mores, as examination of the issue of globalization earlier in this book revealed. Inasmuch as the Internet can share culture, it can also homogenize or even destroy culture.

Apart from the cultural impacts of technology, there is also a dark side of the cyber world wherein hackers, phishing scam artists, and transnational crime groups harness the technology, too. This forms part of Moisés Naím's "wars of globalization" described earlier in this book. Through Trojan horses, criminals and spies gain access to government and private computer networks. Through viruses and denial-of-service attacks, individuals and groups can disrupt governments and corporations. And through spyware or government surveillance programs, the cherished civil liberty of privacy is subverted. No longer only in fiction, the personal, professional, and financial records of one's life can be erased or stolen for malevolent purposes. Thus, for many in the United States and other citizens of developed countries, the ultimate threat to their individual human security comes from cyberspace. Yet cyber security is not just a personal issue but a national security issue, too. The former U.S. director of national intelligence testified to this point: "The growing connectivity between information systems, the Internet, and other infrastructures creates opportunities for attackers to disrupt telecommunications, electrical power, energy pipelines, refineries, financial networks, and other critical infrastructure."[2]

In the cyber world, individual hackers tend to pose the greatest danger to information security, but governments now include cyber war in their planning and operations. The most recent example of this was the cyber attack that accompanied Russia's invasion of Georgia in 2008. As Russian tanks and aircraft were entering Georgian territory, cyber warriors attacked the Georgian Ministry of Defense. Though it had a minimal effect, the attack was a harbinger; future conflicts will have both a physical dimension and a virtual dimension. As governments and militaries embrace technology for efficiency and effect, they also become vulnerable to cyber threats. And as more of society, government, and the economy move online, individuals in developed countries can no longer be isolated from the effects of war. Americans have become accustomed to seeing their military fight wars abroad with little impact on the homeland; cyber war has the potential to change this. Adversaries may disrupt Americans' access to such fundamental necessities as electricity, telecommunications, and water.

In any case, virtual war need not accompany the physical attacks characteristic of warfare. Countries increasingly employ cyber operations outside of warfare, suggesting that it is becoming a unique tool of power. On any given day, foreign governments sponsor regular intrusions into U.S. government networks, hackers steal financial data from banks, and foreign intelligence services conduct cyber espionage. Given the importance of information technology networks and the threats posed to them, there is a growing awareness of cyber security. This chapter defines the cyberspace domain, considers the threats facing information networks and individual citizens, and places cyber security within the national and human security realms.

CYBERSPACE DEFINED

Writer William Gibson coined the term *cyberspace* in a short story published in 1982. Once confined to the cyberpunk literature and science fiction like the movie *The Matrix*, cyberspace entered the real world in the late 1990s, and in 2003 the Bush administration defined cyberspace as the "nervous system—the control system of our country. Cyberspace is composed of hundreds of thousands of interconnected computers, servers, routers, switches, and fiber optic cables that allow our critical infrastructures to work." The U.S. Defense Department later defined cyberspace as "a global domain within the information environment consisting of the interdependent network of information technology infrastructures, including the Internet, telecommunications network, computer systems, and embedded processors and controllers."[3]

Like the physical environment, the cyber environment is all-encompassing. It includes physical hardware such as networks and machines, information such as data and media, the cognitive realm such as the mental processes people use to comprehend their experiences, and the virtual world where people connect socially. When aggregated, what we think of as cyberspace serves as a fifth dimension where people can exist through alternate personae on blogs, social networking sites, and virtual reality games. Larry Johnson, chief executive officer of the New Media

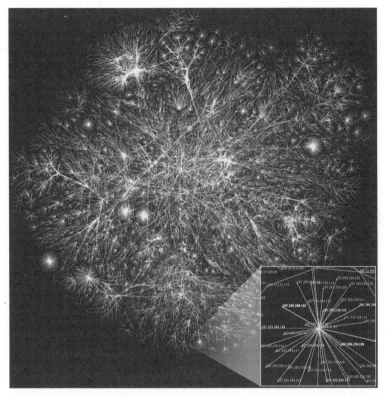

Image 7.1—Partial map of the Internet based on the January 15, 2005, data found on opte.org. Photo credit: Matt Britt, Creative Common.

Consortium, predicts that over the next fifteen years, we will experience the virtual world as an extension of the real one. Johnson believes:

> Virtual worlds are already bridging borders across the globe to bring people of many cultures and languages together in ways very nearly as rich as face-to-face interactions; they are already allowing the visualization of ideas and concepts in three dimensions that is leading to new insights and deeper learning; and they are already allowing people to work, learn, conduct business, shop, and interact in ways that promise to redefine how we think about these activities—and even what we regard as possible.[4]

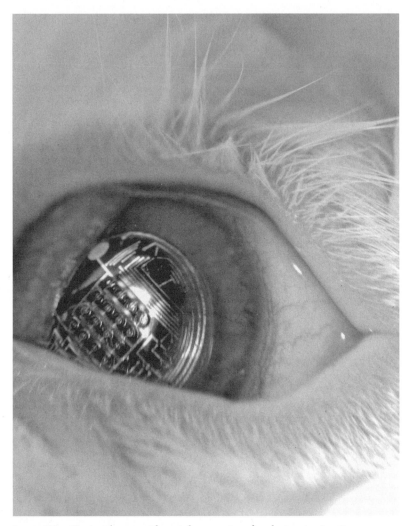

Image 7.2—Contact lenses with metal connectors for electronic circuits were safely worn by rabbits in laboratory tests at the University of Washington. A virtual display like this could be used by drivers or pilots to see a vehicle's speed projected onto the windshield, by video-game companies who could use the contact lenses to completely immerse players in a virtual world without restricting their range of motion, or, in the field of communications, by people on the go who could surf the Internet on a midair virtual display screen that only they would be able to see. Photo credit: Babak Parviz, University of Washington.

FIGURE 7.1. INTERNET USERS IN 2009

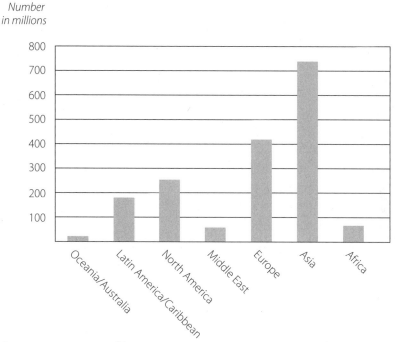

Source: www.internetworldstats.com

Gone are the stereotypes of young male gamers who dominate cyber-space; those who inhabit virtual worlds are middle-aged, employed, and increasingly female. For example, the median age in the virtual world Second Life is thirty-six, and 45 percent are women. The Internet has been the primary means of this interconnectivity, which is both physical and virtual. Due to the highly developed economies and its important role in the information technology sector, the highest Internet penetration rate is in North America. Yet, given its population size and rapid development, Asia has the most users (see Figure 7.1). China has 100 million more Internet users than the United States has people. By the end of 2010 some two billion users were assessed to be using the Internet.

CYBERSPACE AND NATIONAL SECURITY

The link between national security and the Internet has been developing since the Clinton administration in the 1990s. Yet there are significant differences between cyberspace and traditional domains like airspace that make protecting the former difficult. To begin with, no single entity owns the Internet, but individuals, companies, and governments use it. Governments also do not have a monopoly on operating in cyberspace. Anyone with a good computer and Internet connection can operate there. And making it more challenging for governments, most of the cyber expertise resides in information technology companies. Yet all sectors are affected equally by disruptions in cyberspace; a computer virus disruption that occurs through a commercial Web site can slow down the Internet for government and military users as well as for corporations and private citizens.

As it relates to war, the Internet is both a means and a target for militaries. U.S. deputy defense secretary William Lynn underscored how important the information infrastructure is to national defense: "Just like our national dependence [on the Internet], there is simply no exaggerating our military dependence on our information networks: the command and control of our forces, the intelligence and logistics on which they depend, the weapons technologies we develop and field—they all depend on our computer systems and networks. Indeed, our 21st century military simply cannot function without them."[5]

Additionally, governments use the Internet to shape their messages through media outlets hosted throughout the Web. U.S. military commanders use public blogs, and operational units post videos to YouTube. This gives both the military and citizens unprecedented insight from pilots after they bomb a target or from marines as they conduct humanitarian assistance. The transparency is intended to reduce suspicions, counter deceptive claims made by adversaries, and improve the image of the military. The United States sees its center of gravity or vulnerability as popular support, so connecting the military directly to the people is important. Yet there are limits to these potential advantages; the Pentagon is concerned that its personnel can also share too much data through Facebook or project a poor image through YouTube videos, which runs counter to its efforts.

In contrast to traditional war-fighting domains like land, air, or sea, governments are not the only powers in cyberspace. Rather, individuals

---

TABLE 7.1. CYBER THREATS DEFINED

Virus: malicious code that can self-replicate and cause damage to the systems it infects. The code can delete information, infect programs, change the directory structure to run undesirable programs, and infect the vital part of the operating system that ties together how files are stored.

Worm: Similar to a virus, a worm is distinctive for its ability to self-replicate without infecting other files in order to reproduce.

Trojan Horse: stealthy code that executes under the guise of a useful program but performs malicious acts such as the destruction of files, the transmission of private data, and the opening of a back door to allow third-party control of a machine.

Logic Bomb: camouflaged segments of programs that destroy data when certain conditions are met.

Zombie: a computer that has been covertly compromised and is controlled by a third party.

Botnet: a network of zombie machines used by hackers for massive coordinated system attacks.

Denial-of-Service Attack: employing a botnet to send massive simultaneous requests to servers, preventing legitimate use of the servers.

---

can readily harness technology to compete on a global scale. And it is worth noting that virtualization will continue this trend of democratizing the Internet, giving individuals tremendous power unthinkable even ten years ago. Satellite imagery used to be highly classified and limited by the U.S. intelligence community, but now anyone can access imagery from an iPhone using Google Earth. Likewise, the complexity and cost of building a nuclear weapon limit their production to governments, but the same cannot be said for the virtual weapon of mass destruction that can destroy data and networks, undermine international credibility, and disrupt commerce. Malicious activity through worms, viruses, and zombies regularly disrupts Internet activity (see Table 7.1). And there are already many examples of virtual activities impacting the physical world such as terrorists being recruited, radicalized, and trained on the Internet; communications being severed; or power production being disrupted. Illegally armed

groups use cyberspace to move money, conceal identities, and plan operations, which makes it extremely difficult for governments to compete with
them. Consequently, governments are increasingly concerned with the
cyber domain as a new feature within the national security landscape.

In some sense, there has always been an implicit national security purpose for the Internet. After all, it was originally conceived of and funded
by one of the Defense Department's research organizations then known
as the Advanced Research Projects Agency (ARPA). Given the state of
telecommunications and the nonnetworked computer systems that ex-
isted in the 1960s, researchers wanted to create a reliable network where
a user's system or location was unimportant to his or her ability to participate on the network. Charles Herzfeld, ARPA director from 1965 to
1967, explains the genesis of the network:

> The ARPANET was not started to create a Command and Control
> System that would survive a nuclear attack, as many now claim. To
> build such a system was clearly a major military need, but it was
> not ARPA's mission to do this; in fact, we would have been severely
> criticized had we tried. Rather, the ARPANET came out of our
> frustration that there were only a limited number of large, power-
> ful research computers in the country, and that many research
> investigators who should have access to them were geographically
> separated from them.[6]

This vision of a network became a reality in 1969 when a computer link
was established between the University of California–Los Angeles and
Stanford University. At the time, the connection was called "internetwork-
ing," which was shortened to Internet. For thirty years, the Internet was
largely the domain of universities, colleges, and research institutes. But
when Tim Berners-Lee and his colleagues created the World Wide Web
in 1990, commercial and social applications exploded. Within a few short
years, companies like Amazon.com and eBay (1995), Wikipedia (2001),
and Facebook (2004) founded a new industry and changed the way we
live and work. Ongoing trends in Web development tools suggest that the
gap between the virtual and physical worlds is indeed narrowing.

The U.S. government came late to cyberspace. It first emerged as a distinct national security policy area in 1998 when President Clinton signed Presidential Decision Directive 63, which established a White House structure to coordinate government and private action to "eliminate any significant vulnerability to both physical and cyber attacks on our critical infrastructures, including especially our cyber systems." The March 2005 *National Defense Strategy* identified cyberspace as a new theater of operations and assessed cyberspace operations as a potentially disruptive challenge, concluding that in "rare instances, revolutionary technology and associated military innovation can fundamentally alter long-established concepts of warfare." The 2008 *National Defense Strategy* explored the implications of this further, assessing that small groups or individuals "can attack vulnerable points in cyberspace and disrupt commerce and daily life in the United States, causing economic damage, compromising sensitive information and materials, and interrupting critical services such as power and information networks."[7]

In spite of recognizing vulnerabilities and threats to cyberspace, there are clear gaps in how policy and law address these concerns. There are no clear answers on important issues such as how to respond to cyber intrusions, whether computer network attacks constitute a form of warfare, and whether the UN conception of self-defense applies in cyberspace. Yet the threat remains. Deputy defense secretary William Lynn said the Defense Department's culture regarding cybersecurity issues must change because "we're seeing assaults come at an astonishing speed—not hours, minutes or even seconds—but in milliseconds at network speed."[8] Defense officials admitted in 2010 that their systems were being probed by unknown users some 250,000 times an hour, a staggering 6 million times a day.[9] Whereas the Pentagon has a plan to stop an air attack against the United States, there is no corresponding plan to reduce malicious activity.

In an effort to understand the challenges and raise awareness of cyberspace, the Center for Strategic and International Studies bluntly warned in 2008, "America's failure to protect cyberspace is one of the most urgent national security problems facing the new administration." In recognition of this, President Barack Obama declared October 2009 to be National Cybersecurity Awareness Month due to "our Nation's growing dependence on cyber and information-related technologies, coupled with an increasing threat of malicious cyber attacks and loss of privacy."[10]

A month later, a former NATO commander declared, "The cybersecurity threat is real. Adversaries target networks, application software, operating systems, and even the ubiquitous silicon chips inside computers, which are the bedrock of the United States' public and private infrastructure." Retired army general Wesley Clark and Peter Levin argued: "All evidence indicates that the country's defenses are already being pounded, and the need to extend protection from computer networks and software to computer hardware is urgent. The U.S. government can no longer afford to ignore the threat from computer-savvy rivals or technologically advanced terrorist groups, because the consequences of a major breach would be catastrophic."[11]

The global security implications are profound. In recognition, Hamadoun Touré, secretary-general of the United Nations International Telecommunications Union, has warned: "The next world war could take place in the cyberspace and this needs to be avoided. The conventional wars have shown us that first of all, there is no winner in any war and second, the best way to win a war is to avoid it in the first place. So we need to plant the seeds for a safer cyberspace together. And it can only be done at the global level because the criminal needs no longer to be on the crime scene and you can attack many places at the same time in the cyberspace."[12]

With these concerns in mind, the United Nations is working on a no-first-strike policy for its members, which is reminiscent of the policy for nuclear weapons use. This approach certainly makes sense given that the United Nations is organized around the nation-state concept, but it can have little effect on contemporary vulnerabilities to the Internet, where many threats emanate from small groups and nonstate actors. Furthermore, there is an inherent deniability to generating Internet-based attacks, which makes any agreement extremely difficult to monitor or enforce.

THREATS TO THE CYBER DOMAIN

When attempting to examine cyber threats, the point of origin is very difficult to determine. Unlike a missile launch that has a discrete signature

TABLE 7.2: SOURCES OF CYBER INSECURITY

THREAT SOURCE	MOTIVATION
Foreign nations	Foreign intelligence services use cyber tools as part of their information gathering and espionage activities. These include: exploitation and potential disruption or destruction of information infrastructure.
Criminal groups	Criminal groups use cyber intrusions for monetary gain.
Hackers	Hackers sometimes crack into networks for the thrill of the challenge or for bragging rights in the hacker community. While remote cracking once required a fair amount of skill or computer knowledge, hackers can now download attack scripts and protocols from the Internet and launch them against victim sites. Thus, attack tools have become more sophisticated and easier to use.
Hacktivists	These groups and individuals conduct politically motivated attacks, overload e-mail servers, and hack into Web sites to send a political message.
Disgruntled insiders	The disgruntled insider, working from within an organization, is a principal source of computer crimes. Insiders may not need a great deal of knowledge about computer intrusions because their knowledge of a victim system often allows them to gain unrestricted access to cause damage to the system or to steal system data.
Terrorists	Terrorists seek to destroy, incapacitate, or exploit critical infrastructures to threaten national security, cause mass casualties, weaken the U.S. economy, and damage public morale and confidence. The Central Intelligence Agency believes terrorists will stay focused on traditional attack methods, but it anticipates growing cyber threats as a more technically competent generation enters the ranks.

Source: Government Accountability Office, Statement for the Record to the Subcommittee on Terrorism and Homeland Security, Committee on the Judiciary, U.S. Senate; Cybersecurity: Continued Efforts are Needed to Protect Information Systems from Evolving Threats, *November 17, 2009.*

and geographic location, those who employ cyber tactics can easily hide their origin, which makes attribution extremely difficult. James Lewis has argued, "Uncertainty is the most prominent aspect of cyber conflict—in attribution of the attackers [sic] identity, the scope of collateral damage, and the potential effect on the intended target from cyber attack."[13] Thus, when trying to analyze the threats to the cyber domain, it is best to take a comprehensive approach. Accordingly, we can classify threats by *actor* such as individual and government, by *target* such as financial sector or defense department, or by *means* such as virus, bot, or denial of service. In terms of the actor, those who use cyber tactics for nefarious purposes range from individual hackers and organized criminal groups to intelligence services and governments. Table 7.2 captures these sources of cyber insecurity.

As the diversity of actors illustrates, the barriers to entry for cyberspace are low. One needs only a good Internet connection, a decent computer, and the technical know-how to conduct attacks. Unfortunately, all three are cheap, and this helps explain why cyber attacks have become commonplace. The head of the International Telecommunications Union noted, "There is no such thing anymore as a superpower in the cyberspace because every individual is one superpower in itself because it's a human brain that makes a difference in this field. And this is one natural resource that is equally distributed everywhere in the globe." In general reaction to this phenomenon, William Lynn summed up the challenge: "Once the province of nations, the ability to destroy via cyber means now also rests in the hands of small groups and individuals."[14] Thus, in cyberspace, human security and national security are inextricably linked. In spite of this, there is genuine disagreement on whether cyberspace should be treated as a war-fighting domain equivalent to air, space, land, and sea.

So far, criminals constitute the majority of bad actors as they take advantage of the Internet for their illicit purposes. Web-based attacks are the common source of malicious activity, which often happens by exploiting a vulnerable Web application or exploiting some vulnerability present in the underlying host operating system. In general, attackers concentrate their attacks for financial gain by stealing online banking credentials and credit card information. Phishing has become a common way to steal financial information by soliciting confidential information

CONTEMPORARY CHALLENGE

Battling Zombies

It might seem difficult to imagine, but the cyber version of Hollywood's soulless movie zombies is also active in cyberspace. When computers are tied together on a network, their computing power can be used for good and evil. A positive example is the cooperative research program SETI@home, which analyzes radio signals from space. By focusing the computing power of hundreds of thousands of computers, the project creates a virtual supercomputer. While SETI@home is a voluntary program, vulnerable computers can be arrayed in a similar way when they are subverted and transformed into zombies under the control of a malicious entity.

The most common way to create a zombie computer is by infecting it through a bot, which is covertly installed on a user's machine in order to allow an attacker to remotely control it. Often, the installation occurs when host programs are downloaded or carrier attachments are opened. Bots are inexpensive and relatively easy to propagate. In 2008 the computer security company Symantec observed underground-economy advertisements for as little as four cents per bot.[1] In 2008 the results of this were evident in the 10 million or so computers that were bot infected. Once they are transformed into zombie computers, attackers are able to activate them to execute denial-of-service attacks against Web sites, host phishing, attack Web sites, or send out spam e-mail. When an attack is traced, the origin is often masked, since the attack comes from an unwitting victim's zombie computer and not the true attacker. This means analysts must infer the source of attack, as was done when Israel was allegedly attacked in 2009 by at least 5 million computers attributed to Hamas or Hezbollah. Significantly, however, Israeli intelligence experts believe that the attacks were actually engineered by criminals in Russia, who were paid by Hamas or Hezbollah. This case underscores the true complexity of cyber security.[2]

---

1. Symantec Global Internet Security Report, "Trends for 2008," April 2009, available at www.symantec.com/connect/downloads/symantec-global-internet-security-threat-report-trends-2008.

2. "Hamas, Hezbollah Employ Russian Hackers for Cyber Attacks on Israel," Homeland Security Newswire, June 15, 2009, available at http://homelandsecuritynewswire.com/hamas-hezbollah-employ-russian-hackers-cyber-attacks-israel.

from an individual, group, or organization by mimicking (or spoofing) a specific brand. To counter this, cybersecurity specialists can lure hackers to spoofed computer systems to provide disinformation to attackers and study the attack style.

The United States was the top country of attack origin in 2008, accounting for 23 percent of worldwide activity (see Table 7.3).[15] China had the most bot-infected computers in 2008, accounting for 13 percent of the worldwide total. Given the large number of computers in the United States and China, it is not surprising that these two countries top the list of malicious activity. When broken down by region, there are some differences by type of infection. For example, 35 percent of Trojans were reported from North America; 34 percent from Europe, the Middle East, or Africa; 24 percent from Asia-Pacific; and just 6 percent from Latin America. The Asia-Pacific region dominated worm infections with 40 percent, while North America was just 13 percent. The increased proportion of virus infections was linked to the greater proportion of worms reported from the region because viral infection is a common component of worms. It seems that antivirus programs are more prevalent in North America.

CYBER AND WAR

As early as 1993 John Arquilla and David Ronfeldt had forecast that cyber war in the twenty-first century would be the equivalent of Nazi Germany's highly successful blitzkrieg operations in the twentieth century. In war, militaries would use "cyberspace (by operating within or through it) to attack personnel, facilities, or equipment with the intent of degrading, neutralizing, or destroying enemy combat capability, while protecting our own."[16] To date, there has not been a cyber war that meets this definition by producing significant damage or political coercion. Instead, cyber attacks have accompanied traditional warfare with limited impact. Defacement of government Web sites, denial-of-service attacks, and data stealing have been conducted over the Internet but do not constitute warfare. The doctrine and capabilities for cyber war are still developing.[17] But this may not be true for long, and senior military leaders worry about U.S. vulnerabilities and potential irrelevance of current capabilities to cyber threats.

TABLE 7.3: MALICIOUS CYBER ACTIVITY BY COUNTRY

COUNTRY	'08 RANK	'07 RANK	'08 OVERALL PERCENTAGE	'07 OVERALL PERCENTAGE	MALICIOUS CODE RANK	SPAM ZOMBIES RANK	PHISHING WEB SITES HOST RANK	BOT RANK	ATTACK-ORIGIN RANK
UNITED STATES	1	1	23	26	1	3	1	2	1
CHINA	2	2	9	11	2	4	6	1	2
GERMANY	3	3	6	7	12	2	2	4	4
UNITED KINGDOM	4	4	5	4	4	10	5	9	3
BRAZIL	5	8	4	3	16	1	16	5	9
SPAIN	6	6	4	3	10	8	13	3	6
ITALY	7	7	3	3	11	6	14	6	8
FRANCE	8	5	3	4	8	14	9	10	5
TURKEY	9	15	3	2	15	5	24	8	12
POLAND	10	12	3	2	23	9	8	7	17

Source: Symantec Global Internet Security Report, "Trends for 2008," April 2009.

Although cyber war has not yet occurred, the military services have recognized the importance of cyberspace both in peace and in war. For example, the air force has claimed cyberspace as one of its three operating domains (air and space are the others).[18] The navy created the Fleet Cyber Command (Tenth Fleet), while the director of national intelligence created the Joint Interagency Cyber Task Force. At the same time, service capabilities are aggregated under the new U.S. Cyber Command—part of the joint Strategic Command—which is responsible for developing and implementing integrated operations for defense and attack in the cyber domain. In thinking about the future, the U.S. military sees itself as uncomfortably vulnerable in the cyber domain and expects other countries to exploit it. Wesley Clark and Peter Levin argue: "There is no form of military combat more irregular than an electronic attack; it is extremely cheap, is very fast, can be carried out anonymously, and can disrupt or deny critical services precisely at the moment of maximum peril. Everything about the subtlety, complexity, and effectiveness of the assaults already inflicted on the United States' electronic defense indicates that other nations have thought carefully about this form of combat."[19]

China is often identified as a likely opponent in a cyber war. This has as much to do with realist scholars' predictions about the inevitability of war between great powers as it does with Chinese cyber behavior. When speaking about China, Robert K. Knake noted that the Chinese military "plan[s] to thwart U.S. supremacy in any potential conflict we get into with them. They believe they can deter us through cyber warfare." As the Chinese military *PLA Daily* stated, "Internet warfare is of equal significance to land, sea, and air power and requires its own military branch," and "it is essential to have an all-conquering offensive technology and to develop software and technology for net offensives . . . able to launch attacks and countermeasures."[20]

The Chinese seem impressed and inspired by U.S. cyber capabilities and are closely following events. Ming Zhou, a China specialist, noted that "information warfare is not just a theology, they can integrate it into nation-state interests."[21] Ironically, China simultaneously exploits cyberspace for its national security benefits, but is increasingly vulnerable to cyber exploitation. Beyond China, a number of countries that have sophisticated

U.S. Computer Emergency Readiness Team

The U.S. Computer Emergency Readiness Team protects the U.S. Internet infrastructure by coordinating defense against, and response to, cyber attacks. US-CERT is the operational arm of the National Cyber Security Division at the Department of Homeland Security. The NCSD was established by the DHS to serve as the federal government's cornerstone for cybersecurity coordination and preparedness, including implementation of the *National Strategy to Secure Cyberspace*. Information Sharing and Analysis Centers were established to allow critical sectors to share information and work together in an effort to protect our critical infrastructures and minimize vulnerabilities. Included in these centers are banking and finance, emergency services, energy, food and agriculture, government, information technology, real estate, telecommunications, transportation, and water. These sectors are critical to sustaining everyday life for all U.S. citizens.

The biggest threats to civilian infrastructure are through cyber attacks of Supervisory Control and Data Acquisition systems. A SCADA system collects data from remote systems and relays it to a central computer in what is usually a closed loop, requiring little in the way of human intervention. SCADA is widely used in industries that manage remote systems such as electric power, traffic signals, mass transit systems, water management systems, and manufacturing systems. Due to their heavily automated nature, SCADA systems are especially susceptible to computer attack. Control systems, signal hardware, controllers, networks, communications equipment, and software are all vulnerable to determined adversaries. A hacker with even temporary control of a mass transit system, for instance, could cause widespread death and destruction with the click of a mouse. As this example demonstrates, cyber threats pose an extremely difficult challenge for national and human security at all levels, and even the wealthiest governments and human beings may not be able to protect themselves effectively.

cyber national security capabilities include Russia, Israel, India, and France. Accordingly, the U.S. military is wrestling over the meaning of this as it relates to warfare and sees cyberspace as critical to its operations, which requires defensive and probably offensive measures.

CONCLUSION

In its short history, the Internet has been harnessed by individuals and companies to create a new industry, a new social sphere, and a new battle space. At the same time, criminals, other nonstate actors, and intelligence services have benefited as well. As the virtual and physical worlds continue to merge, new threats will develop that take advantage of the vulnerabilities inherent in a relatively open system. When it comes to security, there is tension between the common free space that is the Internet and the government's attempt to police it. This fact was recognized in the 1996 Telecommunications Act: "The policy of the United States [is] . . . to promote the continued development of the Internet and other interactive computer services and other interactive media . . . [and] preserve the vibrant and competitive free market that presently exists for the Internet and other interactive computer services, unfettered by Federal or State regulation." Thirteen years later, however, President Obama declared that "cyber attacks and their viral ability to infect networks, devices, and software must be the concern of all Americans."[22] This might produce the regulation that the 1996 law sought to forestall and ultimately stifle Internet activity. As the United States is the hub for the informational realm, its actions will affect human beings around the world.

Now that cyber security is a focus for national security, a key challenge is understanding "who is in charge." The private sector primarily designs, builds, owns, and operates the Internet, but there is a growing expectation that the government will protect it. The Defense Department is responsible for ensuring the ".mil" domain remains safe, while the Department of Homeland Security oversees security of the ".gov" domain. The ".com" domain is entrusted to the companies who operate there. In recognition of this reality, Richard Harknett and James Stever call for cyber security to rest on a balanced triad of intergovernmental relations, private corporate

THINK AGAIN

Bytes Are Not Bombs

Much like civilian organizations and governments, militaries are increasingly dependent on cyberspace for their operations. Information technology connects ships, aircraft, and ground vehicles to harmonize operations and avoid fratricide. Commanders rely on computer networks to maintain situational awareness and facilitate decision making. Given this dependence, the U.S. military identifies its cyber infrastructure as a critical vulnerability it must protect during war and peace. With very little imagination, it is possible to envision cyber war; that is, using cyber attacks to advance and defend state interests.

Yet this does not mean that the military can or should protect cyberspace. The aim of cyber threat differs substantially from physical warfare; data loss is not the same as human loss. Defacing a Web site is not the functional equivalent of bombing a country's capital. Along these lines, Bruce Schneier sees the United States going down a dangerous path, since "cybersecurity isn't a military problem, or even a government problem—it's a universal problem. All networks, military, government, civilian and commercial, use the same computers, the same networking hardware, the same Internet protocols and the same software packages. We all are the targets of the same attack tools and tactics. It's not even that government targets are somehow more important; these days, most of our nation's critical IT [information technology] infrastructure is in commercial hands."[1] As noted in this chapter, the U.S. government currently places responsibility for the protection of the U.S. Internet infrastructure and its critical sectors under the Department of Homeland Security, via such measures as the Computer Emergency Readiness Team. But just as with other homeland security threats or natural disasters, this department can call upon the Defense Department for support in an emergency. In that case the involvement of DOD would need to be carefully constrained so as to intrude as little as possible into traditionally sacrosanct areas such as citizens' private information and civil liberties.

---

1. Bruce Schneier, "Who Should Be in Charge of Cybersecurity?" *Wall Street Journal*, March 31, 2009.

Image 7.3—The United
States Air Force
monitors its networks at
centers like this one.
Photo credit: U.S. Air
Force photo/Tech. Sgt.
Cecilio Ricardo.

involvement, and active cyber citizenship as a model.[23] Yet it is unclear
how the Department of Defense, Google, and individual users would
manage this relationship.

The U.S. government is not waiting as it becomes more active in cyberspace. The secretary of homeland security is responsible for coordinating critical infrastructure protection, including cyber infrastructure.
Homeland Security Presidential Directive 7 assigned the DHS as the lead
for sharing threat information, assessing vulnerabilities, encouraging appropriate protective action, and developing contingency plans. This ne-
cessitates high levels of cooperation. As the White House's Cyberspace
Policy Review Committee made plain:

> The Federal government should work with the private sector to
> define public-private partnership roles and responsibilities for the
> defense of privately owned critical infrastructure and key re-
> sources. The common defense of privately-owned critical infra-
> structures from armed attack or from physical intrusion or
> sabotage by foreign military forces or international terrorists is a
> core responsibility of the Federal government. Similarly, govern-
> ment plays an important role in protecting these infrastructures
> from criminals or domestic terrorists. The question remains un-
> resolved as to what extent protection of these same infrastructures
> from the same harms by the same actors should be a government

responsibility if the attacks were carried out remotely via computer networks rather than by direct physical action.[24]

In reality, for U.S. citizens and people around the world, the question of who owns what, or who is responsible for what, is probably unimportant. An individual depending on the Internet to do banking just wants secure transactions in the .com domain; an individual trying to find information on charities just wants reliable information in the .org domain; someone trying to find information about driver's license requirements want access to timely, accurate data in the .gov domain; and the student trying to pursue education online wants an effective system in the .edu domain. In other words, most individuals want the cyber world to enhance their human security needs without causing additional vulnerabilities.

Yet there are a myriad of challenges. Attacks may come from such varied bad actors as a foreign intelligence service, a terrorist group, a criminal group, hacktivists, individual hackers, or disgruntled insiders. As this chapter illustrates, a single individual in cyberspace has the power to neutralize defense networks, disrupt civilian infrastructure, and steal identities.[25] As the virtual and physical worlds become closer over the next twenty years, new and unforeseen challenges will emerge. But one fact is certain: Cyber security will remain a key feature of the national and human security landscape, and all governments will struggle to keep pace, just as all citizens will feel compelled to protect their individual security.

To Learn More

Richard A. Clarke and Robert Knake explore cyberspace in *Cyber War: The Next Threat to National Security and What to Do About It* (New York: Ecco, 2010).

Wesley K. Clark and Peter L. Levin offer a plan for cyberspace in "Securing the Information Highway: How to Enhance the United States' Electronic Defenses," *Foreign Affairs* 88, no. 6 (November–December 2009).

Franklin D. Kramer, Stuart H. Starr, and Larry Wentz, eds., examine security issues in *Cyberpower and National Security* (Washington, DC: Potomac Books, 2009).

Gen. Keith B. Alexander considers military issues in "Warfighting in Cyberspace," *Joint Force Quarterly*, no. 46 (3rd Quarter 2007).

To track the growth of Internet usage by country, see www.internetworld
stats.com/.

Examine current malicious cyber activity and the latest national threat advisory level at the United States Computer Emergency Readiness Team, at
www.us-cert.gov/.

The International Telecommunications Union is the leading UN agency for
information and communication technology issues and the global focal point
for governments and the private sector in developing networks and services. Explore how the ITU is connecting the world at www.itu.int/en/pages/default.aspx.

The PBS *Frontline* series explores cyber vulnerabilities at www.pbs.org/
wgbh/pages/frontline/shows/cyberwar/.

Notes

1. Tryhorn, "Nice Talking to You" (see chap. 1, n. 33).

2. Director of National Intelligence, *Annual Threat Assessment of the Intelligence Community for the Senate Armed Services Committee: Statement for the
Record*, March 10, 2009, 39–40.

3. President George W. Bush, *The National Strategy to Secure Cyberspace*
(Washington, DC: White House, February 2003), 1; Christopher J. Castelli,
"Defense Department Adopts New Definition of 'Cyberspace,'" *Inside the Air
Force*, May 23, 2008, available at http://integrator.hanscom.af.mil/2008/May/
05292008/05292008-24.htm.

4. Larry Johnson, "Thru the Looking Glass: Why Virtual Worlds Matter,
Where They Are Heading, and Why We Are All Here," keynote address to the
Federal Consortium on Virtual Worlds, Washington, DC, April 24, 2008.

5. Donna Miles, "Gates Establishes New Cyber Subcommand," *American
Forces Press Service*, June 24, 2009.

6. http://inventors.about.com/library/inventors/bl_Charles_Herzfeld.htm.

7. Presidential Decision Directive 63, "Critical Infrastructure Protection,"
May 22, 1998, sec. 2; U.S. Department of Defense, *The National Defense Strategy
of the United States of America* (Washington, DC: Department of Defense,
March 2005), 3; Secretary of Defense, *National Defense Strategy*; Department
of Defense, *National Defense Strategy* (2008), 7 (see chap. 4, n. 15).

8. Jim Garamone, "Lynn Calls for Collaboration in Establishing Cyber Security," American Forces Press Service, October 1, 2009.

9. Ben Bain, "Military Wrestles with Cyber War Battle Planning," *Federal Computer Week*, July 26, 2010, available at http://fcw.com/articles/2010/07/26/feat-cyber-command-tackles-cyber-war.aspx.

10. CSIS Commission on Cybersecurity for the 44th Presidency, *Securing Cyberspace for the 44th Presidency* (Washington, D.C.: Center for Strategic and International Studies, December 2008), 11, available at http://csis.org/files/media/csis/pubs/081208_securingcyberspace_44.pdf; White House, "Press Release: National Cybersecurity Awareness Month," October 1, 2009, available at www.whitehouse.gov/the_press_office/Presidential-Proclamation-National-Cybersecurity-Awareness-Month/.

11. Wesley K. Clark and Peter L. Levin, "Securing the Information Highway: How to Enhance the United States' Electronic Defenses," *Foreign Affairs* 88, no. 6 (November–December 2009): 10.

12. "ITU Chief Stresses Need for Cooperation to Protect Cyberspace," United Nations Radio, October 6, 2009.

13. James Lewis, "The 'Korean' Cyber Attacks and Their Implications for Cyber Conflict," Center for Strategic and International Studies, October 2009, 1, available at http://csis.org/files/publications/091023_Korean_Cyber_Attacks_And_Their_Implications_For_Cyber_Conflict.pdf.

14. "ITU Chief Stresses Need for Cooperation"; John J. Kruzel, "Cybersecurity Poses Unprecedented Challenge to National Security, Lynn Says," American Forces Press Service, June 15, 2009.

15. Symantec Global Internet Security Report, "Trends for 2008," April 2009, available at www.symantec.com/connect/downloads/symantec-global-internet-security-threat-report-trends-2008.

16. Keith B. Alexander, "Warfighting in Cyberspace," *Joint Force Quarterly*, no. 46 (3rd Quarter 2007): 60.

17. Head of the National Security Agency Gen. Keith Alexander claimed, "We have yet to translate these strategies into operational art through development of joint doctrine for cyberspace" (ibid., 59).

18. U.S. Air Force officials converted more than 43,000 total force enlisted airmen from former communications career fields to cyberspace support on

November 1, 2009. The new specialty is made up of three former career fields: communications-electronics, knowledge operations management, and communications-computer systems. The new cyberspace support career field is broken into eleven new air force specialties: knowledge operations management, cybersystems operations, cyber surety, computer systems programming, client systems, cybertransport systems, RF (radio frequency) transmission systems, spectrum operations, ground radar systems, airfield systems, and cable and antenna systems. The navy did something similar on October 1, 2009, when it created the Fleet Cyber Command (Tenth Fleet) and consolidated several career fields into information dominance.

19. Clark and Levin, "Securing the Information Highway," 2.

20. Robert K. Knake quoted in Ellen Nakashima and John Pomfret, "China Proves to Be an Aggressive Foe in Cyberspace," *Washington Post*, November 11, 2009, available at www.washingtonpost.com/wp-dyn/content/article/2009/11/10/AR2009111017588.html; *PLA Daily* quoted in Alexander, "Warfighting in Cyberspace," 59.

21. Nakashima and Pomfret, "China Proves to Be an Aggressive Foe."

22. 47 USC, Section 230 (b); White House, "National Cybersecurity Awareness Month."

23. Richard J. Harknett and James A. Stever, "The Cybersecurity Triad: Government, Private Sector Partners, and the Engaged Cybersecurity Citizen," *Journal of Homeland Security and Emergency Management* 6, no. 1 (2009).

24. White House, *Cyberspace Policy Review: Assuring a Trusted and Resilient Information and Communications Infrastructure* (Washington, DC: White House, May 2009), 28, available at www.whitehouse.gov/assets/documents/Cyberspace_Policy_Review_final.pdf.

25. At the time of this writing, governments and security and technology experts were still trying to determine who had launched the "Stuxnet" computer worm, a sophisticated and potentially "cyber-superweapon" that demonstrated the capability to infect and attack the hardware that controlled equipment systems for industries in a number of countries. There was even speculation that the Isreali or U.S. government was responsible as the worm was found in significant numbers of computers at the Iranian Bushehr nuclear power plant. See Tom Gjelten, "Cyberworm's Origins Unclear, but Potential Is Not," National Public Radio, September 27, 2010: available at www.npr.org/templates/story/story.php?storyId+130162219.

8

Protecting and Promoting Human Security

Former chairman of the Joint Chiefs of Staff and the sixty-fifth secretary of state, Gen. Colin Powell, has eloquently explained how human security issues today generate national security challenges:

> What I'm not worried about is a world war. What I'm not worried about is a return to some superpower military contest because there are no longer any peer threats to the United States of America. I am worried about the instability we see manifested in places like Iraq, Afghanistan, North Korea and Iran. . . . I am deeply concerned about poverty throughout the world. I am concerned about infectious diseases. I am concerned about all the various problems that create failed states and the angry people that produces. It takes more money, and it takes more considered judgment. The Atlantic Community would do well to redirect more of its energies to these issues.[1]

The concerns expressed by Colin Powell resonate throughout this book. Whereas in the past powerful and expansionist states threatening military actions tended to pose the most serious security challenges, today the greatest threats tend to emerge from, and are enabled by, the least-developed states—whether because of ineffective and corrupt leaders or due to violent armed groups that are beyond any government's control. In weak countries that lack effective and stable institutions, bad actors can find refuge; groups from terrorists to extreme nationalists intent on genocide to drug traffickers and criminal gangs to cyber hackers who use these countries as bases of operation. Undoubtedly, impoverished states are more prone to internal conflict, which in turn further impoverishes these societies. And typically the conflict may spill over legal borders to cause greater regional instability due to ethnic and religious ties between populations. At the same time, problems that can become global concerns such as pandemic diseases are more likely in undeveloped states with weak public health systems and poor living conditions where people and livestock frequently commune. Environmental disasters can more easily occur where governments are corrupt and the majority of the population is not well educated so public scrutiny is minimal. Piracy, too, originates in weak states or essentially ungoverned areas, where individuals may find no other lucrative economic opportunity or effective law enforcement agency to restrain them. This book has highlighted how the forces of globalization help to enable many of these challenges, sometimes transforming them into clear and immediate security threats to the United States and its citizens.

Yet the picture we have attempted to portray in this work is not entirely grim. Globalization has also demonstrated the potential to improve human security, whether because the increasingly integrated global economy proves productive enough to help the poorest states develop out of extreme poverty, because technologies allow the spread of information and education among citizens everywhere and put pressure on ineffective governments to make necessary reforms, or because the Internet enables nongovernmental groups and activists across state borders to cooperate in publicizing problems and creating novel solutions. For instance, there is absolutely no doubt that the human rights protections that U.S. citizens take for granted would not be as widely accepted around the world today without the sustained campaign of the transnational human rights movement, including groups such as Amnesty International. Without the persistent efforts of the global coalition of experts in Transparency

FIGURE 8.1: SPECTRUM OF CHALLENGES

SPECTRUM OF CHALLENGES

Traditional Security Issues	Interrelated Seam Issues	Human Security Issues
Nuclear Attack	Civic Security	Crime
Conventional Attack (land, air, or sea)	Economic Security	Disease
	Environmental Security	Poverty
Civil War	Maritime Security	Corruption
Insurgency	Health Security	Bad Governance
	Cyber Security	Human Rights Abuses

Nonmilitary

Military

Required Capabilities

Governments	International Organizations	NGOs/Social Movements	Individuals

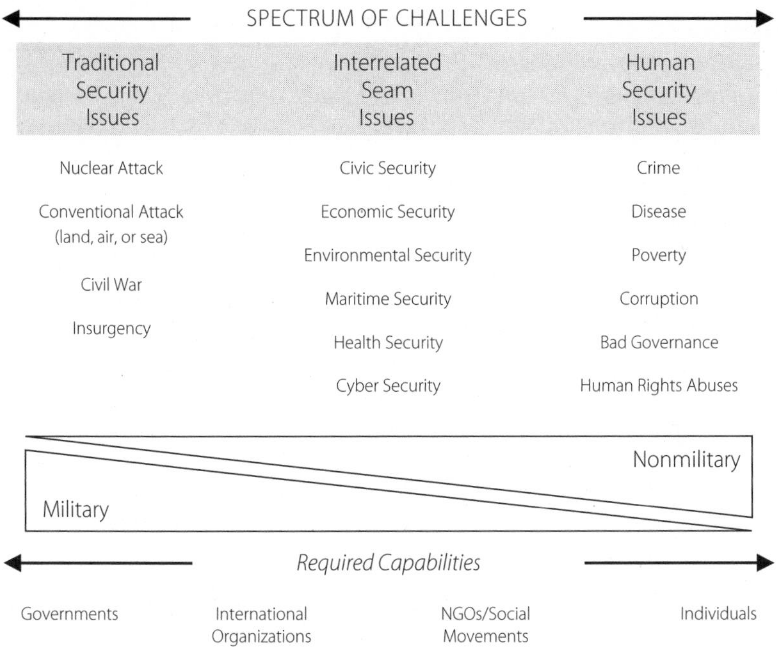

International, many more governments would be able to hide their corruption—one of the principal problems hamstringing good governance. And with no network of scientists, policy experts, and environmental activists, major corporations would be at liberty to pollute and deplete scarce animal and mineral resources.

In this concluding chapter we reflect upon the key features of the many challenges that have been presented throughout the book, integrating them through the construct of protecting and promoting human security. This integration is essential because of the sobering fact that so many of these transnational challenges are inextricably linked and dependent on one another, as they lie across the seams of issue and policy areas. Additionally, these challenges meet at the juncture of domestic and foreign policy bureaucracies, further complicating individual government efforts to alleviate human suffering and improve national security. Figure 8.1 suggests that no issue can be addressed on its own, which makes proposing policy recommendations particularly difficult. Of course, that can make the complexity seem almost overwhelming. Nevertheless, both the international community (whether governments, intergovernmental organizations, or nongovernmental organizations and individual activists) and certainly the U.S. government are faced with doing exactly that, as the concerted U.S. attempt to integrate defense, diplomacy, and development strategies illustrates. To do otherwise is to jeopardize human security for individuals everywhere and for the national security of the United States and its citizens in particular. Christopher Hitchens phrases this warning very effectively in reviewing Gary Bass's book *Freedom's Battle: The Origins of Humanitarian Intervention*, concluding:

> [Bass] makes a sensible case that everyone has a self-interest in the strivings and sufferings of others because the borders between societies are necessarily porous and contingent and are, when one factors in considerations such as the velocity of modern travel, easy access to weaponry, and the spread of disease, becoming ever more so. . . . Afghanistan's internal affairs are now the United States'—in fact, they were already so before Americans understood that. A failed state may not trouble Americans' sleep, but a rogue one can, and the transition from failed state to rogue can be alarmingly abrupt.[2]

But beyond those pragmatic reasons for American citizens to be concerned about human security issues, there are philosophical reasons as well. As Irish rock star and humanitarian activist Bono commented, "America is not just a country but an idea, a great idea about opportunity for all and responsibility to your fellow man. . . . In dangerous, clamorous times, the idea of America rings like a bell."[3] U.S. leadership is necessary around the world to protect and promote human security.

PROTECTING HUMAN SECURITY

Diplomat and human rights advocate Gareth Evans points out that massacres and horrific crimes against civilians have occurred since the birth of mankind, yet only in the wake of the widespread genocide and atrocities of World War II did a sustained movement emerge to protect human rights and, eventually, to support humanitarian intervention on behalf of threatened populations.[4] National interests, domestic politics, and capabilities help explain whether and when external actors will intervene, but today global consensus exists that never again should there be genocide in Rwanda, Yugoslavia, Darfur, Congo, or any other area of the world. This idea has coalesced around an important new norm in international affairs known as "the responsibility to protect." The R2P norm was advocated by the International Commission on Intervention and State Sovereignty in 2001 and formally accepted by more than 150 heads of state at the United Nations Sixtieth Anniversary World Summit in September 2005.[5]

As briefly reviewed in Chapter 1, UN secretary-general Ban Ki-moon outlined the three key elements of R2P in a special report in 2009. First, states have the primary responsibility to protect their populations against genocide, war crimes, ethnic cleansing, and crimes against humanity. Second, the international community should provide assistance to states in building capacity to protect their populations from catastrophe by addressing underlying conditions. Third, the international community should take timely action when states fail to protect their populations (although this provision is not understood to include instances when citizens may be overwhelmed with the violence caused by criminal networks and gangs, a growing problem recognized in Chapter 2). As the secretary-general's report on the responsibility to protect declared, "The strategy stresses the value of prevention, and, when it fails, of early and flexible response tailored to the specific circumstances of each case."[6] Furthermore, the key to prevention was seen in identifying states at risk and developing appropriate responses to aid governments' own efforts to promote development and improve standards of living, as explored in Chapter 3. (It is worth noting here that this type of thinking underlies the U.S. government's commitment to Millennium Challenge Accounts for development aid, an initiative that is examined below.)

Based on these elements, Gareth Evans insists that it is "absolutely not the case" that R2P is just another version of humanitarian intervention— "coercive military intervention for humanitarian purposes."[7] Indeed, the R2P focus is on preventive, positive actions, so as to avoid the possibility

Image 8.1—The U.S. Navy's hospital ship *Mercy* regularly provides medical care and delivers medical supplies throughout the world. Photo credit: James R. McGury, U.S. Navy

of conditions generating genocide or other massive violations of human rights, such as the use of rape as a weapon of war. Evans doubtless felt compelled to make this case because many developing countries continue to be leery about providing a pretext for more powerful countries to intervene in their internal affairs, no matter how praiseworthy their motivations. Yet developing countries and organizations need the assistance of the United States and other countries and organizations to reduce the human security deficits that exist around the world.

Additionally, R2P is predicated on the state in question attempting to help itself with tailored, preventive international assistance across the range of the political-diplomatic, economic, legal, or security sectors.[8] At the same time this does not mean that coercive military action would never be considered in the case of another genocide when the government manifestly cannot, or will not, prevent mass killings—such as Rwanda endured in 1994. The U.S. government has stated as much. In fact, as early as 2006 the U.S. *National Security Strategy* explicitly acknowledged that armed intervention might be necessary on the part of the world community (including the United States) to stop mass atrocities and genocide. And just four years later the U.S. Defense Department's *Quadrennial Defense Review* strategy included the responsibility for the U.S. military to be ready to intervene to end mass atrocities causing large-scale human suffering.[9] This was followed in 2010 by the release of a detailed military planning framework for intervention, *Mass Atrocity Response Operations*, developed in collaboration by the Carr Center for Human Rights Policy, Harvard's Kennedy School of Government, and the U.S. Army's Peacekeeping and Stability Operations Institute.

Of course, it is always a political judgment call to decide whether, and when, international coercive action could actually be successful. Consider the case of Sudan, especially its conflicted region of Darfur. Ambassador Richard Williamson, who served as President George W. Bush's special envoy to Sudan, has termed the situation "genocide in slow motion." He argues that Sudan qualifies as an R2P situation requiring international involvement, as the government has clearly abdicated its responsibility in the face of more than 200,000 deaths from violence or war-related disease and malnutrition, with millions displaced internally. Yet at the same time Williamson maintains that a coercive military intervention would be disastrously counterproductive, as it would harm relief operations and the fragile attempts at peace accords. Nevertheless, other experts such as Gareth Evans believe that sustained political, economic, and legal measures are still necessary and could be effective.[10] Finally, it is also worth noting that one of the reasons so many remain concerned about Sudan is because of its large internally displaced population, in addition to the thousands of Sudanese refugees who have spilled over to burden neighboring impoverished countries like Chad who can barely sustain their own populations.

As with humanitarian intervention attempts, carrying out the R2P mandate to assist governments and vulnerable populations of refugees and displaced peoples can be successful only with a deep understanding of the issues and the context, which naturally includes sensitivity to cultural beliefs and practices. If this is ignored, external efforts are unlikely

Assisting the Most Vulnerable: Refugees and Internally Displaced Persons

A 2009 briefing by then-USAID acting administrator Earl Garst illustrates the complexity of the refugee problem, including defining which people actually constitute legal refugees. According to Garst, there were 17 million internally displaced persons (IDPs) throughout the world in 1997. In spite of economic growth, increased numbers of UN peacekeeping deployments, and more proactive foreign policies, the number increased to 27 million in 2009. Additionally, the number of refugees and stateless persons increased from 15 million persons in 2004 to nearly 22 million by 2008. Finally, there were some 300 million persons who had been affected by natural disasters and been displaced on at least a short-term basis in 2008 (note that these numbers do not include the additional millions of people displaced by massive earthquakes in Haiti, Chile, and China in 2009–2010). Compare these figures to those provided in late 2008 by the UN high commissioner for refugees, Antonio Guterres, who pointed to almost 11.5 million refugees worldwide. There are also more than 27 million people displaced within their own countries; the highest number is in Pakistan as of May 2010, with more than 3 million. Finally, there are perhaps 200 million immigrants in the world.[1] In almost all cases, conflict, often accompanied by persecution, is the underlying condition that forces the mass migration of people.

These disparate figures are cited to underscore the fact that no one is certain of the numbers and that differing factors may be used to distinguish categories. The differences amount to more than semantics, because under international law the status of *refugee* provides more protection and possibility of international assistance than does being an IDP, where the host government still bears the major responsibility. Beginning in 1951, "the UN Refugee Convention set out the criteria for assigning refugee status to people (refugee status is accorded to people forced to leave their countries because of persecution or armed conflict) and the Office of UN High Commissioner for Refugees was established with a mandate to protect and find solutions for refugees."[2] Thus, those individuals officially deemed refugees are entitled to at least some protections under international law and assistance from the

---

1. Eric P. Schwartz and Earl Garst, "Democracy, Human Rights, Refugees: Briefing by Assistant Secretary for Population, Refugees, and Migration Eric Schwartz and USAID Acting Administrator for Africa Earl Garst," *U.S. State Department Daily Digest Bulletin*, September 25, 2009; Antonio Guterres, "Millions Uprooted: Saving Refugees and the Displaced," *Foreign Affairs* 87, no. 5 (2008): 92. The UN Refugee Agency's annual 2009 report placed the number of refugees at 15.2 million, with 27.1 million IDPs, and, overall, 43.3 million persons forcibly displaced (*2009 Global Trends: Refugees, Asylum-Seekers, Returnees, Internally Displaced, and Stateless Persons* [Geneva: UN Refugee Agency, 2010], available at www.unhcr.org/4c11f0be9.html).

2. Guterres, "Millions Uprooted," 90.

United Nations. Of course, that assistance often amounts to families literally spending generations in refugee camps with no hope of returning home due to continuing conflict, whether it is the more than hundreds of thousands of Palestinians still living in camps since a 1948 war or some 120,000 Burundians who have been living in neighboring Tanzania for decades. The sad fact is that probably a third of refugees worldwide are in camps, whereas well over two-thirds of African refugees make their homes in camps.[3]

Image 8.2—Displaced persons in Darfur receive USAID plastic sheeting for use in constructing temporary shelters for war-affected civilian populations during the rainy season. Photo credit: USAID.

Bad as the situation might be for refugees, for IDPs and for those who are often termed economic refugees or migrants (those seeking a better life in other countries, such as Mexicans or Haitians fleeing to the United States), there are no recognized rights under international law. The situation is probably most dire for the estimated six to twelve million "stateless" persons who have no recognized nationality (such as the Roma in Europe) and, thus, no claim to government services or protections. Although member states of the United Nations theoretically have an obligation to fellow human beings, including to those who have been displaced or migrated, in practice the burden of refugees, IDPs, and migrants almost inevitably falls on many of the poorest and most unstable states who harbor them. These countries often lack both the will and certainly the means to help these unfortunate human beings in spite of efforts from developed countries. This is nowhere more true than in post-conflict situations such as Afghanistan, where the UN Refugee Agency has documented large numbers of Afghan IDPs and refugees from Iran and Pakistan, or in areas still experiencing conflict, such as the Darfur region in Sudan, where more than 2 million IDPs suffer constant attacks and pitiful living conditions, causing another 250,000 to seek refuge over the border in extremely poor and unstable Chad.[4] Finally, although no one can foresee the pace or scale of climate change, clearly island nations and regions already experiencing drought and desertification will undoubtedly generate more migrants and refugees, as discussed in Chapter 4, further compounding this global issue.

---

3. "Lost in Limbo," Economist.com, August 27, 2009, available at www.economist.com/world/international/story_id=14302845.

4. "Refugees in Cities Raising Risk of Tension—UNHCR," Reuters, December 7, 2009, available at www.alertnet.org/thenews/newsdesk/GEE5B60TT.htm; UN Refugee Agency, *2009 Global Trends*; Guterres, "Millions Uprooted," 94–95.

to be productive, and even well-intentioned and well-funded development strategies can fail. In the worst case, intervention efforts—military,
political, or economic, or some combination of the three—might actually
cause conditions to deteriorate further, as the United States and the
United Nations have learned at great cost.

While the examples of Iraq, Afghanistan, Pakistan, and even Somalia
might come to mind, it is worth considering a European example here—
Bosnia-Herzegovina. Recall that both the United States and many European countries have been extensively involved military, diplomatically,
and economically in the relatively small state of Bosnia since the early
1990s. Yet, writing in *Foreign Affairs* in 2009, Patrice McMahon and Jon
Western warned that there was clear potential for war in Bosnia again,
leading them to conclude that "if the international community cannot
fulfill its promises in Bosnia—given the country's location in the middle
of Europe, the leverage that the EU and NATO possess there, and the
massive amounts of aid invested thus far—the prospects for international
state building elsewhere are extremely grim." Clearly, it is not enough to
pour in resources and assistance and expect a self-sustaining government
to emerge quickly. In fact, in the wake of the often tenuous situation in
the former regions of Yugoslavia (to include Bosnia and Kosovo), observers such as historian Jerry Muller argue that in some states where
cultural and communal conflict has reached a certain level of violence
and hatred, partition might be the only effective and ultimately humane
solution. In that case the international community's R2P role should be
to provide security and varied types of assistance to help separate and
resettle communal groups as legitimate citizens in appropriate new
homelands.[11]

Nevertheless, as we have reiterated in this book concerning the impact
of globalization, our current borderless world should be viewed not just
with despair but also with optimism. For instance, McMahon and Western also believe that Bosnia could still become a stable state if more attention were paid to its political institutions and power-sharing
arrangements. This is a significant distinction if we heed the arguments
of some experts who propose that it is not the cultural differences that
are the root of conflict but the unjust distribution of wealth and resources

between different ethnic or religious groups.[12] Unfortunately, as noted earlier, it is in the transition period when a country is becoming consolidated and institutionalized, or attempting to move toward democracy, that these differences may become most apparent and a source of conflict (ironically, aided by the increased flow of information). This type of situation is particularly likely where bad leaders may use cultural appeals to maintain their hold on power and to disguise their own lack of good governance and their corrupt rule, as the case of Yugoslav-Serbian leader Slobodan Milošević underscores. But while development expert Paul Collier acknowledges this problem of bad leaders, who are "sometimes psychopaths who have shot their way to power, sometimes crooks who have bought it," he also highlights "the sometimes brave people who, against the odds, are trying to build a better future."[13] It would be difficult to think of a more inspiring example here than Ellen Johnson Sirleaf, elected president of civil war–torn Liberia in 2006 and the first elected woman head of state in Africa. In recognition of her efforts, President George W. Bush awarded her the Presidential Medal of Freedom, the highest civilian award given by the United States, in 2007. As we have attempted to demonstrate in our analysis, individuals like President Sirleaf can make a difference; there are people who continue to struggle for human rights and good governance against great odds. Burmese opposition leader Aung San Suu Kyi, under house arrest for some fifteen years and winner of the 1991 Nobel Peace Prize, is another sterling example. Yet as the concluding section of this book demonstrates, individuals, international and transnational groups, and even governments can make only limited progress in addressing threats that challenge human security without effective integration of policies that institutionalize good governance, democracy, and sustainable development.

PROMOTING HUMAN SECURITY

The increased recognition of the importance of development and international assistance to U.S. national security and global human security was already apparent at the start of the twenty-first century under the George W. Bush administration. Official U.S. development assistance grew from $10 billion in 2000 to $22 billion in 2008.[14] As soon as Barack Obama took office in 2009 he made it clear that development would be considered a central concern, and he mandated a Presidential Study Directive on U.S. Global Development Policy be carried out, with representatives from more than fifteen agencies in the U.S. government that contribute to the development mission. Additionally, the Obama administration pledged to double international assistance during its term in office. For the U.S. State Department, development now stands on its own as a third pillar of foreign policy, along with diplomacy and defense. In her first few months in office in 2009 Secretary of State Clinton directed an intensive, yearlong Quadrennial Diplomacy and Development Review process by the State Department and USAID to assess development policy. The secretary's use of the term QDDR was significant as it mirrors a similar four-year process—the Quadrennial Defense Review referenced above—that the U.S. Department of Defense undertakes to assess defense policy, forces, and risks. In a keynote speech on development in 2010, Secretary of State Clinton proclaimed the following: "The United States seeks a safer, more prosperous, more democratic and more equitable world. We cannot reach that goal when one-third of humankind live in conditions that offer them little chance of building better lives for themselves or their children. We cannot stop terrorism or defeat the ideologies of violent extremism when hundreds of millions of young people see a future with no jobs, no hope, and no way ever to catch up to the developed world."[15]

State Department officials have continued to stress the critical nature of multifaceted development for the success of U.S. foreign policy, highlighting "smart" development as the preferred approach. What this means is improving not only the material conditions of people's lives in terms of health, education, agriculture, and access to food and water, but equally good governance with stable, effective, and accountable political and economic institutions. The importance of the latter fact has been reinforced recently with experiences in Iraq, Afghanistan, and Pakistan.

The Obama administration's policies were designed to expand upon the conclusions reached by the preceding Bush administration, which recognized international assistance to be an important catalyst for devel-

Image 8.3—Even after governments build roads, like this one in Madagascar, it still takes time for modern transportation to arrive. Photo credit: Jennifer Doyle.

opment, but only for certain countries that had already established a level of sound economic policies and accountable government. Otherwise, assistance was seen as ineffective and even detrimental for long-term success, as Chapter 3 earlier described. Thus, the Bush administration determined to assist target states through the Millennium Challenge Corporation (MCC) development fund, whereby countries would reduce poverty through growth, qualifying for individualized funding compacts only if they agreed to design policies linked to certain requirements. For some critics, this amounted to adding yet more strings to badly needed international assistance. However, decades of development assistance experience have taught the United States that how the money is spent, and accounted for, matters. The MCC was seen as one vehicle to control that process, an example of smart development policy that has continued to receive support under the Obama administration.

The Millennium Challenge approach underscores the type of conclusions reached by many experts on development, as explored in Chapter 3. The specifics of development programs cannot be dictated by outsiders but must be ordered by the people involved. As Secretary Clinton has commented, this is "the difference between aid and investment. Through aid, we supply what is needed to people who need it—be it sacks of rice or cartons of medicines. But through investment, we seek to break the cycle of dependence that aid can create by helping countries build their

POLICY SPOTLIGHT

Examining the Millennium Challenge Corporation

According to its Web site, the Millennium Challenge Corporation was specifically created by the U.S. Congress in 2004 at the behest of the Bush administration as "an innovative and independent U.S. foreign aid agency that is helping to lead the fight against global poverty." The focus is on reducing poverty through sustainable economic growth via a performance-based model. The MCC differs from traditional international assistance due to its use of two types of grants: "compacts," which are larger five-year grants, and smaller "threshold programs" grants. Democracy expert Larry Diamond has termed the Millennium Challenge Corporation (also referred to as a Millennium Challenge Account) "one of the Bush Administration's least heralded but most important foreign policy innovations."[1] For Diamond, the key principle of conditionality or aid selectivity is what makes the program work, as it provides support to reforming governments and to citizens in those countries who are trying to pressure their governments for reform, both economic and political. In order to evaluate the requirement that countries be committed to policies of economic freedom, good governance, and investment in their citizens, the MCC examines seventeen indicators, looking for consistency from year to year in areas ranging from respect for civil liberties to immunization rates, from girls' primary education completion rates to trade and fiscal policies. The MCC relies on a variety of governmental and nongovernmental sources for

1. Millennium Challenge Corporation Web site, "About MCC," www.mcc.gov/mcc/about/index.shtml; Diamond, "Democratic Rollback," 47 (see chap. 3, n. 50).

own institutions and their own capacity to deliver essential services. Aid chases need, investment chases opportunity."[16] These comments can all be understood to indicate greater recognition that USAID policies in the past have been oriented too much toward the short term (as noted in Chapter 3's spotlight on USAID) and that sustainable development can

---

Policy Spotlight (*continued*)

its data, including Freedom House, the Heritage Foundation, Transparency International, the World Bank Institute, and UNESCO.

As of May 2010 the MCC had "approved over $7.4 billion in compact and threshold programs worldwide that support country-determined projects in such sectors as: agriculture and irrigation, transportation (roads, bridges, ports), water supply and sanitation, access to health, finance and enterprise development, anticorruption initiatives, land rights and access, [and] access to education."[2] Countries receiving Poverty Reduction Compacts have included Armenia, Benin, El Salvador, Morocco, Nicaragua, Senegal, and Tanzania. Yet in spite of the clearly stated conditionality linkages, at least some governments cannot seem to honor their agreements. For example, in 2008, the MCC cut $61 million from Nicaragua's overall grant of $175 million over concerns about the fairness and transparency of municipal-level elections, and by 2010 that aid had not been restored, as the MCC continued to have reservations about electoral irregularities in the country. Additionally, the corporation cut $10 million to Honduras in 2009 in protest against the disruptive government change that occurred in that country.[3] These results can be viewed positively and negatively—positively in the sense that the MCC is serious about enforcing accountability, or negatively in the sense that some of the neediest whom the aid is designed to assist are losing out (in the Nicaraguan case, direct assistance was provided to some of the poorest regions, including rural farmers). This reinforces the fact that governmental reform, just like development, is a slow, incremental process subject to reversal. Persistence and the long view are crucial to achieve progress.

---

2. Millennium Challenge Corporation Web site.

3. Blake Schmidt, "Nicaragua's Electoral Climate Hasn't Improved, Yohannes Says," *Bloomberg Businessweek*, May 6, 2010, available at www .businessweek.com/ndews/20101-05-06/nicaragua-s-electoral-climate -hasn-t-improved.html.

occur only over the long term. Additionally, there is growing awareness of the need for a "whole-of-government" approach toward development, which integrates all government agencies' efforts above what USAID has authority to accomplish on its own. The draft Presidential Study Directive on Global Development (PSD-7) reportedly was to recommend that the USAID administrator take part in relevant National Security Council meetings and that a high-level development policy coordinating committee be established to oversee development activities within the executive branch.[17] This might square with one of development expert Paul Collier's key recommendations to improve life for the poorest billion people, by elevating development out of governmental development ministries to directly under the head of a government.[18]

Obviously, governmental efforts such as those promoted by the U.S. government, and the multilateral efforts of the United Nations Development Programme, provide the bulk of resources aimed at promoting human security concerns. But that does not mean that transnational social coalitions, nongovernmental groups, and even individuals' actions do not have important ramifications. As with almost all the processes and initiatives we have examined in this book, those effects can be both positive and negative. Many would point to the case of Haiti after the horrific 2010 earthquake as an example of nongovernmental overkill, where international NGOs were providing perhaps 80 percent of the country's basic services. One observer reported in April that barely one cent of each dollar of earthquake aid was allotted to the Haitian government, which was being marginalized, as were popular Haitian organizations. The concern was that there was no accountability to either the Haitian government or its people and that they were being left out of the decision-making process. Yet this observation should be balanced against the worldwide actions of myriad NGOs whose policies are deliberately inclusive, as they encourage the communities they assist to arrive at their own solutions for problems and to sustain them on a long-term basis. For example, Grassroots International, though a small group that disbursed just $1.8 million in cash grants and material aid in 2009, works in collaboration with a network of other groups and directly with small family producers and the most disadvantaged populations from Haiti to the

Gaza Strip and from Brazil to African communities.[19] The potential impact of these international groups is difficult to grasp, considering that estimates range from 40,000 to perhaps 50,000 worldwide. But since these groups often act in concert with domestic nongovernmental organizations, which number in the hundreds of thousands, the implications are enormous.

CONCLUSION

To be sure, promoting human security is not really a novel idea. However, the linkages now made between human security and national security are no longer ignored as they often were in the past. Traditionally, states would provide international assistance to buy influence, even if short-lived and haphazard in nature. Although this is still true in some parts of the world, over the past twenty years there has been an increased urgency to reach out directly to people in need in every region. This is happening for both humanitarian and security reasons. For example, the individual child vulnerable to polio in Afghanistan certainly needs the vaccine, but the children in the rest of the world need polio to be eradicated, too. And whereas states may be motivated at least in part to give assistance because of security concerns, the actions of thousands of citizen-activists across the world who give their time, effort, and money to causes ranging from eliminating land mines and providing microfinance loans for women's groups to writing letters to protest political prisoners and demanding the tropical rain forests be protected must be accounted for, too. Traditional international relations theories such as realism cannot explain the shift or the important roles that nonstate actors play in international security today, although constructivism (and liberalism to some extent) can help to engender thoughtful consideration of these issues.

What should be evident from the nontraditional security issues and cases presented in this book is that the current era of globalization links people and countries across many heretofore dividing seams in unprecedented ways. In contrast to previous eras when different regions or ideologies could be ignored with little effect on U.S. national security, that is increasingly untrue. What happens in countries that range from

Afghanistan to Zimbabwe does impact security in the United States, whether it triggers an incidence of terrorism or generates a pandemic or allows cyber criminals to hack into banks unhindered. One consequence of Thomas Friedman's flat world is that U.S. security is dependent on security in nearly every country of the world. As was evidenced in the attempted terrorist attack on Christmas 2009, it was weak governments and security agencies in Yemen and Nigeria that almost allowed a terrorist to destroy a plane over Detroit. And U.S. citizens in Arizona and Texas are all too aware of the criminal violence posed by warring drug families in Mexico that can threaten their personal security.

Given the changed nature of the security environment, no single solution or policy can address decades of neglect; clearly, long-term international and transnational cooperation is essential. In view of the insecurity present in the maritime domain, the environment, and cyberspace, it is unrealistic to think that a single country can provide for its own security today. For example, any environmental gains made in developed countries can be offset by environmental calamities in developing countries. Likewise, disease prevention and eradication in developed countries can be undermined by poor public health practices and the misuse of antibiotics in developing countries. The international criminal gang that steals the credit card number of a U.S. college student may be based in the relatively ungoverned spaces of Nigeria. And the lack of governance in failing states and resulting ineffective maritime security in East Africa will continue to weaken international commerce through piracy. Though none of these challenges is equivalent to the nuclear threat facing much of the world for four decades after World War II, these challenges threaten state sovereignty and regularly undermine everyone's human security. Fortunately, recognition of this is occurring, albeit slowly.

From our perspective, one of the most promising indications of transforming attitudes that will ultimately strengthen the ability to address human security concerns is visible in the approach of the U.S. Defense Department and its military forces. Secretary of Defense Gates has consistently voiced his support for the State Department and its development mission, including support to increase the latter's budget. In a representative speech to midlevel army officers in 2010, he commented:

When I left the government in 1993 when I retired for the first time . . . there were 16,000 people in the Agency for International Development (AID). It was an expeditionary agency. Those people, most of them expected and wanted to be deployed overseas in developing countries, in harsh circumstances, often with imperfect security. And they were experts in agronomy and rule of law and building water systems and building schools and so on. Now, AID has 3,000 people and is basically a contracting agency. So we have to reestablish, we have to—AID, USIA, these civilian institutions that play such a huge role in our success in the Cold War have to be recreated in some way with the same scale for the 21st century. And we're a long way from being there yet.[20]

For many of us, if traditionally conservative and security-conscious defense sectors are concerned not just with the military budget and forces but equally with supporting civilian agencies and their development mission, there should indeed be optimism!

To Learn More

Gareth Evans offers a comprehensive examination of changing international norms and sovereignty in *The Responsibility to Protect: Ending Mass Atrocity Crimes Once and for All* (Washington, DC: Brookings Institution Press, 2008).

Listen to Colin Powell's characterization of security as he discusses the role of international cooperation to facilitate security at www.acus.org/new_atlanticist/colin-powell-looks-back-and-ahead.

The journal *Prism* publishes articles on efforts to improve governmental coordination during complex operations, which includes humanitarian assistance and development. See http://ccoportal.org/prism.

The U.S. Institute of Peace is a nonpartisan, independent institution established and funded by the U.S. Congress to help prevent and resolve violent conflict around the world and to help build postconflict stability, development, and peace-building experts. View their many projects at www.usip.org/.

Scan the U.S. State Department's Office of the Coordinator for Reconstruction and Stabilization to get an idea of the increasing focus on the civilian

component of nation and peace building; view the Web site at www.state.gov/
s/crs/.

Visit the Web site of the United Nations High Commissioner for Refugees
to get a sense of the immensity of the numbers, problems, and challenges facing
refugees, internally displaced persons, and other stateless persons at www
.unhcr.org/cgi-bin/texis/vtx/home.

The Stanley Foundation is one of numerous private foundations that sponsor research and conferences on global governance, aiming "to connect people
from different backgrounds, often producing clarifying insights and innovative
solutions." View their projects at www.stanleyfoundation.org.

The nongovernmental International Crisis Group was founded in 1995 by
former high-level government officials and policy experts who saw the
tragedies of Somalia, Rwanda, and Bosnia as demonstrating the need for better
prediction and international response to impending conflicts. View their Web
site at www.crisisgroup.org to see why the analysis, policy recommendations,
and advocacy efforts of the Crisis Group are so highly regarded.

Notes

1. "Colin Powell Looks Back and Ahead," interview with Frederick Kempe,
December 14, 2009, available at www.acus.org/new_atlanticist/colin-powell
-looks-back-and-ahead.

2. Christopher Hitchens, "Just Causes: The Case for Humanitarian Intervention," review of *Freedom's Battle: The Origins of Humanitarian Intervention*,
by Gary J. Bass, *Foreign Affairs* 87, no. 5 (2008): 162.

3. Bono, "Rebranding America," *New York Times*, October 18, 2009, available at www.nytimes.com/2009/10/18/opinion/18bono.html.

4. Gareth Evans, *The Responsibility to Protect: Ending Mass Atrocity Crimes
Once and for All* (Washington, DC: Brookings Institution Press, 2008).

5. International Commission on Intervention and State Sovereignty, *The Responsibility to Protect* (Ottawa: International Development Research Centre,
December 2001).

6. United Nations General Assembly, *Implementing the Responsibility to Protect*, 2 (see chap. 1, n. 26).

7. Evans, *Responsibility to Protect*, 56. Evans was at pains to make this case because of the fact that this type of activity had become unpopular among many UN members, not least of which was the United States.

8. Ibid.

9. George W. Bush, *The National Security Strategy of the United States of America* (Washington, DC: White House, March 2006), 17; Robert M. Gates, *Quadrennial Defense Review Report* (Washington, DC: Department of Defense, February 2010), vi.

10. Ambassador Richard W. Williamson, *Sudan and the Implications for Responsibility to Protect*, Policy Analysis Brief (Muscatine, IA: Stanley Foundation, October 2009), 1; Evans, *Responsibility to Protect*, 60–61.

11. Patrice C. McMahon and Jon Western, "The Death of Dayton: How to Stop Bosnia from Falling Apart," *Foreign Affairs* 88, no. 5 (2009): 71; Jerry Muller, "Us and Them: The Enduring Power of Ethnic Nationalism," *Foreign Affairs* 87, no. 2 (2008): 18–35.

12. Dieter Senghaas, "A Clash of Civilizations: An Idée Fixe?" *Journal of Peace Research* 35, no. 1 (1998).

13. Collier, *Bottom Billion*, 4 (see chap. 1, n. 14).

14. Atwood, McPherson, and Natsios, "Arrested Development," 123 (see chap. 3, n. 25).

15. Clinton, "Secretary's Remarks" (see chap. 3, n. 28).

16. Ibid.

17. According to the Modernizing Foreign Assistance Network, "MFAN Statement: Leaked White House Development Document Has Strong Reform Elements," May 3, 2010, available at www.modernizingforeignassistance.org/blog/2010/05/04/mfan-statement-leaked-white-house-development-document-has-strong-reform-elements/.

18. Josh Rogin, "White House Proposed Taking Development Role Away from State," *Cable/Foreign Policy*, May 3, 2010, available at http://thecable.foreign policy.com/posts/2010/05/03/white_house_proposed_taking_development_role_away_from_State.html; Collier, *Bottom Billion*, 188–189.

19. Kevin Edmonds, "NGOs and the Business of Poverty in Haiti," North American Congress on Latin America, April 5, 2010, available at https://nacla.org/node/6501; Grassroots International, *Annual Report, 2009: Land, Water,*

and Food: Resource Rights for All (Jamaica Plain, MA: Grassroots International, 2009).

20. Robert Gates, "Remarks by Secretary Gates at the Command and General Staff College," Fort Leavenworth, KS, May 7, 2010, available at www.defense .gov/transcripts/transcript.aspx?transcriptid=4623.

GLOSSARY

ABC: HIV/AIDS program that emphasizes abstinence, being faithful, and condom usage.

Balance of power: a realist theory that predicts equilibrium in the international system where two or more opposing states constrain one another's actions due to fear of escalation leading to a major war.

Bipolarity: a stage in international affairs where two opposing states dominate the international system (e.g., the United States and the Soviet Union in the cold war era).

Botnet: a network of zombie machines used by hackers for massive coordinated system attacks.

Choke point: a narrow waterway of strategic value that separates two larger bodies of water.

Civic security: the right of all human beings to have their physical security, integrity, and identity secure from violation.

Civil society: the sector of society not controlled by the government or corporations but by citizens, who may form private, voluntary groups for social, economic, educational, humanitarian, and religious purposes, among others.

Climate change: a perspective that maintains that the earth is currently undergoing a slow warming process due primarily to human activity; this process is viewed as generating mainly negative and even catastrophic effects for human beings.

Constructivism: an emerging school of international relations that holds that the international system is constantly being shaped ("constructed") by shared ideas and interactions between peoples and their societies and that this process can result in shared values for better or worse.

Culture: the relatively unchanging norms, values, traditions, and practices of a particular societal group, normally linked to ethnicity, language, religion, and a common history.

Cyberspace: the information environment characterized by computers and their networks, information flowing on the networks, and the interpretations of the information by users.

Democratic peace theory: the belief (seemingly validated by numerous data-supported studies) that as democracies do not go to war with another, establishing more democratic states in the international system would eventually lead to stable peace.

Denial-of-service attack: employing a botnet to send massive simultaneous requests to servers, preventing legitimate use of the servers.

Development: a process that traditionally meant achieving economic growth and progress for societies but has been consistently broadened into a more comprehensive process including the concepts of sustainability, equity, and capacity (and even social and cultural aspects).

Ecomigration: the movement of people primarily due to environmental conditions such as drought, rising sea levels, or desertification.

Economic security: the right of all human beings to adequate resources necessary for survival such as food, shelter, and employment; it essentially equates to the right of human beings to equitable and sustainable development.

Exclusive Economic Zone (EEZ): waters that extend seaward from the low-water mark of a coastal state to two hundred nautical miles.

Failing state: a state at risk of collapse into anarchy because a very weak government, economy, and other institutions cannot effectively protect state borders and the citizenry or provide necessary services and resources.

Food security: the right of all human beings to have access to safe and nutritious food and to be free from hunger.

Globalization: common term used to describe the seemingly dominant trend in the international system that is characterized by constantly accelerating transnational economic, cultural, and information flows, resulting in an increasingly integrated (but sometimes conflicted) world community.

Green revolution: the technological transformation of agricultural practices after World War II into the 1970s, which vastly increased agricultural production in developing countries, allowing them to feed their rapidly growing populations.

Hegemony: a stage of international affairs where one state dominates the international system.

Human rights: the belief that all human beings are inherently entitled to certain rights because they are human beings. There is disagreement about whether human rights should be considered universal or relative (affected by cultural and religious values), but almost all would agree that each person has the right to life and respect for their person and dignity.

Human security: the right of all human beings to respect for their lives and freedoms including freedom from threats (freedom from fear) and freedom to develop (freedom from want).

Human trafficking: the practice of illegally transporting and employing mostly poor women and children (usually by force or trickery) for illicit purposes such as forced labor, debt peonage, and prostitution.

Illegally armed groups: subnational or transnational groups that use violence to fulfill their objectives outside of state control.

Liberalism: a dominant school of international relations that holds that the international system is progressing into a peaceful, just, and prosperous community of (democratic) states and nonstate actors as education and learning influence cooperation for the betterment of all.

Logic bomb: camouflaged segments of programs that destroy data when certain conditions are met.

Microfinance: the practice of providing very small loans to generally poor and marginalized populations (mostly women) so they can establish productive small businesses and escape extreme poverty; it often includes the concept of village-level banks and cooperatives.

Millennium Development Goals (MDGs): A set of eight interrelated and comprehensive development goals—to include twenty-one quantifiable targets and sixty indicators—that member states of the United Nations agreed to achieve by 2015 to address the main development challenges facing the world's peoples.

Multipolarity: a stage in international affairs where more than two opposing states dominate the international system, particularly at the regional level.

Narcotrafficking: the shipment of illegal drugs across national boundaries.

National security: traditional focus on protecting the state's perceived vital and important national interests through integrating military, diplomatic, and economic means.

Nongovernmental organization (NGO): private nonstate actors that develop and implement social, political, and economic policies. These can be solely domestic or international in scope; if international, they are termed INGOs.

Nonstate actor: an individual, group, organization, or company that influences the social, political, economic, or security dimensions of society.

Piracy: an act of boarding or attempting to board any ship in international waters with apparent intent to commit theft or any other crime and with apparent intent or capability to use force in the furtherance of that act.

Predatory state: a state where the government's purpose (even if elected) is to rule in such a fashion as to enrich the leadership and its cronies and not to provide services and resources to the majority of the citizens.

Realism: a dominant school of international relations that holds that in an international system characterized by anarchy and insecurity, states will constantly seek military and other forms of power to protect themselves and to dominate weaker states.

Responsibility to protect (R2P): as outlined by the United Nations, it includes three principles. First, states must protect their populations against genocide, war crimes, ethnic cleansing, and crimes against humanity. Second, the international community should provide assistance to states in building capacity to protect their populations from catastrophe by addressing underlying conditions. Third, the international community should take timely action when states fail to protect their populations.

Rogue state: a term used to refer to states that do not follow conventional, widely accepted norms of state behavior such as respect for diplomatic conventions.

Security assistance: a form of military cooperation that includes education, training, and equipping other countries' militaries.

Social movements: decentralized, usually transnational networks of activists and nongovernmental groups (and sometimes intergovernmental groups) motivated to work together for a cause, often a perceived injustice such as abuse of human rights.

Sovereignty: international legal concept established by the Treaty of Westphalia of 1648 that recognizes the supreme authority of a government within its own defined territory.

Sustainable development: development that meets the needs of the present without compromising the ability of future generations to meet their own needs.

Territorial waters: those waters under government sovereign control and legally recognized as twelve nautical miles from the low-water mark of a coastal state.

Terrorism: acts (or threatened acts) of political and related violence deliberately directed against civilians or civilian targets to instill fear.

3-D approach: shorthand term for U.S. government strategy that integrates defense, development, and diplomacy efforts to achieve foreign policy goals.

Transnational challenge: a challenge that crosses national boundaries and cannot be controlled solely, if at all, by individual states.

Trojan horse: stealthy code that executes under the guise of a useful program but performs malicious acts such as the destruction of files, the transmission of private data, and the opening of a back door to allow third-party control of a machine.

Unipolarity: a stage in international affairs where a single state can dominate the international system.

Virus: malicious code that can self-replicate and cause damage to the systems it infects. The code can delete information, infect programs, change the directory structure to run undesirable programs, and infect the vital part of the operating system that ties together how files are stored.

Weak state: characterized by a government's inability to effectively control its borders, provide security for its citizens, and generate sufficient economic opportunities to improve living standards.

Worm: similar to a virus, a worm is distinctive for its ability to self-replicate without infecting other files in order to reproduce.

Zombie: a computer that has been covertly compromised and is controlled by a third party.

INDEX

ABOUT THE AUTHORS

Derek S. Reveron is the EMC Informationist Chair and professor of national security affairs at the Naval War College in Newport, Rhode Island. His books include *Exporting Security: International Engagement, Security Cooperation, and the Changing Face of the U.S. Military*; *Inside Defense: Understanding the U.S. Military in the 21st Century*; *Flashpoints in the War on Terrorism*; and *America's Viceroys: The Military and U.S. Foreign Policy*. He serves on the editorial boards of the *Naval War College Review* and the *National Intelligence Journal*.

Kathleen A. Mahoney-Norris is professor of national security studies at the USAF's Air Command and Staff College in Montgomery, Alabama. She also teaches Latin American regional security issues at the Air War College. She is coeditor of *Democratization and Human Rights: Challenges and Contradictions* and has written numerous articles and book chapters on civil-military relations, military education issues, and human rights. She serves on the editorial board of *Joint Force Quarterly*.